THE NO B.S. GUIDE TO LINUX

BOB RANKIN

THE NO B.S. GUIDE TO LINUX

no starch press

San Francisco

Printed in the United States of America

1 2 3 4 5 6 7 8 9 10—01 00 99 98 97

 Printed on acid-free recycled paper.

Trademarks
Trademarked names are used throughout this book. Rather than use a trademark symbol with every occurrence of a trademarked name, we are using the names only in an editorial fashion and to the benefit of the trademark owner, with no intention of infringement of the trademark.

Publisher: William Pollock
Project Editor: Karol Jurado
Cover and Interior Design: Derek Yee
Compositor: Derek Yee, Stacie Yamaki
Technical Editors: Mark Bolzern, Andrew Selman
Copyeditor: Gail Nelson
Proofreader: Linda Medoff
Indexer: Nancy Humphreys

Distributed to the book trade in the United States and Canada by Publishers Group West, 4065 Hollis, P.O. Box 8843, Emeryville, California 94662, phone: 800-788-3123 or 510-548-4393, fax: 510-658-1834.

For information on translations or book distributors outside the United States, please contact No Starch Press directly:

no starch press
401 China Basin Street, Suite 108, San Francisco, CA 94107-2192
phone: 415-284-9900; fax: 415-284-9955; info@nostarch.com; www.nostarch.com

Library of Congress Cataloging-in-Publication Data
```
Rankin, Bob.
      The no B.S. guide to Linux / Bob Rankin.
         p.   cm.
      Includes index.
      ISBN 1-886411-04-2 (pbk.)
      1.  Linux.  2. Operating systems (Computers)  I. Title.
   QA76.76.063R365      1997
   005.4'469—dc21                                    97-6234
                                                        CIP
```

BRIEF CONTENTS

CONTENTS

1

2

3

4

5

6

7

8

9

10

11

12

13

FOREWORD

Maybe you've heard that Unix is extremely difficult and takes years and years to master. But a closer look reveals that Unix is much like what you're already used to. DOS took many of its design concepts from Unix, as did OS/2 and Windows NT. So if you have learned to use DOS, then you know almost everything you need to know to use Unix at an above-average level.

Linux (a version of Unix that runs on ordinary PCs) has a lot to offer as a database or application server platform. It is multiuser and multitasking, and can access huge amounts of memory (gigabytes) and huge amounts of disk storage (terabytes). Linux offers virtually everything that Windows NT and OS/2 have been promising for years and may not deliver in a truly stable form for some time to come.

The main reason that Unix has not made a big splash on PCs is that only recently have PCs actually been powerful enough to truly make use of an operating system with the power of Unix. Frankly, Unix didn't really fit well on a 286, just like Microsoft Windows doesn't. However, the new generation of PC operating systems actually requires more horsepower than Unix, while doing less than Unix does.

Linux runs admirably on machines that choke when presented with Windows NT or OS/2. It'll do just fine on a 486/33 with 16MB of RAM and 345MB of hard disk space. And it's also capable of running MS Windows and DOS applications.

At the official introduction of Windows NT, Bill Gates said that NT would be a better Unix than Unix itself. But in order to accomplish this, NT must conform to the same international standards as Unix, and in the process become just another proprietary version of Unix. Don't wait for Microsoft . . . learn Unix now! If NT becomes the success Microsoft hopes it will be, you can jump on it when it's stable and widely distributed.

But don't take my word for it—take a look at the "Help Wanted" ads in your local newspaper, under computers, computer science, or data processing. Look for Unix, AIX, HP/UX, OSF/1, SCO, Solaris, SunOS, DG/UX, Novell UnixWare, C, C++, TCP/IP, NFS, and X Window, among others. In my local newspapers, the overwhelming majority of ads ask for one or more of these things. Wake up and smell the coffee! Thousands of Cobol programmers are out of work or working near minimum wage because they did not adapt. There's no need for you to suffer the same fate, especially considering how easy it is to avoid.

Now that I have whipped up some fear, I want to assure you that the purpose of this book is to alleviate that feeling, and replace it with confidence. By learning Linux on your own PC, you'll be gaining the essential Unix skills to ensure your survival in the computing arena.

WHAT IS LINUX GOOD FOR?

So what is Linux good for anyway? Would you believe me if I said everything? Probably not. But Linux will do virtually anything you can do with any other computer system better, faster, more economically and more reliably. It literally makes better use of your PC hardware. And yes, power does imply education and responsibility, and that is the purpose of this book, to get you rolling to where you are comfortable learning more on your own.

Mark Bolzern is the president and founder of General Computer Services, a consulting, systems integrator, and Unix and Clipper development house. Mark is a certified systems administrator on Novell and LAN Manager and on several versions of Unix, and is considered one of the founders of the Internet because of his pioneering work with communications protocols and ArpaNet. Mark is also President of WorkGroup Solutions, which distributes FlagShip, a full implementation of CA-Clipper on Unix, and Linux Pro, a low-cost PC version of Unix.

INTRODUCTION

ABOUT THIS BOOK

T his book is about Linux, a version of Unix that runs on ordinary personal computers. It's for people who want to learn the basics of installing and using Linux (and thereby Unix) without getting bogged down in too much detail or technobabble.

To be sure, there are other Linux books on the shelf. But you'll find this one is unique because it's short and to the point. Oddly enough, most computer books seem to be written for people who already understand the topic. This book has been carefully crafted and edited so that both the novice and the more experienced computer user will get what they want—Linux on their PC with a minimum of fuss, and the know-how to use it effectively.

Because Unix is the foundation for much of the Internet, many people are using or encountering it nowadays. As the Internet grows, Unix will become more popular, creating an array of new opportunities. If you're simply curious, looking to gain new job skills, or thinking about Linux as a low-cost platform for operating your own Internet server, this book is for you.

WHAT'S INSIDE

You'll find plain-English information here about installing Linux on a personal computer and using it productively. After a brief history and overview of Linux (which happens to be pronounced "LIHN-ucks" and not "LINE-ucks"), the book provides a concise and occasionally light-hearted treatment of

- File systems

- Useful commands

- Text editors

- E-mail tools

- Data manipulation

- Shell programming

- Internet access and tools

- Running your own Linux Web server

The CD-ROM accompanying this book contains **Linux Pro 4.1a** from Workgroup Solutions. Linux Pro (an enhanced version of Red Hat Linux) was selected because it's the most stable Linux product on the market, is very easy to install, and requires minimal configuration.

WHAT'S SO GREAT ABOUT LINUX PRO?

Linux is a superb operating system, no matter which brand you choose. What makes Linux Pro different is the fact that the latest is not always the greatest—often a slightly older product shows the benefits of a longer testing period: it has greater stability and cleaner, more bug-free code. Linux Pro's emphasis on ease of use and installation makes it clear that this is not some thrown-together, public-domain CD.

The Linux Pro CD offers thousands of pages of additional documentation, including the complete electronic version of the *Linux Encyclopedia*, which is also available in print form. (See the catalog pages at the back of this book.)

WHAT IS LINUX?

Linux is a variety of Unix, developed primarily by Linus Torvalds of the University of Helsinki in Finland, and first made publicly available in 1991. News of Linux spread quickly over the Internet, and many other Unix programmers joined the effort to enhance it. Today it is a complete and reliable implementation of the Unix operating system, with the following notable features:

- 32-bit operation (uses all the speed and power of your CPU, unlike 16-bit DOS systems)

- Virtual memory (can use all of your system's RAM; there's no 640K memory limit)

- Fully supports X Window (Unix's standard graphical user interface)

- Supports TCP/IP Networking (allowing connection to the Internet)
- Offers GNU software support (including a huge amount of free Unix software from the GNU Project)

■ **NOTE:** *GNU is one of those recursive acronyms that computer scientists love, and stands for "GNU's Not UNIX." The GNU Project is an effort sponsored by the Free Software Foundation to provide freely available Unix software. See Appendix C for related information.*

Most flavors of Unix require an expensive, high-powered workstation, but Linux is unique in that it runs on personal computers (Intel-based 386, 486, or Pentium machines) and was written totally from scratch without using any of the original AT&T UNIX code. Throughout this book, "UNIX" refers to the original trademarked UNIX invented by AT&T. The term "Unix" is used as a generic term for other variants of the operating system.

Because of that (and because the author is a nice guy), Linux is free. Appendix C has more details on the GNU General Public License—the terms under which Linux may be distributed—but the gist of it is this: you can modify and sell or give away the software as long as you provide full source code and don't impose any restrictions on what others do with it.

WHAT YOU NEED TO USE THIS BOOK

Although it's not essential, a working knowledge of DOS will help you grasp the concepts in this book. You don't need to be a hacker to use Linux, but it is an operating system, and they can be technically challenging. Still, the book aims to provide enough background for most people to tackle just about any Linux problem they may encounter.

A REALLY BRIEF HISTORY OF UNIX

Sometime in the mid-sixties a bunch of geeks at AT&T Bell Labs decided it would be fun to create a new operating system called Multics. (This was no small task, because computers at the time were about the size of a football field and two stories high.) Multics fizzled in 1969 when Bell cut the cord, but some of the geeks continued work on what became known as UNIX; and it became wildly popular inside AT&T.

Since AT&T was not allowed to sell computer software at the time, it gave away UNIX (complete with source code) to any educational institution that would have it. AT&T produced new versions of UNIX called System III and System V in the early eighties, but all the while, geeks at the University of California at Berkeley and other places were busy hacking away on their own versions of Unix based on the AT&T code. Some cross-pollination did occur, but there are still significant differences between the Berkeley (commonly called BSD Unix) and AT&T flavors. In the early 90's, AT&T sold UNIX to Novell, but today it is owned by SCO (Santa Cruz Operation) and marketed as UNIXWare.

Today, there are lots of Unix variants sold or given away by many different companies and universities. While these various flavors can make it difficult to write portable Unix software, efforts to standardize Unix (two of the more notable ones being POSIX and COSE) offer hope for greater compatibility in the future.

Like any operating system, Unix has some cryptic commands and less-than-intuitive aspects. (Three of the most important Unix commands have the peculiar names of *cat, grep,* and *awk*.) Either serious hallucinogens or a warped sense of humor came into play at some point in the creation of Unix. I don't let this bother me, though, taking comfort in my favorite platitude: "Unix was written by geeks on drugs." Seriously, though, Unix is really no more difficult to learn than DOS or Windows—it's just different.

UH, WHAT'S AN OPERATING SYSTEM?

In order for a computer to do anything useful, it needs both application software (programs you use) and an operating system (programs the computer uses). The operating system sits between the physical hardware that makes up a computer (the monitor, keyboard, CPU, hard drive, and so forth) and the end-user software that people use to process documents, play games, and all that good stuff.

My brother Tom and I are both into computers. We're computer programmers by trade, but I'm quick to point out that we produce very different kinds of software. The difference, as I like to explain it, is this: I write software for people, Tom writes software for computers.

We commonly think of the CPU as the brain of a computer, but in reality it can't do much besides crunch numbers and move data around in the computer's memory. The job of the operating system (OS) is twofold:

1. To work with computer hardware to process user requests by

   - Interpreting keystrokes from the keyboard

   - Displaying images on screen

   - Storing files on the hard disk

   - Sending documents to a printer

   - Communicating over a modem

2. To manage the application software's use of memory (RAM) and processor time.

If you've used a multitasking environment like Windows or a multiuser mainframe system, you've seen the concept of "time-slicing" in action. While your computer has only one CPU, which can do only one thing at a time, the OS can make it seem like several people or programs are using the CPU simultaneously. Similarly, even though the real memory (RAM) is shared by all the running applications, the OS can make it seem like you have it all at your disposal, all the time, by sharing it between applications—a technique called *paging*.

The OS time-slices by giving one user or application exclusive use of the hardware for a brief instant, and then doing the same for the next user or application. On systems with adequate horsepower, this approach works so you never even know about that little game of round-robin going on behind the scenes. On a wimpy computer or a mainframe with too many users, it's toe-tappin' time for everybody.

WHERE AM I?

In this introduction to Linux, you've learned the basic tasks of an operating system and how it differs from application software. You're now an expert on Unix history, you understand that Linux is a version of Unix for ordinary PCs, and you can even pronounce it correctly. You don't have a clue about hardware requirements or installation, but that's coming next.

INSTALLING LINUX ON YOUR PC

N ow that you've had a bit of history, it's time for the real fun—installing the Linux operating system on your own personal computer. This chapter assumes that you have a PC currently running some version of DOS, but installing Linux is going to be very different from installing a new DOS or Windows software package. There will be no pointing, clicking, or hand-holding installation programs to guide you through the process. And most important, when you've finished you'll be booting up something entirely different from the DOS-based system you've grown to know and, uh, tolerate.

ABOUT THE CD-ROM

The version of Linux provided on the CD-ROM accompanying this book is Linux Pro 4.1a from Workgroup Solutions. There are many distributions of Linux available, but I chose Linux Pro because it's the most stable and by far the easiest to install.

Other versions of Linux require you to create one or more floppy disks and reboot your system to start the installation. Linux Pro installs directly from the CD-ROM with one simple command. You will have a fully functioning Internet-ready Linux system with a graphical user interface. All the arcane file system, graphical user interface (GUI), and network configuration is done automatically—not the case with other Linux versions.

SAYONARA, DOS?

You'll be running Linux (Unix for your PC), but you can take comfort in the knowledge that your DOS system is still available in case you ever want to return from the Land of Grep and Awk. (These are two Linux commands that sound weird, but are quite useful. You'll learn about them in Chapter 4, "Important Linux Commands"). In fact, you can even access your DOS files directly from Linux, and in some cases run DOS or Windows programs under Linux.

In Chapter 12, "Linux Does DOS and Windows," I'll show you how to keep in touch with DOS while running Linux.

WHAT HARDWARE WILL I NEED?

You don't need an expensive state-of-the-art monster machine to run Linux. Almost any PC with a 386, 486, or Pentium processor will do nicely. That's because Linux, unlike other Unix flavors, is not a disk-chomping, memory-swilling CPU hog. It runs quite happily on a 386SX with 4MB of memory and a 40MB hard drive. Of course it will run faster on a 200-MHz Pentium with 32MB of RAM and a gigabyte hard drive, but that's your choice — you can get to work in a Yugo or a Cadillac.

It's a pretty safe bet that your PC will run Linux if you've already got DOS installed and working, but not every piece of hardware is supported by Linux. Here are the major system components, in terms of compatibility and requirements.

CPU	Intel 80386, 80486, Pentium, or the AMD/Cyrix variants (that is, almost any 386 or better); Linux will emulate a math coprocessor if one is not present; IBM PS/2 (Micro Channel) machines are not supported yet.
Video	Almost any VGA/SVGA card that works with DOS is acceptable.
Floppy	A 3.5-inch floppy drive is required.
Hard Disk	Most MFM, RLL, IDE, and SCSI drives/controllers are supported; a minimum of 200MB of free space is required for the install detailed here, but 300MB is more reasonable for serious usage.
Memory	Minimum 4MB of RAM required, but more memory dramatically improves performance; mixing SIMMs of various speeds (that is, 60ns, 70ns) can cause problems.
CD-ROM	Almost any IDE- or SCSI-based CD-ROM drive will work.
Modem	Required if you want to connect to or host Internet services. The faster the better, but 14.4 Kbps or better is recommended.

- **NOTE:** The **Hardware HOWTO** file for Linux in Appendix B has a more detailed listing of specific devices known to be supported or incompatible. (You should also look on the Internet at http://sunsite. unc.edu/mdw/HOWTO/ to find the latest version of this file and a complete collection of Linux HOWTO files.)

If you don't have a spare PC lying dormant in the closet that fits the bill for your Linux machine, the type of machine you should get depends on whether you want to run Linux for business or pleasure. If you're just experimenting with Linux for fun, you can probably find an old 386 in the classifieds for well under $500. If you're planning on running a busy Web site, a high-end Pentium will set you back about $2000.

The important thing to remember when choosing your Unix machine is that the more RAM you have, the better your system's performance will be. And since memory prices have fallen so much recently, don't skimp.

INSTALLATION IN TEN EASY STEPS

That's it for the preliminaries. Here's an overview of the ten-step installation process you will follow to get up and running with Linux on your PC. It's a good idea to understand what's coming, and to know about the possible gotchas before you start anything so drastic as installing a new operating system, so please read through to the end of this chapter before you begin the process. Trust me, you'll be glad you did!

Here are the steps in brief:

Step 1:   Repartition your hard disk with DOS **FDISK**.

Step 2:   Start the installation with the **INSTALL** command.

Step 3:   Use **cfdisk** to create swap and root partitions.

Step 4:   Define your host name.

Step 5:   Select Linux components to install.

Step 6:   Configure X Window.

Step 7:   Copy Linux files from the CD-ROM to the hard drive.

Step 8:   Configure hardware for Linux.

Step 9:   Install LILO.

Step 10:   Shut down and reboot.

■ *NOTE: You may run into a number of pitfalls during your installation due to quirky hardware, careless keystrokes, or failure to follow these instructions closely. But you can' t really hurt anything if the installation isn' t successful. If you have trouble with your installation, you can always start over and try it again.(If you get really stuck, see Chapter 13, "Learning More About Linux," which lists people and places on the Internet that you can turn to for help.)*

REPARTITION YOUR HARD DISK

Since you're running DOS, it's a given that your hard disk has at least one partition. (A partition is simply a division of your hard disk.) And unless you're very adventurous, it's almost a sure bet that your hard disk has a single DOS partition that occupies the entire disk. Since you need partitions to install multiple operating systems on a single hard disk, you'll have to change the current partitioning of your disk so that there is room for a new partition (or two) for Linux.

Note that in this step you will *not* be creating any Linux partitions, though you will use a DOS utility to reduce the size of an existing partition. (You'll use a Linux utility later to create the Linux partitions.)

You can use two tools to reduce the size of your partition. Which one you choose depends on how much you value the existing data on your DOS disk, and whether or not you're a gambler at heart.

FDISK

The **FDISK** command, which comes with DOS, is the official disk partitioning tool. But since it can't change the size of a partition, it makes you delete your existing partition before it will re-create it as a smaller one. Unfortunately, this means you lose all the data on the disk, so you'll need to do a full backup and restore (along with reinstalling DOS) if you use **FDISK**. **FDISK** is a nuisance, but it works.

FIPS

The alternate utility, **FIPS** (which you'll find in the **install/FIPS** directory on the CD-ROM), can resize an existing partition without deleting it, but it's a "use at your own risk" program. Have a look at the **FIPS** documentation and give it a try if you feel comfortable with it. **FIPS** has been around for several years and is said to be very reliable, but don't call me or my publisher if you choose to use **FIPS** and something screws up.

Regardless of the utility you choose, the amount of space you leave for your Linux partitions will depend on the size of your hard disk, how much space is currently occupied, and how you intend to use Linux. I recommend that you devote 300MB or more to Linux, but you can slide by with only 100MB if space is tight.

■ **NOTE:** *The installation outlined in this chapter requires about 190MB of hard disk space and is the basis of future chapters, so I recommend you follow it pretty closely. If you don' t have that much space available, you can omit the X Window components (about 75MB), but you' ll have a Linux system with no GUI. You could also skip the Emacs and Games components (about 20MB) if you wish, but everything else is mandatory.*

In the example that follows, we'll start with a 300MB hard disk, reduce the DOS partition to 50MB, and use the remaining 250MB for Linux.

If you choose to use **FDISK,** do this:

■ **NOTE:** *This process assumes that you are starting with only one partition. If you have multiple partitions, keep in mind that you don' t necessarily have to delete and re-create all of them. If you have two partitions, you can probably whack a piece off the second one and leave the primary partition untouched. You should leave the unallocated space at the end of your disk for use by Linux.*

1. Back up your hard drive.

2. Create a bootable DOS floppy with the **FORMAT A: /S** command and copy **FDISK.EXE** and **FORMAT.COM** to it.

3. Insert the floppy and restart your system. The computer should boot from the floppy instead of the hard disk. If it doesn't, you may have to fiddle with your machine's CMOS parameters so that it will boot from the floppy first. Typically you can change these settings by pressing the DEL key just after turning on your machine. (See your system manual for help.)

4. Use the **FDISK** utility to delete the existing partition and create a smaller one. (**FDISK** is pretty straightforward, but you should refer to your DOS manual if you've never used it before.)

5. Use the **FORMAT C: /S** command to format the new partition.

6. Finally, restore your hard drive using the backup from step 1. (You did make a backup, right?)

START THE LINUX INSTALLATION WITH THE INSTALL COMMAND

Now that you've partitioned your hard disk, you're ready to begin the Linux Pro installation process. To do so, exit from Windows to the DOS prompt, insert the CD, and enter these commands:

```
D:      (assumes your CD-ROM drive is D)
INSTALL
```

You'll be greeted by a friendly menu-based utility that will guide you through the installation process. **INSTALL** will ask you some questions about your hardware in this start-up phase—here's how to respond. When **INSTALL** says

```
Do you want to use D: as your CD-ROM drive?
```

answer **yes**. (It could say E: or F:, depending on your system setup. That's OK.)

```
Select SCSI Device   (0=None, 1=Adaptec, 2=Buslogic . . .)
```

If you have a SCSI hard drive controller, choose your vendor; otherwise, answer 0.

```
Select Ethernet device (0=None ...)
```

If you have an Ethernet (LAN) card, choose your vendor, otherwise, answer 0. Most people will have a modem instead of an Ethernet card.

```
Select CD-ROM device:
```

Choose your CD-ROM vendor. Your CD-ROM may not be one of the listed choices, but the vendor documentation will tell you if it's compatible with one of them.

Choices for CD-ROM:

If you selected IDE/ATAPI/SCSI above, and you have an IDE drive, choose the **2nd IDE drive** option. Otherwise, choose the **SCSI CD-ROM drive** option. If you selected Panasonic/Matsushita or Sound Blaster, choose the **/dev/spbcd** option.

Do you want to specify any special parameters?

Answer **no**. Let the autoprobe feature determine your CD-ROM drive specs.

Do you want to boot Linux with this configuration?

Answer **yes**. Linux will start and a whole bunch of stuff will flash across the screen. After a minute or two, you'll be prompted to press OK to continue.

Color Yes/No?

Answer **yes** if you have a color monitor, otherwise **no**.

Text or X-based Install

Use the **Text** install option.

CREATE SWAP AND ROOT PARTITIONS

virtual memory

You're now ready to create those Linux partitions on your hard disk that we discussed earlier. Linux uses the swap partition to simulate physical memory (installed RAM), in much the same way that Windows or a Mac uses a chunk of hard drive space to create virtual memory.

physical memory

You need a minimum of 16MB of RAM to run Linux, so if you have less than 16MB of physical memory installed, you have to make up the difference with a swap partition. For example, if you have only 6MB of RAM, you'll need to create a *swap partition* that is at least 10MB in size. In fact, if you have the room on your hard disk, create a 16MB swap partition even if you have 16MB of RAM. (16MB is the maximum size allowed for a swap partition.) The more memory you can muster, the faster Linux will perform.

Once you've created the swap partition, leave the rest of the hard disk for the *root partition*—the portion of your hard disk where all the rest of your files (personal as well as operating system) will be stored.

CREATING THE ROOT PARTITION   Answer **yes** when asked if you need to partition your disk, and the **INSTALL** program will give you the choice of using either **fdisk** or **cfdisk** to create your Linux partitions. Choose the **cfdisk** option. After starting **cfdisk**, confirm that you want to partition the **/dev/hda** disk (or **/dev/sda**, for SCSI hard drives), and you'll see the current partition table. (The actual numbers you get will be different, because this example assumes a 300MB hard disk with an existing DOS partition of 50MB.)

Name	Flags	Part Type	FS Type	Size(MB)
/dev/hda1	Boot	Primary	DOS 16-bit	50
		Pri/Log	Free Space	250

Highlight the **Pri/Log** entry with the cursor keys. Select **NEW** and then **PRIMARY** from the menu at the bottom of the screen to create a new partition, specifying a size of 234MB. (Remember, we need 16MB for the swap partition.) Select **BEGINNING** and then **BOOTABLE** from the menu to finish creating the root partition, and the partition table will appear as below:

Name	Flags	Part Type	FS Type	Size(MB)
/dev/hda1	Boot	Primary	DOS 16-bit	50
/dev/hda2	Boot	Primary	Linux	234
		Pri/Log	Free Space	16

CREATING THE SWAP PARTITION   Great, you've created a second partition (called **/dev/hda2**) for your root file system. Now you'll create a third partition for the swap space. Highlight the **Pri/Log** entry with the cursor keys. Select **NEW** and then **PRIMARY** from the menu at the bottom of the screen to create a new partition, specifying a size of 16MB. Now select **TYPE** and choose **82** to indicate this partition is a Linux swap partition. You have finished partitioning, so your partition table will look like this now:

Name	Flags	Part Type	FS Type	Size(MB)
/dev/hda1	Boot	Primary	DOS 16-bit	50
/dev/hda2	Boot	Primary	Linux	234
/dev/hda3		Primary	Linux Swap	16

■ *NOTE: When you do this on your own, the numbers may be different if you don't have a 300MB disk, or you might choose to leave more or less space for your DOS partition.*

Finish your work in **cfdisk** by selecting **WRITE** and then **QUIT** from the menu. After exiting from **cfdisk**, you'll return to the **INSTALL** utility. Select the **Done with partitioning** option and then select **Continue** (don't reboot now).

■ *NOTE: Don't alter or delete the /dev/hda1 partition with cfdisk. That's your DOS partition, so touching it with a Linux utility would not be safe.*

PREPARE THE SWAP SPACE

Continuing with the installation process, **INSTALL** will ask you to confirm that **/dev/hda3** (or **/dev/sda3** for SCSI) is your swap partition. Check the box to confirm, and Linux will format and prepare the swap space for use.

You've just increased the amount of your system's available RAM by creating a 16MB pool of virtual memory in the swap space. And you didn't have to spend a penny or install new SIMMs!

DEFINE YOUR HOST NAME

network setup

INSTALL will now ask if you'd like to configure for Ethernet TCP/IP networking. If you don't have an Ethernet card, you don't want to. This discussion assumes you're going to connect a stand-alone PC to the Internet with a modem, not a LAN. If your machine is part of an office LAN, check with your local network guru to get the correct IP addresses for the Ethernet setup.

You do need to choose a host name for your system, though. Enter **fritz.com** for now, you can always go back and change the host name later if you think of one you like better.

SELECT THE COMPONENTS TO INSTALL

At this point you've created a root partition to store all of your Linux files, but it's empty. You still need a file system (the physical structure and organization of files on the disk) and a bunch of files to get Linux rolling.

Press the Spacebar to check the box next to **/dev/hda2** (or **/dev/sda2** for SCSI), then press **OK** and **yes,** and Linux will format the file system. This can take several minutes, so keep your hands off the keyboard until the next prompt appears.

Now that you've created the file system, it's time to start putting some files in it. **INSTALL** will show you a long list of packages you can select, each of which is an optional part of the Linux system. Some will be preselected, but make sure you've selected the following packages:

- Applications (15.0MB)

- DOS Compatibility (2.0MB)

- Documentation (6.7MB)

- Emacs (13.7MB)

- Games (6.4MB)

- Mail (6.7MB)

- Multimedia (1.3MB)

- Network Administration (1.6MB)

- Networking (2.1MB)

- Network Servers (4.8MB)

- Printing (0.3MB)

- Serial Communications (2.3MB)

- X Applications (17.2MB)

- X Games (13.6MB)

- X Window (46.3MB)

This will require just under 200MB of hard disk space. As mentioned earlier, you can skip the "X" packages but you won't get the X Window GUI, plus some nifty system configuration tools. If you're a programmer and some of the other packages look interesting, go ahead and select them if you know you have enough disk space. You can always install additional packages later with the **rpm** (text-based) or **glint** (X Window–based) utilities. Press **OK** when you've finished making your selections.

■ *NOTE: INSTALL does not handle a "disk full" condition very well. Instead of exiting gracefully with an explanatory message, it will give you vague "Could not create file" messages over and over, and you'll wind up with an unusable Linux system. It's best to install just the minimum set shown above unless you're certain you have enough space.*

CONFIGURE X WINDOW

INSTALL will now ask what type of graphics card you have in your PC. If you know that you have a specific card such as a Mach32, IBM 8514, or S3, choose it from the list. If you don't know, select either Generic VGA or Generic SVGA, depending on the type of monitor you have. In most cases Generic SVGA will produce the best results, but if you have an older system and you're not sure if it's Super VGA, go with Generic VGA.

INSTALL LINUX FROM CD-ROM TO HARD DISK

We're finally ready for the actual installation of the Linux files to your hard disk. **INSTALL** will ask if you want the option to confirm each package before it is installed. Unless you really know what you're doing, say **no** to this prompt.

A window that looks something like this will appear as the files are copied from the CD-ROM to your hard disk:

```
+------------- Package Installation -----------+
|   Installing: <name of package>              |
|   Package #: 1 of 261                        |
|   *************** 10% *****************       |
+----------------------------------------------+
```

When all the selected packages have been copied, you'll see the message `Package Installation is Complete`. Press **OK** to continue.

CONFIGURE YOUR HARDWARE FOR LINUX

INSTALL will now take you through a series of questions about your hardware in order to configure each device for use with Linux. You'll need to know the following:

• **What type of mouse?**	Probably Microsoft Serial
• **Which port is the mouse on?**	Probably COM1
• **What type of monitor?**	Use "Generic Monitor" if unsure
• **What port is the modem on?**	Probably COM2
• **Type of system clock?**	Probably "Local"
• **Your time zone?**	Can't help you there, sorry
• **Type of keyboard?**	Probably "US"

autoprobe

INSTALL will also ask if you want to "autoprobe" to get the video card settings. Go for it, and say **yes** to all the findings. (Unless you built your own video card from molten silicon, you probably won't know the difference.) INSTALL will ask again if you want to configure for Ethernet networking. Say **no** again.

INSTALL LILO—THE LINUX LOADER

LILO

Next, **INSTALL** will ask if you want to install LILO. You do. LILO (the Linux Loader) lets you boot Linux directly from the hard disk when you power on your PC. Without LILO, you have to create a special floppy disk and boot Linux from it, which is slow and inconvenient.

■ *NOTE: Once you've installed LILO, your system will no longer boot up DOS by default when you power on. But at least LILO is nice enough to give you a choice. Just hold down the C**TRL** key during the boot, and LILO will display a prompt that lets you select which operating system to start.*

Specify that LILO is to be installed on the **/dev/hda** (or **/dev/sda**) disk, and answer **no** to the question about adding parameters. When **INSTALL** asks if you want to select another operating system to start, say **yes** and pick **/dev/hda1** (or **/dev/sda1**) to indicate your DOS partition.

SHUT DOWN AND REBOOT

You're almost at the finish line. **INSTALL** will ask if you want to create any new user accounts. Say **no** (we'll cover that in another chapter). **INSTALL** will also tell you to enter a new password for the **root** user account, but at least on my computer, the prompt never appears. No big deal—you'll learn how to change passwords later.

When you get the `Install complete: Reboot?` message, remove any floppies from the disk drive and select OK. A bunch of messages will show various systems shutting down, and then you'll boot up into your grand and glorious new Linux system.

MOUNTING YOUR CD-ROM DRIVE

After you reboot your system, you'll most likely want to access files on the installation CD or some other CD-ROM disk, either to view some of the helpful documentation found there, or to install additional software packages. But before you can access the CD-ROM drive, you have to mount it. Mounting means you assign a physical device (the CD-ROM) to a directory on your hard disk.

You can mount your CD-ROM drive with a command like this:

```
mount -t iso9660 XXXXX /mnt/cdrom
```

Before you issue that command, you must substitute the device name of your CD-ROM for *XXXXX*. The information below will help you select the correct device name.

CD-ROM TYPE	DEVICE NAME
IDE on Controller 0	/dev/hda or /dev/hdb
IDE on Controller 1	/dev/hdc or /dev/hdd
SCSI Interface	/dev/scd0 or /dev/scd1
Sound Blaster or compatible	/dev/sbpcd

Check your manual to determine what type of CD-ROM drive you have. If you have an IDE drive, either your CD manual or your IDE controller manual will tell you what controller is in use for the CD-ROM drive. (The most common one will be **/dev/hdc**.)

Be especially careful to check the manual if you have a Sound Blaster CD. Some are actually IDE, and some IDE drives are configured to use controller 3. If this is the case, refer to the manual for instructions on how to change the controller, since Linux will not find a CD unless it is on controller 0 or 1. (It's a matter of fooling with the jumpers on the controller card to which your CD is connected.)

ACCESSING FILES ON THE CD-ROM   After you issue the **mount** command, list the files on the CD-ROM to see if the mount worked, using these commands:

```
cd /mnt/cdrom          Switch to the CD directory.
ls                     List the files on the CD.
```

If you try a device name in the mount command and get an error, or your **ls** command doesn't show any files, just pick another device name and try again—you won't hurt anything.

For now, just be happy if you can list the files on the CD-ROM. In Chapter 3, "The Linux File System," you'll learn more about navigating directories, as well as listing and viewing files.

MAKE AN EMERGENCY DISK

Just in case you ever have trouble booting up your Linux system, you should have an emergency Linux boot disk on hand. This will allow you to boot the system using a floppy disk, and access the files on your Linux partition.

After mounting the CD-ROM, you can create the emergency disk like this:

```
cd /mnt/cdrom/images
./mkfloppies.pl
```

Oh, don't forget to put a nice new floppy in the A: drive first, and remove it afterward.

LIVING IN A SHELL

Logging In

Bash (and Other Shells)

Linux Commands

I n order to use Linux—or any Unix-like system, for that matter—
you need to know a few things about shells. A *shell* is a program
that acts as an intermediary between you and the guts of the operating system. In a DOS environment, **COMMAND.COM** acts as your shell.
Linux shells have more interesting names (like **bash, pdksh,** and **tcsh**)
but they do pretty much the same thing. In addition to translating your
commands into something the kernel can understand and act upon,
the shell adds some important functions the base operating system
doesn't supply.

what does a shell do?

Using a Linux shell means working with a command line, which is
much like working from a DOS prompt. There is a GUI for Linux called
X Window that's similar to the Microsoft Windows–Windows 95 interface (see Chapter 7, "The X Window System"), but some Linux tasks
can only be done from the command line. The knowledge of how Linux
works that you'll gain in this chapter will lay the foundation for using
Linux successfully and efficiently. Here's a description of the basic features of all Linux shells, a preview of the functions they perform, and a
rundown on what you'll learn in this chapter.

PROMPTS   A *prompt* is a character or string of characters (such
as **$** or **#**) that the shell displays when it is ready to receive a new
command. You'll learn about the different types of prompts, and
how to customize them to suit you and the way you work.

COMMAND RESOLUTION   When you enter a command, the shell
must determine which program to run in order to perform that
command. You'll learn how shells do this, and how to change the
command resolution process to suit your needs.

multitasking

JOB CONTROL   Linux lets you multitask (run more than one command at a time). You'll learn how to start, list, and stop tasks; and
understand the difference between foreground and background
task execution.

COMMAND HISTORY AND COMPLETION   When you're entering lots
of commands, sometimes you want to repeat the previous command or issue a similar one. You'll learn how to recall and modify
previously entered commands, as well as find out about some
keyboard shortcuts that can automatically complete your commands for you.

WILD CARDS AND ALIASES Wild cards let you process a whole bunch of files at once, instead of repeating the same command for each file. You'll learn how to use two types of wild cards, and how to create aliases for commonly used commands.

PIPING AND I/O REDIRECTION Sending the output of one program directly to another program or to a file can save you time and keystrokes. You'll learn how to pipe program output, and how to make a program get its input from a file instead of the keyboard.

This chapter will look at each one of these functions in detail and teach you how to use them to your advantage. But first—a few shell preliminaries.

LOGGING IN

Unlike DOS, Linux is a multiuser operating system. This means you have to log in before you can use it. When you log in, you're automatically placed in the **bash** shell.

superusers

When you installed Linux you logged in as **root**. The **root** user account is called a *superuser* because it has powers far beyond those of mortal users (and it's not even affected by kryptonite). As **root**, you can access files and change the system in ways other users cannot. But you can also wipe out your entire hard drive in just ten keystrokes.

Unless you plan to install new software or tweak your system, you should log in to Linux as a user other than **root**. Problem is, assuming you've followed the steps I've outlined so far, at this juncture there *are* no other accounts. We'll use the superuser account to change that.

EX NIHILO: ADDING NEW USERS

In the Linux universe, new users do not evolve—they are created by a benevolent superuser. To add a new user account, log in to the **root** account and enter a command like the one below. There's no limit to the number of new users you can add.

`adduser hermie`

After using the **adduser** command, you mut assign a password to the new account before it can be used.

Use this command to set the password:

```
passwd hermie
```

and enter the initial password for **hermie** when prompted.

WHAT VIRTUAL CONSOLES ARE GOOD FOR

Remember that bit about multiple log-ins? While you may not have more than one physical console (a monitor plus a keyboard) connected to your PC, you can use virtual consoles to log in simultaneously to more than one account on your system.

console swapping

You can use virtual consoles to perform two activities in parallel. For example, I used one virtual console to write this chapter, and another to test out the commands as they were introduced. You can even use your mouse to cut and paste text from one virtual console to another. When you start your Linux system and get the log-in prompt, you're looking at console number one. Go ahead and log in as **root** here, then press **ALT-F2**. You should then see another log-in prompt. You can log in as user **hermie** on this console, and then press **ALT-F3** to access a third console, or press **ALT-F1** to return to the first console.

Virtual consoles come in particularly handy if you have a long-running task to perform, like installing a big software package from a CD-ROM—you can pop over to another console and log in again to stay productive while your CD-ROM churns away.

■ *NOTE: You don't have to use a different user account for each console. Linux lets you log in to an account multiple times simultaneously.*

By default, your Linux system already has a bunch of virtual consoles waiting in the wings when you start your system, and pressing **ALT-F***n* at any time will bring the *n*th one up on your screen. (You can also cycle through the consoles with **ALT-LT ARROW** or **ALT-RT ARROW**.)

Multitasking under Linux isn't really much different from having multiple windows active in a Windows 95 or Macintosh system. The major difference is that if you've started multiple consoles, you can only see one at a time on screen, though the others are still working away behind the scenes.

■ **NOTE:** *If you're running Linux in the X Window environment (a GUI for Linux that I'll discuss later), there's no need for virtual consoles because you can have many windows active and visible on the screen.*

STOP THE SYSTEM, I WANT TO GET OFF!

If you're ready to cash in your console and call it a day, use the **logout** command. Entering

```
logout
```

at the command prompt exits your current user account and returns you to the log-in prompt. (To log out from multiple consoles, use **ALT-F***n* to switch between consoles, and then log out from each one.) But note that even if you log out from all of your active consoles, Linux is still running.

shutdown Linux the right way!

If you were to power off your machine at this point, a voice from your computer would drone "You have chosen *unwisely!*" The floor would shake and your PC would glow white hot while your hard disk melted into a pool of molten silicon. Just kidding . . . sometimes the floor doesn't shake, but powering off a running Linux system without using the **shutdown** command will most certainly cause Bad Things to happen to your hard disk. So if you really want to exit Linux, be sure that you're logged in as the **root** user, and enter the command

```
shutdown -h now
```

You'll see some messages indicating that various subsystems are being shut down, and then the computer will reset. When you see a message indicating that shutdown is complete, it's safe to turn off your PC. (Pressing **CTRL-ALT-DELETE** will also safely shut down your system. Just remember to power off as soon as you see your PC's normal bootup screen.)

BASH (AND OTHER SHELLS)

The default Linux shell, **bash**, is popular and offers lots of advanced features. It combines many of the niceties found in the Bourne shell (the original **UNIX** shell) and other modern shells.

But there are alternatives. The KORN shell is popular among many Unix users because it offers a rich scripting (programming) facility. Korn is commercial software, but there is a public domain (free) version for Linux called **pdksh**. Another shell that's popular with C language programmers is the C shell, which exists for Linux as **tcsh**.

The CD-ROM that comes with this book provides both **pdksh** and **tcsh**, and you can try them out by entering their names at your shell prompt. If you decide to make a permanent switch to something other than the default **bash** shell, you must log in as **root** and edit the entry for your user ID in the **/etc/passwd** file.

changing shells
Entries in the **/etc/passwd** file look like the example below. Just change **bash** at the end of the line to **pdksh** or **tcsh**, and you're done. (If you're not familiar with Linux-based text editors, see Chapter 5, "Text Editors.")

```
hermie:x:501:1::/home/hermie:/bin/bash
```

Though there are alternatives, I suggest you familiarize yourself with **bash**'s features first, because **bash** is the most commonly used Linux shell. In the rest of this chapter, we'll go over the basics of working in the **bash** shell, so go ahead and log in as user **hermie** now and follow right along. It'll help a lot to enter the commands as you go, experiment with them on your own, and see the actual output.

LINUX COMMANDS

When you enter a command in Linux, you type a command at a prompt and then press **ENTER**. Commands can be more than one word—some require *switches* (which modify the command's behavior) and/or *file names* (which tell the command what data to act on). Let's dissect the command below (your typing is in boldface):

```
$ ls -l sample.doc
```

The **$** is the command prompt (more on prompts later). The command is **ls**, and we have entered the -**l** switch and a file name, **sample.doc**, along with it. You can tell a switch from a file name because switches always start with a minus or plus sign. The **ls** command will accept a variety of optional switches and can operate with or without file names. (The **ls** command lists your files, like the **dir** command in DOS.)

LINUX COMMANDS ARE CASE SENSITIVE

One of the most important things to remember about entering commands in any Unix environment is that case matters. In DOS, you can type **DIR** or **dir** or even **DiR** and get the same result, but not in Linux. Linux will be quite put out if you type **LS** instead of **ls** to list your files. With file names, you have to be even more careful, since nearly identical files (save for capitalization) can exist in the same directory, though they may have completely different contents—**Cookie_Recipe** and **cookie_recipe** would appear as distinctly different files to Linux, though they may look pretty much the same to you except for the capital letters.

using lowercase

The best rule to follow is this: almost everything in Linux is lowercase, so avoid capital letters when naming your files.

COMMAND PROMPTS CAN VARY

When the Linux shell is ready for a command, you see a command prompt. Unlike DOS, which uses only one prompt, Linux's command prompts vary. For example, when you log in as **root**, your command prompt is the pound (#) sign; but if you try another log-in (like **hermie**), the prompt changes to a dollar sign (**$**).

The **bash** shell uses the different prompts to clue you in to your user privileges. Pay attention to the prompts so you don't inadvertently wipe out important files while logged in to the root account with superuser privileges, for example.

su

It's especially important to mind the prompts if you use the **su** (switch user) command, which allows you to act temporarily as the **root** user while you're logged in as a regular user. Watch how the prompt changes in the following example.

```
$ who am i
hermie
$ su root
Enter password for root: xxxxxxx
# who am i
root
# exit
$ who am i
hermie
```

In this example, entering the command **who am i** tells you who the system thinks you are—hermie. Then, using the **su** command with the addition of **root** we switch to the root user (note the prompt change to the pound sign). The **exit** command exits the root user account and brings us back to hermie; the prompt changes back to a dollar sign.

who am i

In this example we used the prompt and the **who am i** command to show the logged-in user, but customizing your prompt is a better way to keep track of where you are.

For example, the command

```
PS1="\u \$ "
```

changes the prompt so that it displays the user name (\u), followed by the dollar sign (or pound sign, if you're a superuser). You can use other characters to insert the current time, date, or working directory (\t, \d, and \w, respectively). Here's how to use these various options:

PS1="\t \$ " gives: `09:15:24 $`

PS1="\u (\d) \$ " gives: `hermie (Wed Nov 4) $`

PS1="\u (\w) \$ " gives: `hermie (/home/hermie) $`

All you're actually doing here is setting the variable **PS1** (prompt string number one) to a special string of characters. The **bash** shell interprets the value of the **PS1** variable each time it's ready to build the prompt string.

In "Environment Variables," later in this chapter, you'll learn more about special variables such as **PS1** and how to set them automatically each time you log in.

WILD CARDS

Wild cards come in handy when you want to perform an operation on a group of files. As with DOS or Windows, if you want to delete all your files that start with "jan" and end with "txt," you can use the asterisk (*****) wild card character, as in **rm jan*txt**, to delete all such files. (**rm** is the command you'll use to delete files.)

The ****** character tells the shell to find any files that begin with "jan" and end with "txt", regardless of the number of characters between. It will even find files with no characters between, like **jantxt**. Thus, a file named **jan-96.txt** would be deleted, as would **jantxt**.

A more restrictive wild card is the question mark (**?**), which matches any single character. Here are some examples of its use:

> **rm jan-8?.txt** deletes jan-81.txt and jan-82.txt, but not jan-89b.txt

> **rm jan-95.???** deletes jan-95.txt and jan-95.dat, but not jan-95.db

When you use wild cards, the shell finds all matching files and expands the command you entered, so the **rm jan-95.*** command would be the same as typing

```
rm jan-95.txt jan-95.dat jan-95.db
```

Programmers Take Note   In Linux, the shell does wildcard interpretation, and the actual commands (programs) never see the wildcard characters. This provides a convenient and common way for all Linux programs to handle wild cards. In DOS, the program (not the shell) must have the intelligence to handle wild cards. The unhappy result is that you never know which DOS commands will accept wild cards, and each program may interpret them differently—yuck!

COMMAND HISTORY AND EDITING

The **bash** shell remembers what commands you've recently entered so that you can recall and issue them again easily. If you press the **Up-Arrow, bash** places the contents of the previous command on the command line. Repeatedly pressing the Up or Down Arrow navigates through the command history; you can even modify the text in the recalled commands with the Lᴛ Aʀʀᴏᴡ and Rᴛ Aʀʀᴏᴡ, as well as the Iɴsᴇʀᴛ and Dᴇʟᴇᴛᴇ keys, before pressing Eɴᴛᴇʀ to issue the recalled command.

COMMAND COMPLETION: LINUX CAN EVEN READ YOUR MIND

If you're a lazy typist, you'll love this feature. Let's say you have a directory containing the following files:

```
cars-are-fun
cats-are-bad
dogs-are-good
birds-have-lips
```

Typing **rm cat** and then pressing the Tᴀʙ key magically expands your command line to

```
rm cats-are-bad
```

matching a file in your current directory that starts with the word *cat*. The shell looks at what you've typed so far, then checks to see if there is a single file that starts with those characters. If there is, the shell finishes typing that file name for you. If there isn't such a file, or if there is more than one, nothing happens.

You still have to press **Eɴᴛᴇʀ**, but if you remember this nifty feature, you can save a lot of keystrokes and pretend that the computer is actually reading your mind!

ALIASES: CREATE MEANINGFUL SYNONYMS FOR COMMANDS

alias

Defining an alias is another way to minimize your work at the keyboard, and it can also eliminate the need to remember long, awkward commands by creating synonyms that are more meaningful to you. Here are some examples:

```
alias dir='ls -l'
alias dogs='find . -name "*dog*" -print'
```

In this example, the first `alias` tells **bash** that when you enter **dir** on the command line, it should actually execute the **ls-l** command instead. If you're a hard-core DOS user, you could use **alias** to create DOS-like synonyms for many Linux commands.

The second `alias` lets you enter **dogs** instead of that long, ugly **find** command shown above. Don't worry about the **ls** and **find** commands right now. Just keep in mind that the **alias** command can save you some keystrokes or make it easier to remember a command.

.profile

Undoubtedly you will find other clever things to do with the **alias** command and add them to your **.profile** file so they will be available each time you log in. Your **.profile** is a file containing a series of commands that **bash** executes automatically when you log in, similar to **AUTOEXEC.BAT** in the DOS world. (The **/etc/profile** works the same, but it acts on a systemwide level, and not just for one user.)

REDIRECT THE INPUT OR OUTPUT OF LINUX COMMANDS

Another useful **bash** feature is its ability to redirect the input and output of Linux commands. You can save the results of a command in a file instead of displaying the results on screen, or conversely feed data from a file to a program instead of entering data from the keyboard.

Let's look at redirection first. Imagine a fictitious command called **nocats** that prompts the user for a number and then waits for that many lines of text to be entered before processing them. (The program looks at each input line and prints only the ones that do not contain the word *cat*.)

You could feed the program by entering the data from the console (bold text is your typed input, normal text is console output):

```
$ nocats
3
Dogs are much better than those other household animals.
A cat would never beg for jerky treats.
Dogs are pretty stupid, but at least they stick around.
Dogs are much better than those other household animals.
Dogs are pretty stupid, but at least they stick around.
```

redirecting input

Or using a text editor, you could put all the input data in a file called **stuff** and feed the **nocats** program like this:

```
% nocats < stuff
Dogs are much better than those other household animals.
Dogs are pretty stupid, but at least they stick around.
```

redirecting output

The less-than (‹) symbol above causes the program to get input from the **stuff** file instead of waiting for keyboard input. The greater-than (›) symbol, on the other hand, redirects output to a file instead of to the console. Thus the command

```
% nocats < stuff > bother
```

will cause the program **nocats** to read its input from one file (**stuff**) and write it to another (**bother**), without the keyboard or console entering the picture. Note that the **nocats** program doesn't know or care about all this redirection. It still thinks it is reading data from the keyboard and writing to the console—but the shell has temporarily reassigned the input and output to files instead of physical devices.

appending a file

To append to an existing file instead of creating a new one, use » as in this example:

```
zippity > somefile
doodah >> somefile
```

The **zippity** command runs first and the output is placed in a new file called **somefile**. Then **doodah** runs and its output is added (appended) to the **somefile** file.

PIPES: PUMP ONE PROGRAM'S OUTPUT INTO ANOTHER PROGRAM

Linux provides you with a wide array of utilities to manipulate data. You can search, sort, slice, dice, and transform data stored in files in many different ways. A *pipe* (also called a pipeline) is a powerful shell feature that allows you to pump the output of one program directly into another.

For example, say you have a file with information about a group of people, including a name, age, ZIP code, and phone number for each person, that looks like this:

```
Roosevelt    Tommy      38      54579    555-1212
Nixon        Edward     19      37583    246-3457
Roosevelt    Freddie    47      11745    674-6972
Lincoln      Albert     26      26452    916-5763
```

If you wanted to find all the Roosevelts and sort them by ZIP code, you could do it like this:

```
grep Roosevelt people.txt > grep.out
sort +3 grep.out
rm grep.out
```

Since I haven't introduced the **grep** and **sort** commands yet, here's an English translation of what's happening above:

> *Look for lines that contain "Roosevelt" in the **people.txt** file and put them in a file named **grep.out**. Then sort the **grep.out** file on the fourth column and display the results on the console before deleting the **grep.out** file. (Yes, it is odd that the "+3" flag tells **sort** to use the fourth column!)*

But you could avoid creating and deleting the intermediate file (**grep.out**) by combining the operation into one command like this:

```
grep Roosevelt people.txt | sort +3
```

The vertical bar (|) tells the shell that the output of the program on the left (**grep**) should become the input for the program on the right (**sort**). Behind the scenes, the shell may be issuing the exact same three commands as in the previous example, but you don't really care—you've combined three commands into one.

You can have any number of steps in a pipeline, and you can even combine pipes with redirection, as shown in the following:

```
grep Roosevelt people.txt | sort +3 > sort-results
```

Here the same thing happens, except that the end result is stored in a file called **sort-results**.

LISTING PROCESSES

ps

Linux is a multitasking operating system, which means that more than one task can be active at once. To find out what tasks are running on your system concurrently, use the command

```
ps -f
```

UID	PID	PPID	STIME	TTY	TIME	COMD
hermie	24	1	00:35:28	tty1	0:01	bash
hermie	137	24	00:36:39	tty1	0:00	ps -f

The previous output shows for each active task the UID (owning user), PID (process ID), PPID (parent process ID), STIME (when it started), TIME (how long it's been active), and COMD (the actual command line used to start the task). If you examine the PIDs and PPIDs, you can see that **bash** invoked the **ps-f** command, because the PPID of the latter matches the PID of the former.

LAUNCHING TASKS IN THE FOREGROUND AND BACKGROUND

Suppose you have a long-running task (for example, compiling a large program) that you need to run, but you also want to get some other work done. Linux lets you start a task in the background and keep on doing other things from the command prompt. By adding the ampersand (**&**) to the end of any command, you can launch it in the background and get your command prompt back right away. For example,

```
gcc hugepgm.c > outlist &
```

will start **gcc** (the C compiler) as a background task, executing in parallel with other tasks on your system.

- *NOTE: It's a good idea to redirect the output of background tasks to a file, as shown above, since the background task still shares the console with foreground tasks. If you don't, the background task will splash any output it might produce all over your screen while you're editing a file or typing another command.*

task termination

CTRL-Z

fg

bg

If you start up a long-running task and forget to add the ampersand, you can still swap that task into the background. Instead of pressing **CTRL-C** (to terminate the foreground task) and then restarting it in the background, just press **CTRL-Z** after the command starts, then type **bg** and press **ENTER**. You'll get your prompt back, and be able to continue with other work. Use the **fg** command to bring a background task to the foreground.

You might wonder why you'd ever want to swap programs between foreground and background, but this is quite useful if you're using a text editor and you need to pop out to the shell prompt, issue a quick command, and go back to editing. From inside the editor, you could press **CTRL-Z**, then enter the **bg** command to put the editor in the background. Do your thing at the shell prompt, and then enter the **fg** command. Presto—your editor reappears on the screen just the way you left it!

STOP THAT TASK!

Although it's unfortunate, some tasks are unruly and must be killed. If you accidentally entered the (fictitious) command

```
seek_and_destroy &
```

you'd have a background task doing potentially nasty things. Pressing the **Ctrl-C** key would have no effect, since it can only terminate a foreground task. Before this rogue eats your system alive, issue the **ps-f** command to find out the process ID (PID) of the seek_and_destroy task.

```
ps -f
```

UID	PID	PPID	STIME	TTY	TIME	COMD
hermie	24	1	00:35:28	tty1	0:01	bash
hermie	1704	24	00:36:39	tty1	0:00	seek_and_destroy

Note that the offender has a PID of 1704, and quickly issue the command

```
kill 1704
```

to terminate the background task.

kill

You can terminate any active task with the **kill** command, which sends a "terminate gracefully" signal to the running task that allows it to do any necessary cleanup, close files, and so on, before giving up the ghost. Occasionally, though, a task will not respond to the **kill** command, either because a program has become disabled or is coded specifically to ignore it. Time for the heavy artillery. Adding the **-9** flag to the **kill** command, as in

```
kill -9 1704
```

basically sends the "die you gravy-sucking pig" signal to the running task, and forces it to shut down immediately without any chance to do cleanup. Use this flag only as a last resort, since it could cause work in progress (by the soon-to-be-killed task) to be lost.

ENVIRONMENT VARIABLES

Environment variables in the **bash** shell help you in several ways. Certain built-in variables change the shell in ways that make your life a little easier, while you can define other variables to suit your own purposes. Here are some examples of built-in shell variables:

PS1 defines the shell's command-line prompt.

HOME is the home directory for a user.

PATH is a list of directories to search through when looking for a command to execute.

To list the current values of all environment variables, issue the command

```
set
```

echo

or list a specific variable with the **echo** command, prefixing the variable name with a dollar sign (the second line shows the result of the **echo** command).

```
echo $HOME
/home/hermie
```

You've already learned how to customize your shell prompt with the PS1 variable. The **HOME** variable is one you shouldn't mess with, because lots of programs count on it to be able to create or find files in your personal home directory.

UNDERSTANDING THE PATH VARIABLE   As in DOS, the shell uses the PATH variable to locate a command. **PATH** contains a list of directories separated by colons.

```
echo $PATH
/bin:/usr/bin:/usr/local/bin
```

the PATH variable

When you enter a command, the shell looks in each of the directories specified in **PATH** to try and find it. If it can't find the command in any of those directories, you'll get a Command not found message.

If you decide to put your own programs in a **bin** directory under your home directory, you'll have to modify the **PATH** to include that directory, or the system will never find them (unless you happen to be in that directory when you enter the command). Here's how to change your **PATH** variable so it includes your personal bin directory:

changing the PATH

```
PATH=$PATH:$HOME/bin
```

So if **PATH** was set to **/bin:/usr/bin:/usr/local/bin** beforehand, it would now have the value **/bin:/usr/bin:/usr/local/bin:/home/hermie/bin**.

CREATING YOUR OWN SHELL VARIABLES   If you are a programmer, you'll find it handy to create your own shell variables. For example, issue the command

```
code=$HOME/projects/src/spew
```

and then, regardless of what directory you are in, you can issue

```
cd $code
```

cd

to pop over quickly to the directory containing the source code for that way-cool spew program you're developing. (The **cd** command means "change directory.")

A variable assignment like this will work just fine, but its scope (visibility) is limited to the current shell. If you launch a program or enter another shell, that child task will not know about your environment variables unless you export them first.

export

Unless you know for sure that an environment variable will have meaning only in the current shell, it's a good idea to always use **export** when creating variables to ensure they will be global in scope—for example:

```
export PS1="\u \$ "
export code=$HOME/projects/src/spew
```

And be sure to add these commands to your **.profile** file so you won't have to retype them each time you log in.

HOW TO GET HELP

man

Need help figuring out what a command is supposed to do? In an operating system with strange-sounding commands like **awk**, **grep**, and **sed**, it's not surprising. The **man** command (short for manual) is a source of online help for most Linux commands. For example, you can enter

```
man grep
```

to learn all the secrets of the very useful **grep** command. (For a summary of the most-used Linux commands, see Chapter 4, "Important Linux Commands.")

If **man** claims no knowledge of the command in which you're interested, try **help** instead. This command will list all the built-in bash commands with a brief syntax summary.

THE LINUX FILE SYSTEM

W hen you installed Linux, one of the first things you did was create a file system. In the process, you carved out a chunk of hard disk and formatted it so that Linux could use it. You also created a hierarchical (treelike) structure for storing files, to impose some order on the file system to help both you and the Linux system find needed files.

file system

In this chapter, you'll learn how to work with files and directories in a Linux system. You'll understand how the file system is structured to separate system data from personal data and how to navigate through it.

When you have finished this chapter, you'll be creating, deleting, copying, renaming, listing, linking, and protecting your files like a pro. You'll also learn the Nine Deadly Keystrokes—or how to wipe out the entire file system without really trying. (But don't worry, this command can only affect you if you're logged in as **root**.)

Log in as **hermie** and try the examples in this chapter as you read through it. You'll find that the Linux file system is a lot like DOS, only more robust and flexible.

WHAT IS A LINUX FILE?

We've created a structured file system and filled it with a whole bunch of files—without knowing what Linux files are. Here's what files are in the Linux world and how they are named.

TYPES OF FILES

files

In most operating systems, a file is simply a blob of data stored on disk with a unique name. A file could be a list of names and numbers, a cheesecake recipe, or an executable program. But under Linux *everything* is a file. In addition to data and executable files, Linux treats directories and even the various components of your computer as files.

devices

This means there are files that represent your keyboard, console, printer, CD-ROM, and even your system's RAM memory. These special files are called *devices*, and are found in the **/dev** directory (see page 50). (If you look in this directory later on you'll see files such as **/dev/fd0** (a floppy drive), **/dev/tty1** (a console), and others you may be able to identify by their names.) When Linux (or any Unix program) needs to talk to a physical hardware device, it does so by simply reading from or writing to one of these special files.

WHAT'S IN A FILE NAME?

Linux file names can be up to 256 characters long, but you really have to enjoy typing to get to that extreme. You can name a file panda-corporation-financial-reports.y96 if you wish, but you'll probably find that shorter names (and intelligent use of directories) will save lots of time and keystrokes in the course of a day.

When naming files, you can use uppercase and lowercase letters, numbers, and certain special characters. It's a really good idea to stick with letters; numbers; and the dash, dot, and underscore characters to avoid trouble and confusion.

avoid special characters

■ **NOTE:** *Don't use asterisks, backslashes, or question marks in Linux file names—these characters have special meaning to the shell and could cause your commands to do something quite different from what you intended. Also avoid using a dash as the first character of a file name, since most Linux commands will treat it as a switch.*

hidden files

Files starting with a dot are "hidden" files. They behave just like any other file, except that the **ls** (list files) command will not display them unless you explicitly request it to do so. Your **.profile** file is an example of a hidden file.

Also remember that Linux file names are case sensitive, which can be difficult to get used to if you have a DOS background. Linux allows you to have unique files named goodstuff, GOODSTUFF, and GoodStuff in the same directory.

It's best to *always* use lower case in Linux unless you can think of a good reason to use upper or mixed case. Most Unix people use lower case almost exclusively, but aside from this "cultural" point, there's another good reason to use lower case. If you're sharing or accessing a DOS file system with Linux, DOS will not be able to see the files that have upper or mixed case file names.

Unlike under DOS, the dot character (.) has no special meaning. You're not limited to the eight-dot-three (*xxxxxxxx.yyy*) style of naming because Linux treats the dot just like any other character. So you can have a file named Some.Yummy.CHEESECAKE.Recipes if you're so inclined.

Along these lines, Linux executables do not need or use a special extension such as EXE or BAT. Linux will happily run a program file named zippity just as readily as it will run DOODAH.EXE.

And here's another slight difference between Linux and DOS file systems. Linux uses the forward slash (/) in path names, while DOS uses the backslash (\). Don't blame this little quirk on Linux though—the DOS file system was originally modeled after Unix!

DIRECTORIES

A Linux *directory* is a special file that acts as a container for other files and even other directories. You can create directories to hold groups of related files as an alternative to keeping all your files in one huge directory. A Linux file system is like a filing cabinet with a bunch of folders, each of which can contain subfolders and/or files.

After installing Linux and creating a new "hermie" user account, you'll end up with a file system hierarchy like the one shown here.

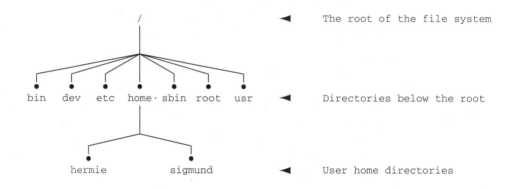

```
                    /                 ◄    The root of the file system


   bin   dev   etc  home· sbin  root  usr  ◄   Directories below the root


         hermie         sigmund        ◄    User home directories
```

As you can see, the file system resembles an upside-down tree, and is very similar to the tree-like directory structure in DOS. The top level is denoted by a slash (/) and is called the **root** directory. Several system-related directories such as **bin, dev,** and **etc** appear below the **root** directory—here's a summary of their purpose in life:

/bin	Contains the Linux system commands and programs (also called *binaries*).
/dev	Contains special device files that correspond to hardware components.

`/etc`	Contains configuration files for Linux and other installed software.
`/home`	Contains the home directories (personal storage) for each user on the system.
`/sbin`	Contains more Linux binaries (special utilities not for general users).
`/root`	The home directory for the **root** user—not to be confused with **/**. Other Linux systems use **/home/root** instead of **/root**.
`/usr`	Contains system programs and other files for general users such as games, online help, and documentation. By convention, a user should not put personal files in this directory.

■ **NOTE:** *Unless you are an All-Knowing Linux Guru, you should never combine or delete any of the directories (or files therein) that appear just below the **root** directory. This could result in your system being unable to boot or operate properly.*

DIRECTORY LINGO

To navigate your Linux file system, there are several terms you should understand.

Current directory   The directory you are in at a given time, sometimes called the *working directory*. The **pwd** (print working directory) command will tell you the name of the current directory.

Subdirectory   A directory within the current directory.

Parent directory   The directory above the current one. Every directory except the top level has a parent. If you are in the **/usr/spool directory**, then **/usr** is the parent.

Home directory   A user's personal directory. For example, if your user name is **hermie**, your home directory is **/home/hermie**. The user has complete control over all files stored in directories beneath the home directory.

Root directory The top of the file system, denoted by a slash. Only subdirectories appear below this directory. (Don't confuse this with **/root**, the home directory for the **root** user.)

Absolute file name A file name that is valid no matter where you are in the file hierarchy. In practice, this means it must start with a slash and specify the full path to the file. For example, **/home/ hermie/recipes/sludge_fudge** is an absolute file name, while **sludge_fudge** is not.

Relative file name A *relative file name* specifies a file relative to the current directory. For example, if you were in hermie's home directory, **/home/hermie/**, you would reference that healthy fudge recipe as **recipes/sludge_fudge**.

TREE CLIMBING

cd

You can move from one directory to another using the **cd** command. For example, if you are in your home directory (**/home/hermie**) and want to switch to the recipes directory (**/home/hermie/recipes**), the following command does the trick:

```
cd recipes
```

In order to switch back to your home directory, you could type

```
cd /home/hermie
```

But there are two shortcuts you will find useful. The first is the use of the double-dot (..) notation, as in

```
cd ..
```

This will move you one level up, to the parent directory. You can even do things like

```
cd ../secrets
```

single-dot

double-dot

to move up to the parent and then go back down to a directory that is at the same level as the current one. This double-dot notation is not specific to the **cd** command, though. You can use it with any Linux command that needs a file name as input. You might also see the single-dot (.) notation, which means "this directory." It wouldn't make much sense to enter **cd .** because you'd still be in the same directory, but there are other commands (notably the **find** command, described in Chapter 4, "Important Linux Commands") where it's convenient to use the single dot as shorthand for the current directory name.

Another directory navigation shortcut involves using **$HOME**. No matter what directory you are in, the following command will return you to your personal **recipes** directory.

```
cd $HOME/recipes
```

tilde

And if you want to change to another user's home directory, you can use the tilde (~) notation. In the examples below, the tilde character is shorthand for "the home directory of." You must put the name of a user on your system immediately after the tilde.

For example, **cd ~sigmund** means "change to sigmund's home directory"; **cd ~edbo/stuff** means "change to edbo's stuff directory."

The single dot, double dot, and tilde notations are useful in conjunction with the **cd** command, but they can also be used in any Linux command where you need to enter a file or directory name.

■ *TIP: One common mistake people make in navigating Linux directories is using a slash in front of file names when it is not needed. Suppose you have a **bin** directory under your home directory. If you were at **/home/hermie** and you entered **cd /bin**, you'd end up at the bin underneath the **root** directory—oops. (Linux understands the slash before **bin** as telling it to go to the **root** directory first, and then to the **bin** directory just below the root.) The correct way to reach the **bin** directory under **/home/hermie** is to type **cd bin** from within your home directory (**/home/hermie**). Don't use a leading slash unless you're sure you want to start at the top (root) of the file tree.*

LISTING FILES

The **ls** command lists all the files in a directory. For example

ls

ls	Lists the files in the current directory.
ls recipes	Lists the files in another directory using relative addressing.

ls /usr/bin Lists the files in another directory using absolute addressing.

By default, **ls** prints a simple, columnar list of your files. But it will list your files in many different formats if you give it one or more flags on the command line. In order to use any one of them, simply type the **ls** command at your prompt, followed by a space, and then add a switch by typing a minus, followed by the flag, as in

```
$ ls -F
```

Here are some of the most commonly used **ls** flags.

a	List all files, including hidden ones.
l	Show file list in long format, including file details like size, time stamp, and owner.
F	Add a slash after the name for directories, an asterisk for executables, and an "at" sign (**@**) for linked files.
r	Reverse the sort order (alphabetic or time).
t	Sort the list by the time each file was created.

Here's a look at the contents of a directory named `animals`, using some of these flags.

```
$ ls -F animals
   cat_info       cow_info       dog_info
   pig_info       slugs/         zippity*
```

In this case, **ls** returns just the file names in columnar format, but with a few marks, thanks to the **-F** flag. The slash suffix on `slugs` indicates it is a directory, while `zippity` is identified as an executable.

```
$ ls -al animals
-rw-r--r--    1 hermie   users      1758 Mar 17 23:17 .hoohah
-rw-r--r--    1 hermie   users     45090 Mar 23 23:17 cat_info
-rw-r--r--    1 hermie   users     64183 Feb 14 22:07 cow_info
-rw-r--r--    1 hermie   users    115032 Jan 06 11:14 dog_info
-rw-r--r--    1 hermie   users       248 Jan 16 09:18 pig_info
drwxr-xr-x    1 hermie   users      1024 Feb 28 06:12 slugs
-rwxr-xr-x    1 hermie   users     45198 Jan 23 11:14 zippity
```

.hoohah

Here **ls** has displayed all files in the `animals` directory, including the hidden `hoohah` file. In addition to the file name, the file's permissions, owner, group, size in bytes, and the date and time of last modification are displayed. (More on permissions later in this chapter.)

```
$ ls -lrt animals
-rw-r--r--   1 hermie   users    115032 Jan 06 11:14 dog_info
-rw-r--r--   1 hermie   users       248 Jan 16 09:18 pig_info
-rwxr-xr-x   1 hermie   users     45198 Jan 23 11:14 zippity
-rw-r--r--   1 hermie   users     64183 Feb 14 22:07 cow_info
drwxr-xr-x   1 hermie   users      1024 Feb 28 06:12 slugs
-rw-r--r--   1 hermie   users     45090 Mar 23 23:17 cat_info
```

This time we got the files sorted by time stamp, in reverse order. If you have lots of files in a directory, this is a handy way to find out which are the oldest and newest. Also notice that we combined the **-l, -r,** and **-t** switches into **-lrt** in the command above. We could just as well have issued ls **-l -r -t animals**.

DISPLAYING FILES

You know how to get a list of files. But what if you want to take a peek at a file's contents? Several commands, including **cat, more,** and **less,** can be used to display files. Let's see how they work in this example:

```
$ cat pig_info
Pigs make great pets, but they are not dogs or cats. Maybe
somewhere in between. I tend to believe that they have more
personality. They do require significant amounts of attention,
love, and scratches. But they aren't always snuggly in return.
```

cat

The **cat** command (short for "concatenate") shown in this example is like the DOS **type** command. In response to the command **cat pig_info,** the system simply splatters the file on screen. If there is more data in the file than will fit on one screen, the contents whiz by before you can see it. The **more** command solves this problem by displaying the file screen by screen:

```
$ more dog_info
Affectionately known as the "Toller," the Nova Scotian Duck
Tolling Retriever was once called the Little River Duck Dog,
since it was developed in the Little River district of Yarmouth
County, Nova Scotia. This engaging dog is a specialist with
waterfowl. Tolling, or luring, is the practice of tricking ducks
into gunshot range. Hunters had long observed this behavior
--More--(01%)
```

The **more** command pauses when the screen fills up and waits for you to press the SPACEBAR before it rolls out another screenful of text. A legend at the bottom of the screen tells you what percentage of the file has been displayed so far. You can press CTRL-C to quit more before reaching the end of the file.

The **less** command works like **more** except that it lets you move both forward and backward in the file while the command is running—use the **B** key on your keyboard to back up one screen and use the SPACEBAR to move forward and show the next screen.

Although all of these commands will let you view the contents of a file in different ways, none allow you to change the data in the file. If you want to view and update a file, use one of the text editors discussed in Chapter 5, "Text Editors."

COPYING FILES

cp

Copying files under Linux is similar to copying files under DOS. Here's an example using the **cp** (copy) command:

```
$ cp goulash recipes/hungarian
$ cp stuff stuff.bak
```

The first example copies the **goulash** file from the current directory and stores it in your **recipes/hungarian** directory. The second example creates a file called **stuff.bak** in the current directory that is identical to the source file **stuff**.

■ *NOTE: The cp command will overwrite files with the same name without warning. To be prompted before overwriting, use the -i flag like so:*

```
$ cp-i goulash recipes/hungarian
cp: overwrite recipes/hungarian/goulash (y/n)?
```

RENAMING FILES

mv

Use the **mv** command to rename a file or move it to another directory, like so:

```
$ mv stuff junk
$ mv junk trashcan
```

The first example renames the file stuff as **junk**, while the second moves the file junk into a directory called **trashcan**.

■ *NOTE: The **mv** command will wipe out files without warning. To be prompted before overwriting, use the -i flag like so:*

```
$ mv -i stuff junk
mv: overwrite junk (y/n)?
```

CREATING FILES

touch

If you want to create a new file rather than copy an existing one, use the **touch** command:

```
$ touch new.file
```

This creates a new, empty file.

If you issue the **ls -l new.file** command, you can verify that the file has a size of zero bytes. It might seem silly to create an empty file, but you can use them to verify that you have permission to create files in a certain directory, and some programs insist upon a control or log file even if it's empty. (The **touch** command will also update the time and date stamp on an existing file.)

echo

If you'd rather create a new file with data in it, like a line of text, use the **echo** command:

```
$ echo "Remember to buy oatmeal cookies." > reminder
```

This will create a file named **reminder** with just one line in it (the text in quotes). The **echo** command normally just prints a line to the screen, but here we've directed the output to a file. (This command also works in DOS.)

If you want to create a multiline file, use the **cat** command (similar to the DOS **type** command):

```
$ cat > fox.socks
Through three cheese trees three free fleas flew.
While these fleas flew, freezy breeze blew.
Freezy breeze made these three trees freeze.
Freezy trees made these trees' cheese freeze.
That's what made these three free fleas sneeze.
^D
```

The first line in this example tells Linux what to name the new file **fox.socks**. The typed lines that follow will become the contents of this new file. Pressing **CTRL-D** tells Linux that the file is done, and the **cat** command transfers your typing to the new file.

DELETING FILES

rm

Ready to do a little damage? The **rm** command removes a file (assuming you have permission to do so) without even saying *hasta la vista*. Be sure you really want to delete your files before you use **rm** because once the files are gone, they're not coming back. For example,

```
$ rm wallet
```

immediately deletes the file named **wallet** in the current directory without prompting. If you want to be prompted before the deletion, use the **-i** flag.

■ *NOTE: There is one little safety feature in **rm**—it won't delete a directory (unless you use the **-r** flag).*

One other **rm** flag is **-f,** which translates roughly to "Don't ask me any questions, just delete the files." While **rm** normally asks for confirmation before deleting a write-protected file, the **-f** (force) flag overrides this prompt.

Be careful with the **rm** command, since the multiuser nature of Linux does not allow for undelete as in DOS. As soon as you let go of the space occupied by a file, the operating system is likely to use it for something else.

CREATING DIRECTORIES

mkdir

If you've got a bunch of related files scattered in your home directory, why not create a directory for them? Use the **mkdir** command as follows:

```
$ mkdir cooking
```

This creates a new directory named **cooking** in the current directory, into which you can move all those recipes for easy retrieval.

DELETING DIRECTORIES

rmdir

If you created a directory named "spelunking" six months ago, and now you're not so keen on crawling through slimy caves, the **rmdir** command may be able to help.

```
$ rmdir spelunking
```

This command removes the specified directory, but only if it's empty. If the directory contains files or subdirectories, you'll have to delete them using **rm** first.

One alternative to painstakingly removing all the contents of a directory that you just want to make disappear is to use the **rm -r** command. The **-r** flag gives **rm** license to kill directories, their files, and even their subdirectories. Be very sure you understand what's about to happen before using a command like

```
$ rm -r spelunking
```

Let's just say that careless use of the **-r** flag might end your spelunking hobby prematurely.

WILD CARDS

Wild cards come in quite handy when you want to operate on more than one file at a time. You can use wild cards with any of the commands in this chapter to list, copy, rename, or delete groups of files or directories.

The asterisk (*****) character will match any number of characters in a file name, so consider these examples in light of the **animals** directory we used earlier.

```
$ ls -l c*
-rw-r--r--    1 hermie    users        45090 Mar 23 23:17 cat_info
-rw-r--r--    1 hermie    users        64183 Feb 14 22:07 cow_info
$ mv *inf* ../docs
$ rm -f *
```

The first command lists only those files that begin with the letter "c." The second will move files with the term *inf* anywhere in the name to another directory. The third command will delete all (nonhidden) files from the current directory.

***wild card
expansion***

■ ***NOTE:*** *The expansion of the wild card is done by the shell, not the command you are running. What this means is that when you enter the command*

```
rm -f *
```

the shell expands the wild card by replacing it with all files that match, and actually ends up executing this command:

```
rm -f cat_info cow_info dog_info pig_info slugs zippity
```

This might seem a bit arcane, but it's actually important. Since the shell handles the wild cards in Linux, you don't have to worry about which commands accept wild cards and which don't. This is quite different from DOS, where only certain commands work with wild cards.

Here's a little pop quiz: what will be left in the **animals** directory if you execute the **rm** command shown above? Try it and then use the **ls -al** command—you may be surprised at the answer.

DON'T TRY THIS AT HOME

At the beginning of this chapter, I promised to reveal the Nine Deadly Keystrokes that could wipe out your entire file system. Given what you know now about the **rm** command and the structure of the Linux file system, perhaps you can see that the command

```
rm -rf /
```

would be something to avoid at all costs, if you were logged in as root. But don't let this scare you—it's just a reminder to be careful when deleting files. You can avoid nasty surprises like this by running the **pwd** and **ls** commands before you delete anything. (Try to **ls** the same file or directory that you're going to delete.) Then you'll always be sure what directory you're in and what files are about to be deleted.

And in general, it's a good idea to log in as root only when you're doing system administration tasks such as adding new users or installing software. Create another account and use it for all your normal everyday Linux tasks.

CONTROLLING ACCESS TO YOUR FILES

If you share a Linux (or Unix) system you will undoubtedly have private files that you want to keep private, as well as files that you want to be public. You can control access to your files by setting the permission flags and ownership for your files.

HOW TO TELL WHAT ACCESS YOUR FILES HAVE

When we discussed using the **ls** command, you may have been wondering about that gibberish in the first few columns of the **ls -l** command (stuff like **--rw, r--,** and so on). Here's an example of output from the **ls -l** command showing the contents of a directory:

Permissions	User	Group	Size	Date	Name
-rw-r-----	1 hermie	users	64183	Feb 14 22:07	cow_info
-rw-r-----	1 hermie	users	115032	Jan 06 11:14	dog_info
-rw-r--r--	1 hermie	users	248	Jan 16 09:18	pig_info
-rw-r--r--	1 hermie	users	64183	Feb 14 22:07	cow_info
-rwx--x---	1 hermie	users	45198	Jan 23 11:14	zippity
drwxr-x---	1 hermie	friends	1024	Feb 28 06:12	slugs

For each file you see listed a set of permissions; the owning user; a group name; and the size, creation date, and name of the file. We'll focus on the permission first by dissecting the file access permissions for the dog_info file. Specifically, these permissions are shown in the string of characters preceding the file in the first column, -rw-r-----. Note that the permissions data is made up of ten characters, each of which has meaning.

In order to understand how to read file permissions, let's start by splitting apart those ten characters for cow_info:

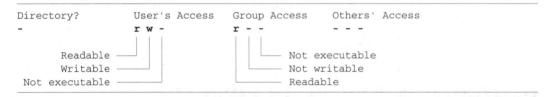

The character in the first position, a dash (–), indicates that this is a file and not a directory. Directories are marked with a **d**, as in drwxr-x--- (this precedes the directory slugs).

The next three characters (rw-) tell us whether the file's owner (hermie) can read, write, and execute the file. An **r** in the first position means that the file can be read; a **w** in the second position means that the file can be written to (updated); and if the third character is an **x** the file can be executed (run). In all three cases, if a hyphen appears in place of an r, w, or x, that specific privilege is removed. For example, rw– means that the file can be read and written to, but not executed.

The next sets of three characters define read, write, and execute access for the users in a particular group (the users group in this case), along the same lines as above. For example, the characters r–– that appear in these positions for dog_info tell us the users group can read this file but can't write to or execute it.

The final set of three characters—all hyphens, in this case—defines access for those who are not the owner or in the listed group. This one's easy: no one outside the listed group has any kind of access to this file.

■ *NOTE: Groups are a convenient way to give a set of users the same access to a bunch of files. Only a superuser can add to or remove users from groups. To find out what groups you belong to, use the* groups *command.*

In sum, access to the **dog_info** file is controlled like so: the user (hermie) can read and update the file, but cannot execute it. People in the users group can only read the file, and everybody else on the system gets no access at all.

Here's another example. The characters that precede the file `zippity`,

```
-rwx--x---   1 hermie   users      45198 Jan 23 11:14 zippity
```

tell us that this file is readable, writable, and executable by hermie, can only be executed by those in the users group, and that others outside the users group have no access to it.

■ *NOTE: You can give execute permission to any file, but it doesn't make sense to do so unless the file is actually a program.*

If you look at the listing for `slugs`,

```
drwxr--x---  1 hermie   friends     1024 Feb 28 06:12 slugs
```

you can see first that it's a directory (signified by the **d** in the first position). User hermie has read and write access, which in the case of a directory translates into the ability to list files and to create and delete files. Hermie also has execute access, which in the case of a directory means the ability to **cd** into it. Those in the friends group can list files in the directory and use **cd** to make it the current directory, while others have no access whatsoever to the directory.

chgrp

■ *NOTE: Unless you are administering a large UNIX system with lots of users, groups are not very important. In these examples, "users" is just the name of a group that all users belong to by default in a Linux system. If your primary group is "users," all files you create will show that as the group name, unless you use the* chgrp *com-*

*mand to change it. If you're curious, use the **man chgrp** command to find out more.*

USE CHMOD TO CHANGE A FILE'S PERMISSIONS

chmod

Fine, you can decipher the permissions for a file or directory, but what if you want to change them? Maybe you've decided that the **pig_info** file is a little too sensitive for just anybody to view, or that you should allow all users to execute the **zippity** program. The **chmod** (change mode) command can take care of that. The general form of the **chmod** command is

```
chmod <permission flags> <file or directory name(s)>
```

To tell **chmod** the new permissions for a file, you can use any combination of these permission flag characters:

Who It Applies To (pick one or more)	Access Change (pick one)	Access Type (pick one or more)
u for the owner	**+** grant access	**r** for read access
g the group	**-** deny access	**w** for write access
o for all others		**x** for execute access

Here are some examples:

`chmod o-r pig_info`	Removes read access from all others.
`chmod g+rw pig_info`	Grants read and write access to group.
`chmod ugo+x zippity`	Grants execute access to everybody.

In effect, you're saying "change the mode for *these people* by *adding/removing* their access to *read/write/execute* the file named *whatever*." Just pick the proper combination of flags in each of the three columns, depending on what type of access you want for the file.

■ **NOTE:** *If you give* **chmod** *a directory instead of a file name, the permissions have slightly different meanings. For a directory, read access means that you can list the files with the* **ls** *command; write access allows you to create or delete files; and execute access gives you the ability to change to that directory with the* **cd** *command.*

TRANSFER OWNERSHIP OF A FILE USING CHOWN

chown

You can transfer ownership of a file or directory (if you move it into another user's directory) using the **chown** command.

To tell chown what to do, just give it the new owner and the file name, as in

```
chown sigmund zippity
```

This will make **sigmund** the owner of **zippity**. Once you've transferred ownership, sigmund will be able to set the file's permissions (with **chmod**) if he wants to.

IMPORTANT LINUX COMMANDS

Working from a Linux command line is not always intuitive, especially since there are hundreds of different commands with a myriad of switches and flags to make things even more confusing. You certainly don't need to know all of them to make good use of your Linux system, but there is a certain set of indispensable tools with which you should be familiar.

We've covered a handful of commands in previous chapters that let you work with the shell and your file system. The commands covered in this chapter will complement what you've learned and give you some essential tools to manage your Linux environment. (You'll also be able to use these commands on other Unix-based systems.) You'll pick up other important commands in Chapter 6, but you should first master this starter set to build the skills that will help you perform common Linux tasks more easily.

IF YOU NEED HELP, ASK THE MAN

Assuming you can remember the right command for a particular job, it's tougher still to remember all the switches associated with that command. The **man** command (short for manual) will help you on both counts by displaying pages from online manuals and telling you which commands may be relevant to the task at hand.

Say you want to change your password but you don't know the command to do it. You can use the **man** command plus the keyword flag, **-k**, to search by keyword **password** for relevant commands:

```
$ man -k password
passwd    passwd (1)   - change login password
pwck      pwck (1m)    - password/group file checkers
vipw      vipw (1b)    - edit the password file
```

You can probably deduce that **passwd** is the correct command. But before blindly issuing any Linux command, you should know the proper syntax and understand what the command might do to you first. Using **man** with a command name will display all you need to know (probably more) about a command. For example, entering **man passwd** will display

```
$ man passwd
passwd(1)        User Commands        passwd(1)
NAME
   passwd - change login password and attributes
SYNOPSIS
   passwd [ name ]
   passwd [ -d | -l ] [ -f ] [ -n min ] [ -w warn ]
          [ -x max ] name
   passwd -s [ -a ]
   passwd -s [ name ]

DESCRIPTION
   The passwd command changes the password or lists
   attributes associated with the user's login name.
--More--(5%)
```

(The **man** command pauses after each screenful and waits for you to press the SPACEBAR before continuing.) The word More at the bottom of each page indicates how much of the help has so far been displayed. The terms in square brackets are optional parameters (**-d**, **-l**, **-f**, for example); vertical bars indicate that the terms on either side are mutually exclusive—you can only use one at a time.

USE PASSWD TO CHANGE YOUR PASSWORD

You can use the **passwd** command to change your log-in password, and as you can tell from the **man** output above, you have quite a few options. Here are some of the most common.

passwd	Change your own password.
passwd sleepy	Change sleepy's password.
passwd -d sleepy	Delete sleepy's password.

When you enter one of these commands to change a password, you will be prompted for the old (current) password and a new password. Your new password should be at least six characters long and not too easy for someone else to guess. Oh, and writing it down on a scrap of paper taped to your monitor is not recommended either. :-)

If you share your Linux system with multiple users, or you have a dial-in modem attached, password security for each account is particularly important. But if you're the only one who will ever lay a finger on your system, you might want to delete your password, thus removing the need to enter it each time you log in. It's your call, but you never know when your five-year-old will wander by the keyboard!

By the way, you might get the idea from the commands above that users can go around changing each other's passwords at will, but that's not the case. Only a superuser (such as **root**) can change or delete another user's password.

SWITCHING USERS WITH SU

Even if you have no schizophrenic tendencies, sometimes you'll want to become someone else while using Linux. For example, if you're logged in as **hermie** and you need to do something quickly that requires superuser authority, just enter the command

```
$ su-
```

In response to the **su** (switch user) command, you'll be prompted for the root account password. If you enter the password correctly, your prompt will change from a dollar sign to a pound sign (to reflect your status as **root**), and you will assume the powers of the **root** user. Issue the **exit** command to resume your previous identity.

You can also use **su** to become any user on the system, not just root. For example, to become sigmund you would enter this command:

```
$ su- sigmund
```

When you use **su** to assume the powers of another user temporarily, the **.profile** for that user is not executed. So it's not really the same as logging in, because your environment variables, aliases, and home directory will not change. This would be like starting DOS without running the **AUTOEXEC.BAT** file—things wouldn't work the same, because your personal setup commands (**PATH** and so on) would not run.

But why would you want to use **su** when you can have multiple logins via virtual consoles (see Chapter 2, "Living In a Shell")? Because it's sometimes quicker or more convenient to switch between users using **su,** and because you may have no virtual consoles available— you may be using all of them or, if you're logged into the machine via a modem, virtual consoles may not be available to you.

TELL ME WHO IS LOGGED IN

If you want to know which users are currently logged in to your Linux system, which consoles they're using, and the dates and times they logged in, issue the **who** command. You'll see output something like this:

```
$ who
root      tty1    Nov 2 17:57
hermie    tty3    Nov 2 18:43
sigmund   tty2    Nov 2 18:08
```

In the output above, the term `tty` stands for "teletype." In the olden days of computing, a terminal was just a keyboard with an attached printer, so you read everything off the teletype.

If you've logged in with multiple virtual consoles and changed your identity on any of them, you may have some trouble figuring out who you are—or at least what user is logged into the console you're on. If you find yourself in such an identity crisis, try this variant of the **who** command:

```
$ who am i
```

WHAT'S TODAY'S DATE?

Use the **date** command to print the current date and time. If you add the **-u** flag, the results will be for the Greenwich mean time zone. And if you log in as a superuser, you can even change the date or time. Now, that's power! (The command syntax for each option is shown below.)

```
$ date                              print the date and time
Sat Nov 2 20:09:43 EST 1997
$ date -u                           print the GMT date and time
Sun Nov 3 01:09:45 GMT 1997
$ date 0503                         set the clock to 5:03AM
```

IS THERE AN ECHO IN HERE?

The **echo** command displays a message on screen and is primarily useful for programmers writing shell scripts (see Chapter 8, "Rolling Your Own"). But anyone can use **echo** to show the value of environment variables. Here are some examples:

```
$ echo $PATH
/usr/bin:/usr/local/bin
$ echo My name is $USER - Home directory=$HOME.
My name is hermie - Home directory=/home/hermie.
```

The **echo** command is very similar to the DOS command of the same name, except that the DOS **echo** command cannot display environment variables—it just displays a message.

WHAT GOOD IS A SPELL CHECKER?

Always run your important documents through a spell checker. It will plane lee mark four you're revue, miss steaks ewe mite knot sea. However, it probably won't do much for poor grammar or sentences like that one! Linux has a rudimentary spelling checker, which you can invoke thus:

`$ spell important.txt`	A regular spelling check on the file **important.txt**.
`$ spell -b important.txt`	A spelling check using British spelling rules.

If **spell** finds words that do not appear in its dictionary, it will print them on the console. (Commercial word processors with built-in spell checkers are also available for LInux—see Chapter 7 for details.)

CONFIGURING YOUR SYSTEM FOR PRINTING

Linux Pro comes with a nice graphical printer configuration utility that will create the necessary system files to set up your printer. Start the

X Window GUI with the **startx** command and double-click on the **Printer Config** icon in the **Control Panel** window, then follow these steps:

1. Select the **Add** button (the Printer Type window appears as shown below).

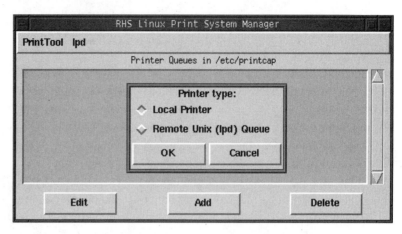

2. Pick **Local Printer**, then press **OK** (a second pop-up appears as shown below).

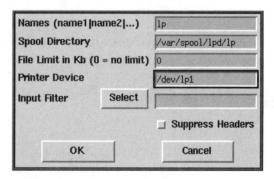

3. In the Names field, enter **lp**.

4. In the Spool Directory field, enter **/var/spool/lpd/lp**.

5. In the File Limit field, enter **o** (zero).

6. In the Printer Device field, enter **/dev/lp1**.

7. Press the **Select** button next to the Input Filter field (a third pop-up appears, as shown below).

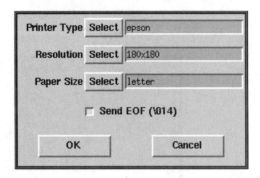

8. Press **Select** and choose your printer type from the list.

9. In the Resolution field, enter **180 x 180** (or **360 x 360**).

10. In the Paper Size field, enter **letter.**

11. Check the **Send EOF** box and press **OK** (the second pop-up returns as shown on the previous page).

12. Check the **Suppress Headers** box and press **OK.**

Now restart the Linux printer subsystem. Select **lpd** from the action bar and click on **restart lpd**. That's it; now you can try printing.

PUTTING IT IN PRINT

Now that your system is ready for printing and your important document is free of spelling errors, why not print a copy for posterity? In Linux the print command is **lpr,** so you might enter a command like this:

```
$ lpr paperless-office.txt
```

The **lpr** command makes a copy of your file and stuffs it in the system's print queue (a process called *spooling*), so you can change or delete the original file without harming your printout.

The **lpr** command will accept two optional flags, described here:

-r   Delete the file after printing.

-s   No spooling (don't make a temporary copy for printing).

The **-r** flag tells the system to delete the file after printing, and **-s** tells it to print directly from the original file instead of spooling to the print queue. Of course, if you specify the **-s** flag you can't modify or delete the original file while it's printing; but it can save a bit of time (since no copy is made) when the original file is big.

Here are some examples using the **-r** and **-s** flags:

`$ lpr -r humongous`	Delete file *humongous* after printing.
`$ lpr -s humongous`	Print file *humongous* without spooling.
`$ lpr -r -s humongous`	Print file *humongous* without spooling, then delete it.

■ *NOTE: Some printers under Linux exhibit a staircase effect as shown below, with each line starting in the column where the last line ended, instead of starting in the first column:*

```
this is line one
                this is line two
                                this is line three
```

If this happens with your printer, see the **Printing-Usage-HOWTO** file on the CD-ROM in the **doc/HOWTO** directory.

CUSTOMIZING YOUR PRINTOUTS

The **lpr** command is a no-frills way to print your files; it doesn't do any fancy formatting, it just dumps your file on the printer. If you'd like to format your printout (paginate, add a title, set margins, or control the page length), you can use the **pr** command in conjunction with **lpr**. By default, **pr** will add page numbers and a title consisting of the file's name and the date and time it was last modified. But you can do lots of other fancy formatting. Here are some of the options that **pr** supports:

`-d`	Double-space the printout.
`-h <my title>`	Specify a title for the page header (default is the file name).
`-ln`	Set the page length to *n* lines (default is 66).

`-on`	Set the margin to *n* characters (default is 8).
`-t`	Suppress the page header.
`-2 | -3 | -4`	Print output in two, three, or four columns (like a newspaper).

Typically, the output from **pr** is sent only to your printer (by piping the output to **lpr,** as shown in the examples below); but if you leave off the **lpr** step, you'll see the output on screen instead. Here are some examples using the **pr** command to print a file named **panda97.txt,** for example, with no options specified, just adding page numbers and the default title (file name and date):

```
$ pr panda97.txt | lpr
```

Here we've specified a more meaningful title for the printout:

```
$ pr -h "Financial Report" panda97.dat | lpr
```

And now we set the page length to 55, the margin to 5 spaces, and double-space:

```
$ pr -h "Financial Report" -155 -o5 -d panda97.dat | lpr
```

STOP THE PRESSES!

If you send a file to the printer by mistake, you might be able to snatch it from the print queue before it's too late. First use **lpq** to find the job number:

```
$ lpq
Rank Owner   Job  Files            Total Size
1st  hermie  17   really-humongous 2317678 bytes
```

In the example above, the job number is 17. Once you know the job number, enlist the assistance of **lprm** to remove that file from the queue as follows (using job 17 as an example):

```
$ lprm 17
```

PRINTING POSTSCRIPT FILES

Postscript is a complex formatting language that certain laser printers can interpret to produce really nice-looking documents. But if you send a Postscript file to a printer that doesn't understand the Postscript language, your printout will be pages of incomprehensible gibberish. And unless you shelled out megabucks for your laser printer, chances are it won't print a Postscript file.

■ *TIP: You can tell a Postscript file by the file name and the contents. If the file name ends with* **.ps** *and the first line of the file starts with the percent sign (%), you can be sure it's Postscript.*

It gets worse. Most of the documentation for Linux comes in Postscript format, which suggests that you may not be able to print it unless you have Postscript capability. But all is not lost. The version of Linux included with this book has a nifty program called Ghostscript that can read a Postscript file and either show it on screen or print it on your printer, even if the printer doesn't have built-in Postscript support.

To view a Postscript file on screen, enter a command like this (**qwerty.ps** is a sample file name):

```
$ gs qwerty.ps
```

■ *NOTE: You must start the X Window software (with the **startx** command) before running this command.*

Assuming you followed the instructions above to set up your printer, you can print a Postscript file with the **lpr** command, just like any other file. The system will invoke Ghostscript behind the scenes and send the file to your printer.

USE CAT TO JOIN FILES

The **cat** command's primary function is to catenate or join files, but you can use it to display a file on screen, too. The **cat** command takes one or more files that you specify, smashes them together, and then sends the resulting file to the standard output device (without changing either of the original files).

The standard output device is your screen, but by using the greater-than (>) operator you can redirect **cat**'s output to another file. Here are some examples:

`$ cat food`	Display the **food** file on screen.
`$ cat scratch fever`	Join the files **scratch** and **fever**, then display them on screen.
`$ cat eats bird > DetailsAt11`	Join the files **eats** and **bird**, and save them in the file **DetailsAt11**.

Note that the original files that **cat** joins are not modified. For example, say the file **eats** contained the lines

```
The Owl and the Pussy-Cat went to sea
In a beautiful pea-green boat.
```

and the file **bird** contained these lines:

```
They took some honey, and plenty of money
Wrapped up in a five-pound note.
```

After the above command, neither file would change, but a new file called **DetailsAt11** would be created, containing all four lines:

```
The Owl and the Pussy-Cat went to sea
In a beautiful pea-green boat.
They took some honey, and plenty of money
Wrapped up in a five-pound note.
```

SEARCH FOR FILES WITH FIND

Linux's tree-structured file system is great for organizing your files, but a plethora of directories and subdirectories can make it easy to lose track of specific files. To search for a file named **cookie**, you'd use the **find** command like this:

```
$ find / -name "cookie" -print
```

This command tells **find** to start looking in the **root** directory of the file system (**/**) for files named (**-name**) **cookie,** and then to print (**-print**) the full name of each file it finds.

If you leave off the **-print** flag, find will merrily search and then throw the results in the *bit bucket.* (This is a fictitious device attached to all computers. When the operating system deletes a file or discards data, it is said to be thrown in the bit bucket.)

This is a departure from the rule of thumb that Linux commands will print their output on the screen unless you specify otherwise.

Starting from the root could take a long time, since **find** will search every single directory on the system. You can shorten the search time by telling **find** where to start searching if you know that the file you want lies along a certain path. Here are a few examples:

`$ find . -name "cookie" -print`	Start looking in the current directory.
`$ find ~sigmund -name "cookie" -print`	Start looking in sigmund's home directory.
`$ find /etc -name "cookie" -print`	Start looking in the **/etc** directory.

If you can't remember the exact name of the file you're after, but you have some sort of clue about it (for example, it has the word *cow* in it), you can use wild cards to search:

`$ find . -name "cow*" -print`	Look for files beginning with the word "cow."
`$ find . -name "*cow" -print`	Look for files ending with the word "cow."
`$ find . -name "*cow*" -print`	Look for files with "cow" anywhere.

Finding the right files is one thing, but doing something useful with the found files would be a big plus. You can use the **-exec** flag to apply a command to each of the found files. The following example will send all the files it finds to the printer (**lpr**):

```
$ find . -name "*.txt" -exec lpr {} \;
```

The set of brackets ({ }) is a placeholder that represents the name of each file found, and the slash-semicolon (\;) is a bit of magic that signals the end of the command. So if you had files in the current directory named **sample1.txt** and **sample2.txt**, the **find** command would issue the following commands for you:

```
lpr sample1.txt
lpr sample2.txt
```

You can apply any command you like to the found files.

Using **find** with the -**exec** flag is a convenient way to copy, move, print, and even delete groups of files that may be scattered across many different directories. A word of caution, though: if you're going to apply some potentially dangerous command (like **rm**) to your files, use the -**ok** flag instead of -**exec**. It works the same way, except it prompts you to confirm each command before executing it. Here's an example:

```
$ find . -name "*.txt" -ok mv {} junkdir \;
mv sample1.txt junkdir    ok? (y/n)
mv sample2.txt junkdir    ok? (y/n)
```

The **find** command found two matching files, constructed the commands shown above by substituting a file name for the brackets, and then asked for confirmation before executing the commands.

WHAT'S THE DIFFERENCE BETWEEN TWO FILES?

If when you use **find** you discover that there are two files with suspiciously similar names, you might want to know whether they really contain the same information. The **diff** command will compare two files and give you the lowdown on just how different they are. Here's an example of how you would use the command, and the output you might get from it:

```
$ diff cookies.old cookies.new
5c5
< One cup vanilla extract
---
> One teaspoon vanilla extract
7d6
< Six ounces chopped liver
21a22
> Note: The previous version of this recipe had a few errors!
```

The **diff** output is actually a description of how to transform the old file into the new one. Here, **diff** is telling you three things:

1. The fifth line of the file has undergone a change. The 5c5 says to replace line five of the old file with line five of the new file. Both the old and new text are displayed, separated by a line of three dashes. (The less-than (‹) notation means "remove this line" and the greater-than (›) sign means "add this line.")

2. Line seven of the old file does not appear in the new file. The 7d6 says to delete line seven from the old file, and the files will then be in sync, starting at line six of the new file. The text to be deleted is displayed on the next line.

3. A line was added to the new file. The 21a22 says to add a new line after line 21 of the old file. The text to be added is displayed on the final line of the output.

Two useful flags you can specify when comparing files are **-b** (*ignore blanks*) and **-i** (*ignore case*). You can use them separately or combine them. The ignore blanks feature is especially useful when you're comparing the source code for two programs, since indentation changes are rarely significant. For example, here's how you might compare two programs, **ur2cool.c** and **ur2cool.backup**:

```
$ diff -b -i ur2cool.c ur2cool.backup
```

Don't worry if you have some difficulty understanding the output of the **diff** command. It's cryptic because it was designed to be used by computers, not humans. (Some source code control systems used by programmers use **diff** to keep a record of what changes were made to a program over time.)

Do pay attention, though, to the less-than and greater-than indicators to see at a glance what was added or deleted; and be happy if you manage to get a general feeling for how the files differ.

REMIND ME AT SIX

Linux provides a really handy way to schedule future events to run automatically. You can use the **at** command to schedule reminders or administrative tasks, or to run a command later when the computer won't be busy. Once you specify the time (and optional date) for your event, **at** prompts you for the command to run. After entering your command, press **CTRL-D** to finish. Here are some examples:

```
$ at 8:15am Jul 14
echo "Remember to call Ruth about the Amalgamated Contract!"
^D
$ at midnight Friday
cp project/source backup
^D
```

To find out what events you have already scheduled with at, enter:

```
$ at -l
Date                  Owner   Queue   Job#
08:15:00 07/14/97     root    c       1
00:00:00 01/10/97     root    c       2
```

To cancel an event scheduled with at, use the **-r** switch and a job number (which you can find using the at -l command). For example, to cancel job number 2 you would enter:

```
$ at -r 2
```

LINKING FILES TOGETHER

The **ln** command lets a file on your disk be accessed with more than one file name by *hard linking* a new file name to it. When you hard link a file, you create a new file name and connect it with the original file. Hard linking can let two users share the same file, or provide a more convenient way of referencing files buried deep in a series of directories.

Here's an example. Suppose hermie and sigmund are working on the Top Secret Snowgun Project, and the formula for the Snowgun is stored in **/home/hermie/projects/snowgun/formula.txt**. Sigmund doesn't want to type that long ugly filename every time he needs to update the file, so he can create a hard link to the file like this:

```
ln /home/hermie/projects/snowgun/formula.txt sgformula
```

The command above would link the file name **sgformula** to the file **formula.txt** contained at the end of that directory string. There's still only one copy of the snowgun formula (formula.txt) on the disk, but now sigmund can access it quickly with the name **sgformula** (assuming hermie gives him write permission to the file). Interestingly, if hermie deletes his **projects/snowgun/formula.txt** file, Linux will not remove the file from the file system because sigmund still has a link to it.

Think of the **ln** command as creating a kind of nickname for a file. By the way, there is no parallel to this file linking concept in the DOS world—you'd have to create a second copy of the file and keep them in synch manually to get a similar result.

HARD AND SYMBOLIC LINKS

The type of link we just created is called a hard link, but there's another type called a symbolic link. *Symbolic links* (also called *symlinks*) work like hard links, but you can do a bit more with them. If you want to create a link to a directory (as opposed to a file) you must create a symlink. Symlinks are also required when linking to a file on a different disk partition or on a network. To create a symbolic link, add the **-s** parameter to the **ln** command like this:

```
ln -s /dev/fd0 A:
ln -s /etc/httpd/conf web
```

The first example allows you to access the floppy drive as **A:** just like in DOS, and the second creates a directory entry called **web** that can be used instead of **/etc/httpd/conf**.

WRAPPING UP

Learning Unix would be hard if you tried to master everything it has to offer all at once. But then so would DOS, and especially Windows. In fact, Windows' configuration files are more complex than Unix's. When you first learned DOS, there were only a dozen or so commands that you needed to understand—you could learn the rest as needed. It's the same with Unix. You need only learn more if you want to get more out of Unix.

Also, though you may not realize it, DOS is a kind of subset of Unix. DOS adopted from Unix the idea of a hierarchical filesystem, as well as the concept of filters and piping. Moreover, each command that you learned in DOS has a direct parallel in Unix. (See the table of DOS/Unix equivalences in Chapter 12, "Linux Does DOS and Windows".)

TEXT EDITORS

For most people, a text editor is the most basic and often-used computer tool. If you want to write a letter, send e-mail, or compose a computer program, you use a text editor to enter your prose and save it in a file.

Although they perform the same basic functions, a text editor and a word processor (such as Word or WordPerfect) are slightly different in nature. In general, a text editor is like a very basic word processing program—it can't do fancy stuff like fonts, underlining, and boldface. A text editor is useful for entering, updating, and storing text, but you need a word processor to create really sharp-looking documents.

Aside from their differing looks and abilities, text editors and word processors store data in different formats. Text editors store files in plain-text (ASCII) format, which means the files can be read by any other text editor or program, while word processors store them in specially coded formats that can only be read by that program. (Actually, most popular word processors can read files created by other programs, but they don't always show the same formatting.)

This chapter focuses on three Linux text editors (vi, emacs, and pico) commonly used to create and modify files. You'll get an introduction to each one here, and then you can decide which one is best for you.

THE VI EDITOR

editors and religion

The **vi** editor comes with every version of Linux or Unix. I think it's a terribly unfriendly beast of an editor, but many hardcore Unix wizards would rather fight than switch. The old maxim rings true—editors are like religions, only people feel stronger about their editors. Anyway, you should know about **vi** because someday you're likely to find yourself on a system where you have no other choice but to use it.

Using **vi** is similar to using other editors in that you can see your file on screen (this is not the case with a line editor, for example), move from point to point in the file, and make changes. But that's where the similarities end. Cryptic commands, a frustrating user interface, and the absence of prompts can all drive you up a wall. Still, if you focus on a few basics, you'll get the job done.

COMMAND AND INPUT MODE

The hardest thing to understand about **vi** is the concept of *modes*. When using **vi** you're always in either Command or Input mode. Unfortunately **vi** gives you no clue as to its current mode. In Command mode, you can move the cursor, search for characters, or delete existing text. But to enter or edit new text you have to switch to Input mode.

use the Esc key to switch modes

When you start **vi** you're in Command mode. To enter Input mode, type the letter **a** (lowercase only) to signal that you want to add text after the cursor position. Press **Esc** to switch back to Command mode at any time. (If you were already in Command mode, **vi** beeps.)

Here's how to create a file from scratch using **vi**. To start, create a new file named **cow.joke** by typing

```
vi cow.joke
```

You'll see a screen that looks like Figure 5-1.

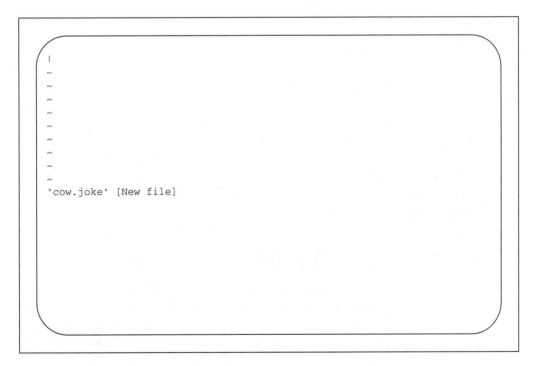

FIGURE 5.1: *The vi editor screen*

ADDING NEW TEXT TO YOUR FILE

Your cursor (shown as the vertical bar at the top) is in the upper left-hand corner of the screen, and the message at the bottom tells you that a new file called **cow.joke** was just created. The tilde (~) characters in the first column are just placeholders for empty lines.

Now type the letter **a** to enter Input mode, and type in the lines shown in Figure 5-2. Press **ENTER** at the end of each line to go on to the next.

```
Jane: Knock, knock...
Bill: Who's there?
Jane: The Interrupting Cow.
Bill: The Interrupting Cow wh...
Jane: MOOOOOO!
|
~
~
~
~
"cow.joke" [New file]
```

FIGURE 5.2: *Creating a file with vi*

SAVING YOUR WORK

So far, so good—let's save this little masterpiece. You're still in Input mode, so press **Esc** to enter Command mode, then type **ZZ** (to put your file to sleep). You won't see any Z's on screen, but after you've entered the second Z your file will disappear, your Linux command prompt will return, and you'll see this message indicating that your file was successfully saved:

```
"cow.joke" 6 lines, 113 characters
```

Congratulations—you've just survived your first encounter with **vi**. You know that the **a** command switches to Input mode, **Esc** gets you back to Command mode, and **ZZ** saves the file, but you'll have to expand this limited repertoire to get any real work done.

COMMON VI COMMANDS

Have a look at this list of common **vi** commands (there are many more, but these will at least allow you to get some basic work done). Then we'll do one more exercise before moving on.

■ **NOTE:** *As with all of Linux,* **vi** *commands are case sensitive.*

Cursor Positioning

→	Move cursor one space right.
←	Move cursor one space left.
↑	Move cursor up one line.
↓	Move cursor down one line.
CTRL-F	Move forward one screen.
CTRL-B	Move backward one screen.
$	Move cursor to end of line.
^	Move cursor to beginning of line.
/	Search for a character string.
x	Delete the character at the cursor position.
dd	Delete the current line.

Entering Input Mode

---

a   Add text after the cursor.

i   Insert text before the cursor.

R   Replace text starting at the cursor.

o   Insert a new line after the current one.

Entering Command Mode

Esc   Switch from Input mode to Command mode.

To Leave or Save Your File

ZZ   Save file and exit.

:q!   Quit without saving.

TRY OUT SOME MORE COMMANDS

Here's another example to try out some of the commands above. Enter the command below to fire up **vi** again, and you should see the file as we left it in Figure 5.2.

```
vi cow.joke
```

CHANGING TEXT   Let's change Bill's name to Biff on the second line. To do so, use the arrow keys to position your cursor on the third character of line two (the letter l in Bill), then press **x** twice (to delete the two l's). Now press **i** (to enter Input mode) and then type **ff** to complete the change from Bill to Biff.

■ *TIP: Be careful not to press the arrow keys while you're in Input mode—you can only position the cursor in Command mode. Yuck.*

You could also have used the **R** command to do this job of replacing text, so use it to change the other Bill now. Press **Esc** to enter Command mode, then type **/Bill** to search for the word "Bill." The cursor should move to line four, right to where Bill is found.

Now position your cursor on the third character (the letter **l**) and press **R** to replace the characters, followed by **ff**. Both Bills should now be Biffs.

ADDING AND DELETING LINES   Here's how to add or delete a line. Press **Esc** to enter Command mode, then press the **o** key to add a new line. You're in Input mode again, so you can type whatever you like on this new line. But that would ruin the joke, so delete this new line by pressing **Esc** and then entering the **dd** command. The line you just added should go away.

QUITTING WITHOUT SAVING YOUR CHANGES   Hmmm . . . "Biff" just doesn't have that wholesome ring to it, so let's forget about all the changes we've made in this editing session and exit **vi** without saving the file. Make sure you're in Command mode, enter the **:q!** command, and then press **ENTER**. Your Linux prompt should return, and the **cow.joke** file will be just as it was before.

PARTING WORDS ABOUT VI

Using **vi** can be frustrating, but it really isn't rocket science once you get used to the concept of the two modes, and get the hang of when it's okay to move your cursor or enter text. If you're ever unsure about which mode you're in, just remember that pressing Esc always returns you to Command mode. If you were already in Command mode, **vi** will beep.

There are some powerful (but arcane) commands that diehard **vi** users use to get things done quickly in this relic-of-the-sixties text editor. The **man vi** command will tell you a lot more about **vi** if you decide you want to become proficient.

discuss vi in comp.editors

The Usenet newsgroup *comp.editors* is a good place to discuss **vi** or ask questions. You can find the vi FAQ (Frequently Asked Questions) file on the Web at *http://www.macom.co.il/vi/index.html*

THE EMACS EDITOR

The **emacs** editor is not part of Linux, but since it is one of the GNU utilities, it's on the CD-ROM that comes with this book. If you selected all the suggested packages when you installed Linux, **emacs** should already be on your system. If not, you can install it by mounting the Disk 1 CD-ROM and running the **glint** command after starting the X Window GUI.

emacs is modeless

The **emacs** editor is a lot easier to use than **vi**. There are no silly modes to trip you up—when you want to enter text you just position the cursor and type. Gee, what a great idea. It also has built-in help.

But while **emacs** is a vast improvement over **vi**, you'll still have to remember quite a few commands to be productive, and you'll probably get a little lost. If you get into a situation where **emacs** seems to be stuck, or you don't know what to do, press **CTRL-G** and things will return to normal. (**CTRL-G** cancels the current operation in **emacs**.)

Let's try creating a file from scratch using **emacs**. To start, enter the command

```
$ emacs bulb.joke
```

In response, you should see a screen that looks like the one shown in Figure 5-3.

ADDING NEW TEXT TO YOUR FILE

Your cursor (shown as the vertical bar in Figure 5-3) is in the upper left-hand corner of the screen, and the message at the bottom tells you that a new file called **bulb.joke** was just created. The body of the file is blank (not tildes, as with the vi editor).

To enter new text, just start typing! There's no need to press any special keys first. Go ahead and enter the text shown in Figure 5-4. (Press **ENTER** at the end of each line.)

SAVING YOUR WORK

To save your work without leaving emacs, press **CTRL-X** (for exit) and then **CTRL-S** (for save). A message at the bottom of the screen should confirm that the file was written to disk. It's a good idea to save your work every few minutes, just so you don't lose it all if the system suddenly crashes.

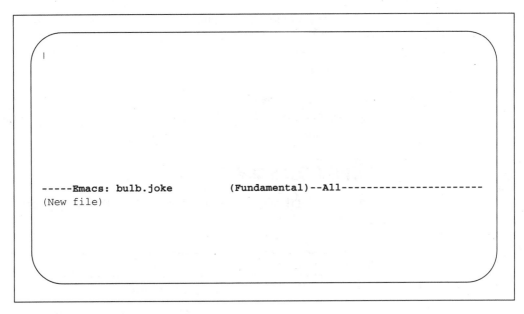

FIGURE 5.3: *Starting the emacs editor*

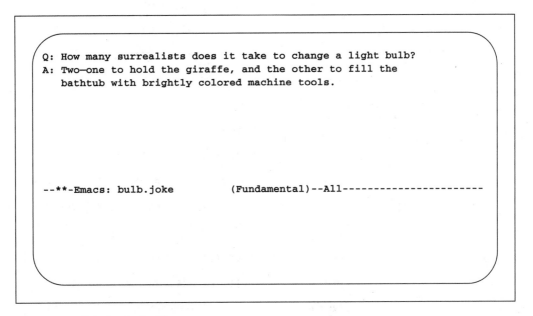

FIGURE 5.4: *Entering text with emacs*

To save your file and exit **emacs**, press **CTRL-X** and then **CTRL-C**. A prompt like

---

Save file bulb.joke? (y, n, !, ., q, C-r or C-h)

---

should appear at the bottom of the screen. Type the letter **y** to save your file and exit the editor. After leaving **emacs**, you'll be back at the Linux command prompt. (I'll discuss the other choices later.)

COMMON EMACS COMMANDS

Have a look at this list of **emacs** commands, and then we'll do one more exercise before moving on.

Cursor Positioning

→	Move cursor one space right (also **CTRL-N**).
←	Move cursor one space left (also **CTRL-P**).
↑	Move cursor up one line (also **CTRL-F**).
↓	Move cursor down one line (also **CTRL-B**).
CTRL-V	Move forward one screen (also **PGUP**).
ESC-V	Move backward one screen (also **PGDN**).
ESC-‹	Move to beginning of file.
ESC-›	Move to end of file.
ESC-F	Move cursor to next word.
ESC-B	Move cursor back one word.
HOME	Move cursor to beginning of line (also **CTRL-A**).
END	Move cursor to end of line (also **CTRL-E**).
DEL	Delete character at cursor (also **CTRL-D**).
CTRL-K	Delete to end of line.
CTRL-Y	Undelete the last thing you deleted.
CTRL-X + U	Undo the last command.
CTRL-S	Perform a search (forward).

Ctrl-R	Perform a search (backward).
Ctrl-H	View online help.
Ctrl-H + T	View emacs tutorial.

To Leave or Save Your File

Ctrl-X + Ctrl-S	Save your file and exit.
Ctrl-X + Ctrl-C	Quit without saving.

Unlike **vi** commands, **emacs** commands are not case sensitive, so whether you enter Ctrl-H or Ctrl-h, for example, you'll get the same result. There are many other **emacs** commands, but the starter set above should be enough to get you rolling.

Here's another example to let you try out some of these **emacs** commands. Enter the command below to fire up **emacs** again and you should see the file as we left it in Figure 5.4.

```
emacs bulb.joke
```

CHANGING TEXT AND MOVING THROUGH YOUR DOCUMENT

To change text that's already in the file, you first need to reach it. You can move through your file in different ways. The arrow keys provide the simplest way, and they work just like you'd expect them to—they move you character by character through your file.

If you want to jump to the beginning or end of the current line, use the **Home** and **End** keys, respectively. You can jump from word to word using **Ctrl-F** and **Ctrl-B**. Or you can scroll page by page using **Ctrl-V** (next page) and **Esc-V** (previous page). On some keyboards, the **PgUp** and **PgDn** keys work, too.

Text that you enter is inserted to the left of the cursor, and any text to the right of cursor is pushed to the right as you type. You can use the **Del** key (or **Ctrl-D**) to delete one character at a time, or press **Ctrl-K** to delete all characters from the cursor to the end of the line.

SEARCHING FOR TEXT

When you're working in a big file, you'll often want to locate a certain string of text. You can either scroll through the file until your eye catches it, or you can use **Ctrl-S** to search using **emacs'** less than elegant search tool.

As soon as you press **Ctrl-S** you can start to enter the text you want to find, but don't type too fast! As you enter your search string, **emacs** immediately moves the cursor to a word in the file that matches what you've entered so far, so if you type too fast you may miss something.

Try It   Starting at the top of the file, press **Ctrl-S** and then type the letter **b**. The cursor should jump to the word `bathtub` right away. If you now type an **r** after the b, emacs searches for "br" and the cursor should jump to the word `brightly`. You can search backward, too, by using **Ctrl-R** instead of **Ctrl-S**.

ADDING AND DELETING LINES

Let's practice adding and deleting lines now. To add a new line to your file, move the cursor to the end of a line (press **End** or use the **Rt Arrow** key), then press **Enter**. A new blank line should appear after the current line. Pressing **Enter** with the cursor at the beginning or end of a line adds a new blank line before the current line; pressing **Enter** with the cursor anywhere else on a line splits the line at that point (as it does with most any word processor).

To delete a line, move to the beginning of the line (with the **Home** key) and press **Ctrl-K**. The line will become blank, but it will not go away. To delete the blank line from the file, press **Ctrl-K** again or press the **Del** key.

CUT AND PASTE WITH EMACS

If you ever want to move a block of text from one spot in your file to another, you can use **Ctrl-K** (kill) along with **Ctrl-Y** (yank) to get the job done. When you press **Ctrl-Y** the last thing you "killed" with **Ctrl-K** will be yanked back into the file. So to move a block of text, just kill one or more lines with **Ctrl-K,** then put your cursor at the spot where you'd like to place the text and press **Ctrl-Y** to yank it back.

For example, here's how to move the first line of the **bulb.joke** file to the end. With your cursor on the first character of the first line, press **CTRL-K** twice. (Line one disappears.) Press the DN ARROW twice to move your cursor to the third line of the file, which is blank now. Press **CTRL-Y** once to paste the deleted line at line three, and then press **CTRL-Y** again.

You should now have two copies of the deleted line at the end of your file, which should look like Figure 5.5.

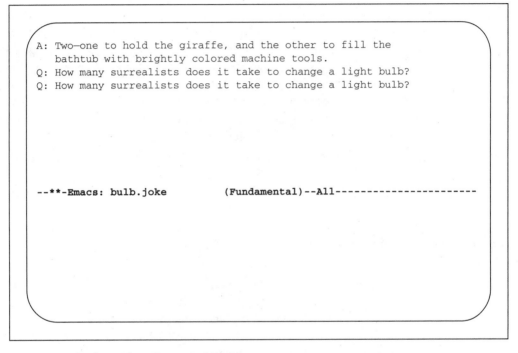

```
A: Two—one to hold the giraffe, and the other to fill the
   bathtub with brightly colored machine tools.
Q: How many surrealists does it take to change a light bulb?
Q: How many surrealists does it take to change a light bulb?




--**-Emacs: bulb.joke        (Fundamental)--All----------------------
```

FIGURE 5.5: *Cutting and pasting text with emacs*

QUITTING WITHOUT SAVING YOUR CHANGES

To leave **emacs** without saving your changes, press **CTRL-X**, then **CTRL-C**. A prompt like

```
Save file bulb.joke? (y, n, !, ., q, C-r or C-h)
```

will appear at the bottom of the screen.

Press **n** and then answer **yes** when **emacs** asks

```
Modified buffers exist; exit anyway? (yes or no)
```

Your Linux prompt will return and the **bulb.joke** file will be just as it was before you started editing.

PARTING WORDS ABOUT EMACS

We haven't even scratched the surface of what you can do with the **emacs** editor. As its name suggests, you can write your own macros to add functionality to the editor or to automate repetitive editing tasks.

Take the time to go through the **emacs** tutorial (accessed by pressing **CTRL-H + T**) to get an idea of all the things you can do with it. While it's not easy to learn all the various CTRL and ESC commands, if you're a programmer (or even if you dabble) **emacs'** customizability makes it your best bet as a text editor.

discuss emacs
in comp.emacs

The Usenet newsgroup *comp.emacs* is a good place to discuss **emacs** or ask questions. You can find the **emacs** FAQ file on the Web at *ftp://rtfm.mit.edu/pub/usenet/comp.emacs*.

THE PICO EDITOR

Pico, short for Pine Composer, started life as the built-in editor for the Pine e-mail program. Lots of people use Pico as a text editor because they also use the friendly Pine program for e-mail.

The Pico text editor doesn't have a lot of fancy features, but it's a welcome alternative to the **vi** or **emacs** editors because learning it is quick and easy. Cursor movement and text entry are straightforward, and—best of all—you don't have to learn any arcane commands: all commands are listed in a handy menu at the bottom of the screen.

To start **pico,** enter a command like this:

```
pico bulb.joke
```

In response, you should see the file **bulb.joke** displayed on your screen in **pico,** ready for editing.

```
  UW PICO(tm) 4.3                                              File: bulb.joke

  Q: How many surrealists does it take to screw in a light bulb?
  A: Two—one to hold the giraffe, and the other to fill the
     bathtub with brightly colored machine tools.




                              [ Read 3 lines ]
  ^G Help   ^O WriteOut   ^R Read File ^Y Prev Pg   ^K Cut Text    ^C Cur Pos
  ^X Exit   ^J Justify    ^W Where is  ^V Next Pg   ^U UnCut Text ^T To Spell
```

FIGURE 5.6:   *The pico editor*

GETTING AROUND IN PICO

Before we explore **pico** commands, here's a summary of how to navigate your way around a file in **pico**.

Cursor Positioning

→	Move cursor one space right (also **CTRL-N**).
←	Move cursor one space left (also **CTRL-P**).
↑	Move cursor up one line (also **CTRL-F**).
↓	Move cursor down one line (also **CTRL-B**).
DEL	Delete character at cursor (also **CTRL-D**).
CTRL-Y	Move backward one screen (also **F7**).
CTRL-V	Move forward one screen (also **F8**).

Cᴛʀʟ-A	Move cursor to beginning of line.
Cᴛʀʟ-E	Move cursor to end of line.

With the exception of the Cᴛʀʟ-Y (page down) command, text entry and cursor handling are identical to that of the **emacs** editor, so we won't cover that again here.

THE PICO MENU

When you start **pico,** you'll see this menu of commands:

```
^G Help   ^O WriteOut  ^R Read File ^Y Prev Pg   ^K Cut Text    ^C Cur Pos
^X Exit   ^J Justify   ^W Where is  ^V Next Pg   ^U UnCut Text ^T To Spell
```

Here's a list of what they mean (the circumflex (^) stands for Cᴛʀʟ).

PICO COMMANDS

Cᴛʀʟ-G	Display help screens.
Cᴛʀʟ-O	Write file to disk.
Cᴛʀʟ-R	Read another file.
Cᴛʀʟ-K	Cut line or marked text.
Cᴛʀʟ-C	Display cursor position.
Cᴛʀʟ-X	Exit from pico.
Cᴛʀʟ-J	Reflow the paragraph.
Cᴛʀʟ-W	Search for text.
Cᴛʀʟ-U	Paste (uncut) text.
Cᴛʀʟ-T	Run spelling checker.

SAVING AND EXITING

Saving your file is easy with **pico**—just press **Cᴛʀʟ-O** to write your file to disk and remain in the editor, or press **Cᴛʀʟ-X** and respond **y** to the **"Save Modified Buffer?"** prompt to save and exit.

If you want to exit from **pico** without saving your file, press **CTRL-X** and respond **n** to the **"Save Modified Buffer?"** prompt.

INSERTING ANOTHER FILE

To insert another file into the one you're currently editing, position the cursor where you want to insert the file, press **CTRL-R**, and enter the name of the file you wish to insert at the prompt that appears on your screen:

```
Insert file from home directory: _____
^G Get Help   ^T To Files
^C Cancel
```

If you can't remember the name of the file to insert, press **CTRL-T** to display a list of all your files. If you ultimately decide not to insert it, press **CTRL-C** to cancel.

CUT AND PASTE WITH PICO

If all you want to do is cut and paste a line of text, you can use the **CTRL-K** key to delete the current line and **CTRL-U** to paste it somewhere else. The Pico text editor also lets you cut and paste blocks of text. Put your cursor on the word "light" on the first line of the **bulb.joke** file, and press **CTRL-^** (the circumflex is the shifted **6** key).

Nothing happens right away, but as you move the cursor it highlights a block of text. Move the cursor to the end of the word "giraffe" on the next line—your file should look like Figure 5-7.

Once you've marked a block of text, **CTRL-K** acts a bit differently from before. Instead of deleting the entire line where the cursor is located, it deletes the highlighted block. You can then use **CTRL-U** to paste the deleted block elsewhere.

■ *TIP: You don' t have to paste the deleted text right away, or ever. CTRL-K can be used simply as a handy way of deleting unwanted text. (Deleted text goes to an invisible clipboard, and it disappears once you delete more text.)*

```
  UW PICO(tm) 4.3                                        File: bulb.joke

  Q: How many surrealists does it take to screw in a light bulb?
  A: Two—one to hold the giraffe, and the other to fill the
     bathtub with brightly colored machine tools.
```

FIGURE 5.7:   *Marking text for cut and paste*

BELLS AND WHISTLES

justifying text

The Pico text editor has a few nifty features you might not expect to find in a simple text editor. For example, **CTRL-J** will justify the sentences in the current paragraph. Type in a bunch of short sentences on separate lines and try it. If you don't like the results, **CTRL-U** will undo the operation.

spell checking

Pico also has a built-in spelling checker you can call up with **CTRL-T** from within a file. If **pico** doesn't find any dubious words in the current document, nothing much happens except that the message Done checking spelling appears at the bottom of the screen.

And if you'd like to know exactly where you are within a file (on which line and at which character), or if you'd like a quick character or line count, press **CTRL-C** and look in the message area at the bottom of the screen for something like this:

```
line 2 of 4 (50%), character 65 of 173 (37%)
```

PARTING WORDS ABOUT PICO

Pico is my personal favorite in text editors because it's easy to use and starts up quickly. Pico is under constant development at the University of Washington. For more information, you can visit the Pine Information Center on the Web at *http://www.washington.edu/pine*— you can even download the latest version of pico for Linux there.

SLICING AND DICING

HEAD

TAIL

SORT

UNIQ

CUT

GREP

SED

AWK

FIND

Pipe Fitting

O ne of the nice things about Linux is that it comes with a bunch of tools to help you manipulate files and data without writing programs. For example, if you want to search inside a bunch of files, pull out all lines that contain a certain keyword, sort those lines, eliminate duplicates, and then print just the third column of each line — it's really not much trouble using the tools described in this chapter.

Writing a C program to do that would not be a trivial exercise, even for an experienced programmer. But you can use these slicing-and-dicing tools like building blocks to manipulate data and produce reports without a computer science degree.

Following is a description of how each tool works, and at the end of the chapter you'll find some tips on how to combine them into even more powerful commands.

HEAD

The **head** command displays the first few lines at the top of a file. It can be useful when you want a quick peek at a large file, as an alternative to opening it up with a text editor. By default, **head** will show the first ten lines of a file, but you can also tell it how many lines to display.

`head some.file`	Show first ten lines of *some.file*
`head -5 some.file`	Show first five lines of *some.file*

TAIL

The **tail** command displays the last few lines of a file. Like **head**, it can save you time, because it's a lot quicker than calling up a file with a text editor and scrolling all the way down to the bottom. By default, **tail** will show the last ten lines of a file, but you can also tell it how many lines to display:

`tail some.file`	Show last ten lines of *some.file*
`tail -3 some.file`	Show last three lines of *some.file*

Here's a practical example of how to use the **tail** command. Many Linux programs put diagnostic messages in the **/var/syslog/messages** file when they run, so this file can get pretty large after a while. To see if your most recent command issued any messages, look at the tail end of this file with the **tail /var/syslog/messages** command.

SORT

The **sort** command sorts a file according to fields—the individual pieces of data on each line. By default, **sort** will assume that the fields are just words separated by blanks, but you can specify an alternative field delimiter if you want (such as commas or colons). Output from **sort** is printed to the screen, unless you redirect it to a file.

If you had a file like the one below containing information on people who contributed to your presidential reelection campaign, you might want to sort it by last name, donation amount, or location.

```
Bay Ching 500000 China
Jack Arta 250000 Indonesia
Cruella Lumper 725000 Malaysia
```

Let's take this sample donors file and sort it according to the donation amount. (Using a text editor, enter those three lines into a file and save it with **donor.data** as the file name.) Below, you can see the command to sort the file on the third field (donation amount) and the output from the command:

```
$ sort +2 -3 donors.data
Jack Arta 250000 Indonesia
Bay Ching 500000 China
Cruella Lumper 725000 Malaysia
```

The syntax of the **sort** command is pretty strange, but if you study the examples below, you should be able to adapt one of them for your own use. The general form of the **sort** command is:

sort ‹*flags*› ‹*sort fields*› ‹*file name*›

The most common flags are as follows:

-f Make all lines uppercase before sorting (so "Bill" and "bill" are treated the same).

-r Sort in reverse order (so "Z" starts the list instead of "A").

-t*X*	Use *X* as the field delimiter (replace *X* with a comma or other character).
-u	Suppress all but one line in each set of lines with equal sort fields (so if you sort on a field containing last names, only one "Smith" will show even if there are several).

Specify the sort keys like this:

+*M*	Start at the first character of the *M*+1th field.
-*N*	End at the last character of the *N*th field (if -*N* is omitted, assume end of line).

Looks weird, huh? Let's look at a few more examples with the sample **company.data** file shown below, and you'll get the hang of it. (Each line of the file contains four fields: first name, last name, serial number, and department name.)

```
Jan Itorre 406378 Sales
Jim Nasium 031762 Marketing
Mel Ancholie 636496 Research
Ed Jucacion 396082 Sales
```

To sort the file on the third field (serial number) in reverse order and save the results in **sorted.data,** use this command:

```
$ sort -r +2 -3 company.data > sorted.data
Mel Ancholie 636496 Research
Jan Itorre 406378 Sales
Ed Jucacion 396082 Sales
Jim Nasium 031762 Marketing
```

Now let's look at a situation where the fields are separated by colons instead of spaces. In this case we will use the -**t:** flag to tell the **sort** command how to find the fields on each line. Let's start with this file:

```
Itorre, Jan:406378:Sales
Nasium, Jim:031762:Marketing
Ancholie, Mel:636496:Research
Jucacion, Ed:396082:Sales
```

To sort the file on the second field (serial number), use this command:

```
$ sort -t: +1 -2 company.data
Nasium, Jim:031762:Marketing
Jucacion, Ed:396082:Sales
Itorre, Jan:406378:Sales
Ancholie, Mel:636496:Research
```

To sort the file on the third field (department name) and suppress the duplicates, use this command:

```
$ sort -t: -u +2 company.data
Nasium, Jim:031762:Marketing
Ancholie, Mel:636496:Research
Itorre, Jan:406378:Sales
```

Note that the line for "Ed Jucacion" did not print, because he's in Sales, and we asked the command (with the **-u** flag) to suppress lines that were the same in the sort field.

There are lots of fancy (and a few obscure) things you can do with the **sort** command. If you need to do any sorting that's not quite as straightforward as these examples, try the **man sort** command for more information.

UNIQ

The **uniq** command reads the input file and compares adjacent lines. Any line that is the same as the one before it will be discarded. In other words, duplicates are discarded, leaving only the unique lines in the file.

Let's say you're a publisher with an inventory of all your books in the **my.books** file shown below:

```
Atopic Dermatitis for Dummies
Atopic Dermatitis for Dummies
Chronic Rhinitis Unleashed
Chronic Rhinitis Unleashed
Chronic Rhinitis Unleashed
Learn Nasal Endoscopy in 21 Days
```

To remove all the duplicates from the list of books, use this command:

```
% uniq my.books
Atopic Dermatitis for Dummies
Chronic Rhinitis Unleashed
Learn Nasal Endoscopy in 21 Days
```

If you want to print only the book titles that are *not* duplicated (to find out which books you have only one copy of), add the **-u** flag like this:

```
% uniq -u my.books
Learn Nasal Endoscopy in 21 Days
```

Conversely, you might want to exclude the titles that appear only once. If so, add the **-d** flag like this:

```
% uniq -d my.books
Atopic Dermatitis for Dummies
Chronic Rhinitis Unleashed
```

Now let's take inventory! To summarize the list of books and add a count of how many times each one appears in the list, add the **-c** flag like this:

```
% uniq -c my.books
2 Atopic Dermatitis for Dummies
3 Chronic Rhinitis Unleashed
1 Learn Nasal Endoscopy in 21 Days
```

Note that the **uniq** command does not sort the input file, so you may want to use the **sort** command to prepare the data for **uniq** in advance. (See the end of this chapter for an example.) Here's a recap of the flags you can use with the **uniq** command:

-u   Only print lines that appear *once* in the input file.

-d   Only print the lines that appear *more than once* in the input file.

-c   Precede each output line with a count of how many times it was found.

CUT

The **cut** command takes a vertical slice of a file, printing only the specified columns or fields. Like the **sort** command, **cut** defines a field as a word set off by blanks, unless you specify your own delimiter. It's easiest to think of a column as just the *n*th character on each line. In other words, "column five" consists of the fifth character of each line.

Consider a slight variation on the **company.data** file we've been playing with in this chapter:

```
406378:Sales:Itorre:Jan
031762:Marketing:Nasium:Jim
636496:Research:Ancholie:Mel
396082:Sales:Jucacion:Ed
```

If you want to print just columns 1 to 6 of each line (the employee serial numbers), use the **-c1-6** flag, as in this command:

```
$ cut -c1-6 company.data
406378
031762
636496
396082
```

If you want to print just columns 8 and 4 of each line (the first letter of the department and the fourth digit of the serial number), use the **-c8,4** flag, as in this command:

```
$ cut -c8,4 company.data
S3
M7
R4
S0
```

And since this file obviously has fields delimited by colons, we can pick out just the first and last names by specifying the -**d:** and -**f4,3** flags, like this:

```
$ cut -d: -f4,3 company.data
Jan Itorre
Jim Nasium
Mel Ancholie
Ed Jucacion
```

Here is a summary of the most common flags for the **cut** command:

`-c [n | n,m | n-m]`	Specify a single column, multiple columns (separated by a comma), or a range of columns (separated by a dash).
`-f [n | n,m | n-m]`	Specify a single field, multiple fields (separated by a comma), or a range of fields (separated by a dash).
`-dc`	Specify the field delimiter.
`-s`	Suppress (don't print) lines not containing the delimiter.

GREP

The **grep** command selects and prints lines from a file (or a bunch of files) that match a pattern. Let's say your friend Bill sent you an e-mail recently with his phone number, and you want to call him ASAP to order some books. Instead of launching your e-mail program and sifting through all the messages, you can scan your in-box file like this:

```
$ grep 'number' /var/mail/hermie
can call No Starch Press at 800/420-7240. Office hours are
noted that recently, an alarming number of alien spacecrafts
among colleagues at a number of different organizations
```

Here, **grep** has pulled out just the lines that contain the word "number." The first line is obviously what you were after, while the others just happened to match the pattern. The general form of the **grep** command is this:

```
grep <flags> <pattern> <files>
```

The most useful **grep** flags are shown below:

`-i`	Ignore uppercase and lowercase when comparing.
`-v`	Print only lines that do *not* match the pattern.

`-c`	Print only a count of the matching lines.
`-n`	Display the line number before each matching line.

When **grep** does its pattern matching, it expects you to provide a *regular expression* for the pattern. Regular expressions can be very simple or quite complex, so we won't get into a lot of details here. Here are the most common types of regular expressions:

abc	Match lines containing the string "abc" anywhere.
^abc	Match lines starting with "abc."
abc$	Match lines ending with "abc."
a..c	Match lines containing "a" and "c" separated by any two characters (the dot matches any single character).
a.*c	Match lines containing "a" and "c" separated by any number of characters (the dot-asterisk means match zero or more characters).

Here are a sample **poem.txt** file and some **grep** commands to demonstrate regular-expression pattern matching:

```
Mary had a little lamb
Mary fried a lot of spam
Jack ate a Spam sandwich
Jill had a lamb spamwich
```

To print all lines containing "spam" (respecting uppercase and lowercase):

```
% grep 'spam' poem.txt
Mary fried a lot of spam
Jill had a lamb spamwich
```

To print all lines containing "spam" (ignoring uppercase and lowercase):

```
% grep -i 'spam' poem.txt
Mary fried a lot of spam
Jack ate a Spam sandwich
Jill had a lamb spamwich
```

To print just the number of lines containing the word "spam" (ignoring uppercase and lowercase):

```
% grep -c 'spam' poem.txt
3
```

To print all lines *not* containing "spam" (ignoring uppercase and lowercase):

```
% grep -i -v 'spam' poem.txt
Mary had a little lamb
```

To print all lines starting with "Mary":

```
% grep '^Mary' poem.txt
Mary had a little lamb
Mary fried a lot of spam
```

To print all lines ending with "ich":

```
% grep 'ich$' poem.txt
Jack ate a Spam sandwich
Jill had a lamb spamwich
```

To print all lines containing "had" followed by "lamb":

```
% grep 'had.*lamb' poem.txt
Mary had a little lamb
Jill had a lamb spamwich
```

If you want to learn more about regular expressions, start with the **man regexp** command. There's also a good book called *Mastering Regular Expressions*, by Jeffrey Friedl, published by O'Reilly & Associates.

SED

You can use the **sed** command to change all occurrences of one string to another inside a file, just like the search and replace feature in your word processor; **sed** can also delete a range of lines from a file. The general forms of the **sed** command are

```
sed 's/<oldstring>/
<newstring>/g' <file>      Substitution

sed '<start>,
<end>d' <file>             Deletion
```

Let's start with a substitution example. If you want to change all occurrences of "lamb" to "ham" in the **poem.txt** file from the **grep** example, do this:

```
% sed 's/lamb/ham/g' poem.txt
Mary had a little ham
Mary fried a lot of spam
Jack ate a Spam sandwich
Jill had a ham spamwich
```

In the quoted string, the "s" means "substitute," and the "g" means a "global" change. You can also leave off the "g" (to change only the first occurrence on each line) or specify a number instead (to change the first *n* occurrences on each line).

Now let's try an example involving deletion of lines. The values for **start** and **end** can be either a line number, or a pattern to match. All lines from the **start** line to the **end** line are removed from the file. This example will delete starting at line 2, up to and including line 3:

```
% sed '2,3d' poem.txt
Mary had a little lamb
Jill had a lamb spamwich
```

This example will delete starting at line 1, up to and including the next line containing "Jack":

```
% sed '1,/Jack/d' poem.txt
Jill had a lamb spamwich
```

The most common use of **sed** is to change one string of text to another string of text. But I should mention that the strings that **sed** uses for search and delete are actually regular expressions. This means you can do pattern matching, just as with **grep**. Although you'll probably never need to do anything like this, here's an example, anyway. To change any occurrences of "lamb" at the end of a line to "ham," do this:

```
% sed 's/lamb$/ham/g' poem.txt
Mary had a little ham
Mary fried a lot of spam
Jack ate a Spam sandwich
Jill had a lamb spamwich
```

Use the **man sed** command for more information on using **sed**.

AWK

The **awk** command combines the functions of **grep** and **sed**, making it one of the most powerful Unix commands. Using **awk,** you can substitute words from an input file's lines into a template, or perform calculations on numbers inside a file. (In case you're wondering how **awk** got such an offbeat name, it's derived from the surnames of the three programmers who invented it.)

To use **awk,** you write a miniature program in a C-like language that transforms each line of the input file. We'll concentrate only on the **print** function inside **awk,** since that's the most useful and the least confusing of all the things awk can do. The general form of the **awk** command is

```
awk <pattern> '{print <stuff>}' <file>
```

In this case, *stuff* is going to be some combination of text, special variables that represent each word in the input line, and perhaps a mathematical operator or two. As **awk** processes each line of the input file, each word on the line is assigned to variables named $1 (the first word), $2 (the second word), and so on. (The variable $0 contains the entire line.)

Let's start with a file, **words.data,** that contains these lines:

```
nail hammer wood
pedal foot car
clown pie circus
```

Now we'll use the **print** function in **awk** to plug the words from each input line into a template, like this:

```
% awk '{print "Hit the",$1,"with your",$2}' words.data
Hit the nail with your hammer
Hit the pedal with your foot
Hit the clown with your pie
```

Say some of the data in your input file is numeric, as in the **grades.data** file shown here:

```
Rogers 87 100 95
Lambchop 66 89 76
Barney 12 36 27
```

You can perform calculations like this:

```
$ awk '{print "Avg for",$1,"is",($2+$3+$4)/3}' grades.data
Avg for Rogers is 94
Avg for Lambchop is 77
Avg for Barney is 25
```

So far we haven't specified any value for **pattern** in these examples, but if you want to exclude lines from being processed, you can do something like this:

```
% awk /^clown/ '{print "See the",$1,"at the",$3}' words.data
See the clown at the circus
```

Here, we told **awk** to consider only the input lines that start with "clown." But this is just the tip of the **awk** iceberg—entire books have been written on this command. If you are a programmer, try the **man awk** command.

FIND

The **find** command locates files in many different ways. Unlike the rest of the commands in this chapter, **find** does not look at the contents of a file—it only helps you find files that meet certain criteria, such as name, size, age, and type. The general form of the **find** command is

```
find <starting point> <search criteria> <action>
```

The *starting point* is the name of the directory where **find** should start looking for files; **find** examines all files in this directory (and any subdirectories) to see if they meet the *search criteria*. If so, it will take the specified *action* on each found file. Here are some of the most useful search criteria options:

-name *pattern*	Find files with names that match the pattern.
-size [+|-] *n*	Find files larger or smaller than a certain size.
-atime [+|-] *n*	Find files accessed before or after a certain date.

-mtime [+|-] *n*	Find files modified before or after a certain date.
-type *filetype*	Find just regular files, or only directories.

And here are the actions that can be applied to found files:

-print	Print just the names of matching files.
-ls	Print the names, dates, sizes, and so on of matching files.
-exec *command*	Execute a command with the file name as input.
-ok *command*	Same as **-exec**, but asks for confirmation first.

That all might look a bit confusing, so here are some examples to bring it down to earth. To find files (starting in the current directory) with names ending with ".data" and print their names, try this:

```
$ find . -name *.data -print
company.data
donor.data
grades.data
sorted.data
words.data
```

To find files larger than 40K, and print the file names and details (use a minus sign instead of a plus sign to find files smaller than a certain size), issue this command:

```
$ find . -size +40k -ls
-rw-rw-r-- hermie users  56720 Jan 16 12:42 bigfile
-rw-rw-r-- hermie users 415206 Feb 27 21:37 largefile
-rw-rw-r-- hermie users 3915428 Jan 07 05:23 hugefile
```

To find files ending with ".txt" that are smaller than 100K:

```
$ find . -name *.txt -size -100k -ls
-rw-rw-r-- hermie users  26720 Feb 06 23:52 recipes.txt
-rw-rw-r-- hermie users    506 Feb 18 18:45 poem.txt
```

To find files that have not been accessed for over 30 days and delete them (by sending their names to the **rm** command):

```
find . -atime +30 -exec rm {} \;
```

To find directories (starting in the "junk" directory) and conditionally delete them (by sending their names to the **rmdir** command):

```
find junk -type d -ok rmdir {} \;
```

PIPE FITTING

Throughout this chapter we've discussed how to manipulate a file with many different tools. But you can use each of these tools in a more powerful way by combining them into pipelines. Back in Chapter 2, "Living in a Shell," you learned how to pump the output from one command to another by redirecting the input or output of those commands.

Following are several examples that show how to combine the power of the tools described in this chapter.

- Find files that have not been accessed for over 30 days and print the first five lines of each:

```
find . -atime +30 -exec head -5 {} \;
```

- Find out if there is a process running named **netscape**:

```
ps | grep netscape
```

- Print only the second and third lines of a file:

```
head -3 some.file | tail -2
```

Note that the usage changes slightly when a command is in the second or subsequent stages of a pipeline. There is no input file specified, because the previous stage feeds the command.

At the beginning of this chapter, I said that it would be no problem to search inside a bunch of files, pull out all lines that contain a certain keyword, sort those lines, eliminate duplicates, and then print just the third column of each line. Here's proof that you can do it all on one line:

```
grep 'stuff' *.data | sort +1 -2 | uniq | cut -f3
```

Seems almost too easy, doesn't it? Beats the heck out of writing a program several hundred lines long if you only want to run it once! Now let's use the rest of the commands from this chapter in another pipeline.

Start by creating the file **odds.ends** containing the lines shown below:

```
Ford Cat 47
IBM Lion 152
Xerox Slug 31
Zenith Bear 26
Intel Cat 133
Hershey Lynx 28
Apple Panda 74
```

Then execute the following command. (The backslash at the end of a line tells the shell that you are continuing a command on the next line.) Can you figure out what the output will be?

```
head -5 odds.ends | sed s/Cat/Tigger/g | \
awk /Tigger/ '{print "Buy",$1,"from","$2","at",$3}' | \
tail -1
```

The correct answer is "Buy Intel from Tigger at 133"—can you prove it?

THE X WINDOW SYSTEM

So far, everything we've done in Linux has been text based. No pretty pictures, no pointing and clicking—just a command prompt and words on a screen. But most Unix systems have a graphical user interface called the X Window System (commonly referred to as X) that provides many of the same features you'll be familiar with if you use Windows 95.

I'm going to assume you're familiar with GUI basics like mouse handling and terms such as *window*, *icon*, etc. If you've used any version of Microsoft Windows or even a Mac, the X interface will be very easy to learn and use.

Linux Pro comes with **XFree86**, an implementation of X for PCs that was done by a group at MIT. **XFree86** also includes **fvwm**, the Freeware Window Manager that looks very much like Motif—the most popular window manager for X-based systems.

STARTING X

When you installed Linux according to the instructions in Chapter 1, "Installing Linux on Your PC," the **INSTALL** program asked you a bunch of questions about your monitor, video card, and mouse. This was done to configure your system for running X, so you should be able to start the GUI now by entering the command

```
startx
```

A bunch of stuff will flash across your screen, and then you'll see a gray background take over the entire screen. After a minute or so, several windows will appear, and you'll see the mouse cursor, a small black "X."

HELP, IT DIDN'T WORK!

If X fails to start (you never got the gray background) look closely at the messages on your screen. You may see something indicating an "unsupported chipset" or some other configuration error. If you get the gray background but there's nothing there (or just the "X" cursor) then press **CTRL-ALT-BKSP** to return to the command prompt and examine the messages. (If you issue the command **startx ›xlog 2›&1** you can capture all the messages in a file named **xlog** and then view it with a text editor.)

It's possible that your video card is not supported by the version of **XFree86** that came on the CD-ROM, but enhancements and support for additional cards are always in the works. See the XFree86 Home Page at *http://www.XFree86.org/* for information on supported video cards, or how to download and install the very latest code.

But before you run off and download anything, there's a chance that you can fix the problem by reconfiguring your X system. To try that, enter these commands while logged in as **root**:

```
cp /etc/X11/XF86config /etc/X11/XF86config.bak
Xconfigurator
```

This will make a backup copy of your X configuration file and then step you through the setup process again. When you've finished, try the **startx** command again. If it still doesn't work, you might have success by trying different options in the **Xconfigurator** program.

If you still have problems getting X to work, your best bet is to get another video card or try a commercial X Window product such as Xi Graphic's Accellerated-X server or Metro-X from MetroLink (*http://www.metrolink.com*). Both of these products support a wider range of video hardware than **Xfree86**, are easier to install, and will probably provide better performance. (See *http://www.linuxmall.com* for more information.)

USING X

Using X is a lot like using Windows 95 — you can have several applications open in different windows on the screen, and move from one to another using your mouse. Here are some examples of windows you'll see on your X display.

ELEMENTS OF AN X WINDOW

The figures show the features that you'll find in most every window while running X, namely the Minimize/Maximize buttons, title bar, grab handles, and so on, that are also present in the Microsoft Windows GUI.

FIGURE 7-1: *X Calculator*

Not every window will have all these features because X is "policy independent": windows under X don't have to look the same, as they do in other GUIs. For example, you can see that the Calculator window (Figure 7-1) has no Minimize button, and the Clock window (Figure 7-2) has no frame or title bar at all. As they say, consistency is the hobgoblin of little minds.

FIGURE 7-2: *Clock*

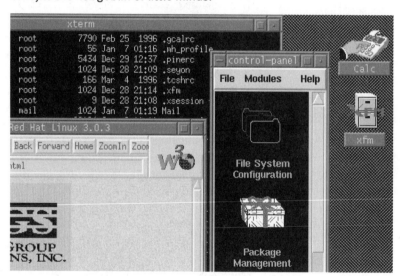

FIGURE 7-3: *Sample X Display*

Refer to Figure 7-3 as we explore some of the ways you can interact with an X window. (I've used "LMB" and "RMB" as abbreviations for "left mouse button" and "right mouse button" in the table on the next page.)

Feature	Location	Function
Control bar	Upper left	Click with LMB to reveal system menu (the only important option here is Quit or Close) or double-click to Close.
Title bar	Top middle	Click with LMB to bring window to front, or click with RMB to send window to rear. You can also move a window by dragging while holding down LMB on the title bar.
Maximize button	Top right (square inside button)	Click with LMB to make the window occupy the whole screen. Click again to resume former size.
Minimize button	Top right (dot inside button)	Click with LMB to iconize the window. Icons appear on the far right of the display. Double-click an icon to restore it to a window.
Grab handles	All four corners	Hold down LMB and drag to resize the window.

THE XTERM WINDOW

From the title bar in Figure 7-4, you can see that this is an **xterm** (X Terminal) window. An **xterm** window is where you find your Linux command prompt (much like a DOS prompt under Windows 95), and it acts just like the virtual console you were using before you entered the **startx** command. But there are a few nice things you can do with an **xterm** that you can't do with a plain text-based virtual console.

Change the font   Hold down CTRL and click with RMB in the window background and a "VT Fonts" pop-up will appear, from which you can select several different font sizes, ranging from Unreadable to Huge.

Scrolling   Click inside the scroll bars on the left side of the window to scroll the display up (RMB) or down (LMB).

Cut & paste   Mark text by dragging with LMB in the xterm window, then press the middle button to paste it on the xterm command line, or in any other window where you can enter text. (Press both LMB and RMB together if you have a 2-button mouse.)

```
                                          xterm
[root@cybarena /root]# ls -al
total 33
drwxr-xr-x    5 root     root         1024 Jan  7 00:39 .
drwxr-xr-x   17 root     root         1024 Jan  7 00:14 ..
-rw-rw-r--    1 root     root            8 Jan  7 00:04 .X
-rwxr-xr-x    1 root     root          322 Sep  6  1995 .Xclients
-rw-r--r--    1 root     root         1126 Aug 23  1995 .Xdefaults
-rw-rw-r--    1 root     root         2918 Jan  7 00:11 .bash_history
-rw-r--r--    1 root     root           24 Jul 13  1994 .bash_logout
-rw-r--r--    1 root     root          238 Aug 23  1995 .bash_profile
-rw-r--r--    1 root     root          176 Aug 23  1995 .bashrc
-rw-r--r--    1 root     root          180 Mar  4  1996 .cshrc
-rw-r--r--    1 root     root         7790 Feb 25  1996 .gcalrc
-rw-rw-r--    1 root     root         5434 Dec 29 12:37 .pinerc
drwxr-xr-x    2 root     root         1024 Dec 28 21:09 .seyon
-rw-r--r--    1 root     root          166 Mar  4  1996 .tcshrc
drwxr-xr-x    2 root     root         1024 Dec 28 21:14 .xfm
lrwxrwxrwx    1 root     root            9 Dec 28 21:08 .xsession -> .Xclients
drwx------    2 root     root         1024 Dec 29 12:37 mail
-rwxr-xr-x    1 root     root          831 Jan  5 00:49 ppp.dip
-rw-------    1 root     root            0 Dec 29 13:41 tt.swp
-rw-rw-r--    1 root     root           51 Jan  5 00:51 ttt
[root@cybarena /root]# █
```

FIGURE 7-4: *Sample X Display*

STARTING A NEW WINDOW

There are three ways to start a new window on your X display. The easiest is to enter the name of an X program in an **xterm** window, followed by an ampersand. For example:

    xterm &   Start another xterm window

    xcalc &   Start an xcalc (Calculator window)

If you remember the discussion of foreground and background tasks from Chapter 2, "Living in a Shell," you'll know that the ampersand makes Linux launch the program in the background (in its own window) so it won't tie up **xterm**. (Not every command you issue from an **xterm** will cause a new window to open—only programs that are written specifically to run under X will do this.)

The second way to open a new window is by double-clicking a program's icon. For example, clicking the **Package Management** icon in **control-panel** (Figure 7-5) launches **glint,** a tool you can use to install or remove software packages. (You could do the same thing by typing **glint &** at an **xterm** command prompt.) Note that **control-panel** is only available when you're running X as the **root** user.

The third way to open a new window is to use the handy pop-up menus that appear when you press the LMB while the pointer is in the gray X background (not over any icon or window).

When you hold the button down you'll see the **Program Menu** pop-up, as shown in Figure 7-6.

As you move the mouse over an item in the menu, it will be highlighted. Releasing the mouse when an item that is highlighted launches the highlighted program. Selecting menu items with arrows to the right of the text will bring up cascading menus. For example, when you move the pointer over **Applications**, the menu in Figure 7-7 appears.

FIGURE 7-5: *Control Panel*

CLOSING A WINDOW

Because each new window you open consumes more system resources (like memory and processor power), having too many windows open at one time will tend to slow down your system. It's a good idea to close windows that you're not using.

You can close a window by double clicking the control bar in the upper-left corner, but that may not allow the program running in that window to exit gracefully. Instead, check first to see if there is an action bar with a **Quit** or **File+Close** option and use that if it's available.

FIGURE 7-6: *Program Menu*

The **Xterm** windows are a little different, since they don't have an action bar, and double-clicking the control bar could terminate a program that was doing something important. If you must close an **xterm** window with a running program, try pressing **CTRL-C** to interrupt the program before using the control bar method. If there's nothing running in the **xterm,** you can enter the **exit** command to close the window.

LEAVING X WINDOW

There seems to be more than one way to do everything in X, and exiting is no exception. The

FIGURE 7-7: *Applications pop-up*

best way to exit is to hold down the LMB while in the gray background to get the Program Menu pop-up shown in Figure 7-8 and then select the **Exit Fvwm** option.

Incredulous, X will display another pop-up menu asking **Really Quit Fvwm?** (Figure 7-9).

Select **Yes, Really Quit** to leave or **No, Don't Quit** to stay in X.

If you get stuck and the mouse will not respond, you can also leave X by pressing **CTRL-ALT-BKSP**.

FIGURE 7-8: *Program Menu pop-up*

FIGURE 7-9: *Exit FVWM pop-up*

CUSTOMIZING X WINDOW

X is customizable in many ways. You can configure it to launch whatever windows you like upon startup, change the pop-up menus, and even redefine the mouse buttons if you're left-handed.

CONFIGURING X STARTUP

When you start X you get a set of windows that includes an **xterm**, the Arena browser, a clock, and the Control Panel. If you'd like to change that set of windows, just edit your **.Xclients** file. Here's an example:

`#!/bin/bash`	Comment
`# xmodmap -e 'pointer = 3 2 1'`	Left-handed mouse
`xterm &`	Start an **xterm**

`xclock -geometry +0+0 &`	Start clock at upper left
`control-panel &`	Start the Control Panel
`arena /usr/doc/HTML/index.html &`	Start Arena with file name
`exec fvwm`	Start window manager

The first line is magic, so don't worry about it for now. If you're left-handed, you might want to uncomment (remove the **#** from) the second line, as it will swap the left and right mouse buttons. The next four lines launch the specified programs, and the last line starts the **fvwm** window manager. X won't run without a window manager, so this line is mandatory.

You can add or delete startup commands from this file, and you can also use several flags to modify the appearance or positioning of a window:

`-geometry +`*XXX*`+`*YYY*	Specify the window position. Values of *XXX* and *YYY* are determined by your screen resolution (i.e.: 1024 x 768) and are offsets from the top-left corner.
`-iconic`	Starts the program as an icon instead of a window.
`-title "my title"`	Specify a title for the window.
`-bg`	Specify the background color for a window.
`-fg`	Specify the foreground color for a window.

■ **NOTE:** *Look in the file **/usr/lib/X11/rgb.txt** for a list of all the colors you can use.*

Here are some examples of how to use these flags:

`xclock -geometry +50+50 &`	Start xclock at new location

xfm -iconic &	Start xfm as an icon
xterm -title "Console 1" &	Start first xterm
xterm -title "Console 2" &	Start second xterm
xterm -bg Black -fg Wheat &	Start xterm with new colors

If you don't already have a **.Xclients** file, you can create one with a text editor. But be aware that this file has to be both readable and executable, so you may need to set the permissions with this command:

```
chmod ug+rx .Xclients
```

CHANGING POP-UP MENUS

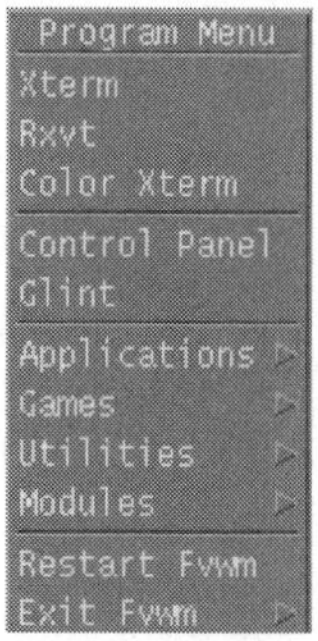

You can change the pop-up menus that appear when you press the LMB in the X background. To do so you'll need to copy the **/etc/X11/fvwm/ system.fvwmrc** file to your home directory, name it **.fvwmrc,** and edit the appropriate Pop-up sections.

There are several hundred lines in this file, most of which you don't want to touch. To alter the Program Menu pop-up (Figure 7-10), find the section that looks like this:

FIGURE 7-10: *Program Menu pop-up*

```
Pop-up "Utilities"
 Title  "Program Menu"
 Exec   "Xterm"              exec xterm -e bash &
 Exec   "Rxvt"              exec rxvt -bg Black -fg Wheat &
 Exec   "Color Xterm"       exec xterm-color &
 Nop      " "
 Exec   "Control Panel"      exec control-panel &
 Exec   "Glint"             exec glint &
 Nop      " "
 Pop-up "Applications"       Apps
 Pop-up "Games"             Games
 Pop-up "Utilities"         Utils
 Pop-up "Modules"           Module-Pop-up
 Nop      " "
 Restart "Restart Fvwm"      fvwm
 Pop-up "Exit Fvwm"         Quit-Verify
EndPop-up
```

The section starts with the keyword Pop-up "Utilities" and ends with EndPop-up. Here's a description of what the lines in between are all about:

Title	Defines the title for the pop-up.
Exec	The label for the pop-up menu item appears in quotes, followed by the command to execute when the item is selected.
Pop-up	Points to a submenu. You must have another Pop-up/EndPop-up section to define it (see below).
Nop	Creates a separator line in the menu.
Restart	Similar to **exec,** a special command to restart the window manager.

From this series of commands you can see why this menu looks the way it does, and why the secondary menus appear when you select "Applications" or "Utilities". For example, the line reading

```
Pop-up    "Utilities"    Utils
```

refers to another section in the file that looks like this:

```
Pop-up "Utils"
  Exec    "Calculator"    exec xcalc &
  Exec    "Xman"          exec xman &
  Exec    "Xmag"          exec xmag &
  Exec    "xosview"       exec xosview &
EndPop-up
```

This menu has only Exec statements and no submenus. You can add, delete, or change the Exec and Pop-up statements in the Pop-up/Endpopup sections to change the items that appear on the pop-ups. For example, if you want to add your favorite spreadsheet program to the "Utilities" pop-up and add a submenu for your graphics programs, you might change the example above to look like this:

```
Pop-up "Utils"
  Exec   "Calculator"       exec xcalc &
  Exec   "Spreadsheet"      exec xspread &
  Pop-up "Graphics Stuff"   Graphics
  Exec   "Xman"             exec xman &
  Exec   "Xmag"             exec xmag &
  Exec   "xosview"          exec xosview &
EndPop-up
```

The new pop-up menus will not become active until you restart the window manager. (You can do this by selecting **Restart Fvwm** from the **Program Menu** pop-up.)

X APPLICATIONS

Lots of cool X applications come with Linux Pro, including productivity and system administration tools, games, and other utilities. Here's a list of some you might find helpful.

ARENA

Arena is a graphical web browser. Not as powerful as Netscape, but it gets the job done. When you start X, Arena displays a page with links to a bunch of helpful Linux resources and help files. Unless you have an Internet connection, Arena will only be able to access local files.

If you've ever used Netscape, you probably won't like Arena very much (shown here).

You can download Netscape for Linux at the Linux Mall (*http://www.linuxmall.com*). See Chapter 11, "Connecting to the Internet," for details on how to establish a SLIP/PPP connection to the Internet.

FILE MANAGER

Much like its Windows cousin, this program (Figure 7-11) lets you navigate your file system with a mouse. Double-clicking on a folder displays its contents, double-clicking a program launches it in a new window, and double-clicking a text file displays it in the **emacs** editor. Start File Manager from the Program Menu pop-up shown in Figure 7-12, or use the **xfm** command from an **xterm** window.

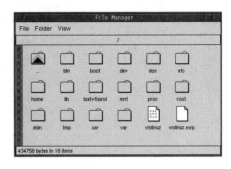

FIGURE 7-11: *File Manager*

FIGURE 7-12: *Program Menu pop-up*

CONTROL PANEL

This window (shown at right) has icons for launching various system administration tools. If it's not already running, issue the **control-panel** command from an **xterm** window. Here are some of the tools you can use:

- **File System Configuration** to mount and unmount disks, floppies, and CD-ROMs

- **Package Management** to install software from CD-ROM, or remove software

- **Modem Configuration** to set up your modem for use with Linux
- **User/Group Configuration** to add or delete users and groups
- **Printer Configuration** to set up your printer for use with Linux
- **Network Configuration** to set up Ethernet and SLIP/PPP connections
- **Time & Date** to set your system's time and date

CLOCK

A simple analog clock. Issue the **xclock** command from an **xterm** window, or start it via the Program Menu pop-up. (See Figure 7-2.)

CALCULATOR

A basic calculator. Issue the **xcalc** command from an **xterm** window, or start it via the Program Menu pop-up. (See Figure 7-1.)

EXMH

A graphical e-mail program. Issue the **exmh** command from an **xterm** window, or start it via the Program Menu pop-up.

XV

A powerful utility that can display and manipulate many different types of graphic files. Also does image conversions and screen snapshots. Issue the **xv** command from an **xterm** window, or start via the Program Menu pop-up.

XFIG AND XPAINT

Both of these are tools to help you create artwork, a bit like the MacDraw or Windows Paintbrush programs. Issue the **xfig** or **xpaint** command from an **xterm** window, or start them via the Program Menu pop-up.

GAMES

Lots of games are available for Linux! If you installed all the packages recommended in Chapter 1, you can try any of these games by typing the program name in an **xterm** command prompt.

gnuchess   Play chess against a worthy opponent—your computer.

xbill   Wipe out all the miniature "Bills" running around on the screen before they install deadly software on all the workstations—hilarious!

xboing   A fast-paced shoot 'em up in space game.

xchomp   A variation on the PacMan theme.

xdemineur   The Minesweeper game.

xdoom   The popular Doom game—hours of bloody fun.

xgammon   Play backgammon with your PC.

xlander   Land a spacecraft on the moon or die trying.

xrubik   Rubik's Cube—twist and shout.

xtetris   That irritating "falling blocks" game. There's also **xhextris**, which uses falling hexagons instead of blocks.

COMMERCIAL APPLICATIONS

The Linux Pro CD comes with a ton of great freeware and shareware. Part of the Linux tradition is that operating system software should be freely available, and the ad hoc team of Unix wizards that continually keep making Linux better is to be commended.

But alas, not all software can be given away for free—programmers have to make a living somehow. In fact, the development and sale of well-supported commercial Linux products is key to marketplace acceptance of Linux as a serious business tool.

APPLIXWARE

ApplixWare is a graphical office suite for Linux that includes word processing, spreadsheet, presentation graphics, e-mail, and tools to develop your own graphical applications.

The ApplixWare suite is the leading office product for Unix platforms, and the features compare quite favorably to popular Windows-based packages such as Microsoft Office and Lotus SmartSuite.

THE LINUX MALL

In the back of the book you'll find information on other commercial Linux products that you may find useful. I recommend that you also visit the Linux Mall online at *http://www.linuxmall.com* and browse their comprehensive collection of Linux products.

ROLLING YOUR OWN — LINUX PROGRAMMING

Basic Shell Programming

Other Linux Programming Languages

Even if you think you're not a programmer, Linux has some features to make your life a bit easier. Any time you have a repetitive task that involves Linux commands or changing the contents of a file, you should think about automating it with a program.

If you've ever written a word processor macro or a spreadsheet formula, you're a programmer. By taking advantage of Linux's built-in programming features, you can automate repetitive tasks and build simple interactive applications without a degree in computer science.

This chapter covers basic shell script programming and introduces you to other more powerful programming tools available in Linux Pro, such as Perl and the C and C++ programming languages.

BASIC SHELL PROGRAMMING

The **bash** shell is your main port of entry to Linux, since the shell interprets everything you enter on the command line before passing it off to the operating system for execution. But in addition to providing the niceties of command resolution, wildcard handling, and piping, **bash** has its own powerful built-in programming language.

A *shell script* is a program written for **bash**. The simplest shell script is a sequence of Linux commands; but when you add the power of variables and flow control, you can do a lot more with it. Shell scripts are similar to DOS batch files (those files that end in .BAT), but shell scripts are more powerful and actually easier to create.

Shell scripts are interpreted, which means that the shell reads each line and acts on it immediately. This process differs from that of a formal programming language like C or C++, where the program is compiled and optimized for faster execution. So there's a tradeoff—it's easier to create quick little shell scripts; but if the task at hand requires serious number crunching or complicated logic, a compiled language is better.

- **NOTE:** *All of the shell script syntax and examples in this chapter will work in both the **bash** and Korn (**pdksh**) shells. The C Shell (**tcsh**) has subtle differences in many areas, so scripts written for one shell may not work in another. If you decide to use the C shell instead of **bash**, use the **man tcsh** command for more info on writing shell scripts for that environment.*

CREATING A SHELL SCRIPT

To create a shell script, use a text editor and enter your Linux commands as if you were typing them at the command prompt. For example:

```
cd /tmp
echo "Removing temp files..."
ls -al
rm junk*
```

If you save those four lines in a file named **deltemp,** you will have a simple shell script that automates the process of switching to the **/tmp** directory, listing all the files there, and deleting the ones that start with the word "junk."

EXECUTING A SHELL SCRIPT

So how do you run this little wonder of technology? In DOS, all you have to do is name a file with a .BAT extension and it'll be recognized as an executable file—not so with Linux. Since Linux attaches no meanings to file extensions, you have to mark the file as executable by using the **chmod** command, like so:

```
$ chmod +x deltemp
```

The **x** marks the file as executable; if you list the permissions for the **deltemp** file afterward, you will see the **x** in position four, confirming this:

```
$ ls -l deltemp
-rwx------   1 hermie other    55 Feb 19 14:02 deltemp
```

If you want other users to be able to run this script, give them both read and execute permission, like so:

```
$ chmod ugo+rx deltemp
$ ls -l deltemp
-rwxr-xr-x   1 hermie other    55 Feb 19 14:04 deltemp
```

Now the permissions show that any user can view or execute the **deltemp** script, but only you can modify it. To run the script, enter its name at the command prompt, prefixed with **. /** as shown below.

```
$ ./deltemp
```

- **NOTE:** *If the current directory is in the PATH, you can omit the **. /** before the name.*

But there's one important thing you should know about running shell scripts this way. When you enter the shell script name and tell **bash** to run it, a subshell is created for the execution of the script. This subshell inherits all the shell environment variables, including the current directory, but you lose any changes made to that environment when the script terminates.

What's the practical meaning of this? Well, you might expect that the current directory would be **/tmp** after you've run the **deltemp** script, but it's not. You'll still be in hermie's home directory. And if we had set an environment variable inside the script, its value would be good only during the execution of the script. Here's an example to demonstrate this point. Create an executable **setvar** script with these lines:

```
PS1='My Prompt: '
echo $PS1
```

Now watch how the values of the current directory and the PS1 variable change:

```
$ PS1='Bash Me! '
$ echo $PS1
Bash Me!                        PS1 before setvar
$ setvar
My Prompt:                      PS1 during setvar
$ echo $PS1
Bash Me!                        PS1 after setvar
```

It looks like this script is absolutely useless for the intended purpose of setting the environment variable. But a little trick will make it work the way you want. Run the script by prefixing the name with a dot and a space, like so:

```
. setvar
```

This tells **bash** to run the **setvar** script in the current shell environment, instead of creating a temporary subshell. Verify for yourself that the command prompt does in fact change to My Prompt: after running this script.

VARIABLES AND QUOTING

A variable in a shell script is a way to reference a numeric or character value. And unlike formal programming languages, a shell script doesn't require you to declare a type for your variables. So you could assign a number to the variable **stuff,** and then use it again in the same script to hold a string of characters. To access the value (contents) of a variable, prefix it with a dollar sign.

```
stuff=5
stuff='chocolate truffles'
```

Don't put any spaces before or after the equal sign, or you'll get an error. And if you want to assign a string that contains spaces, you will need to put quotation marks around the string.

This is a good time to note that there are several distinct ways to use quotes in a shell script. Let's look at the difference between single quotes, double quotes, and the backslash character; then follow up with some examples.

- Single quotes ('), as in the above example, will always get you exactly what's inside the quotes—any characters that might otherwise have special meaning to the shell (like the dollar sign or the backslash) are treated literally.

- Use double quotes (") when you want to assign a string that contains special characters the shell should act on.

- The backslash (\) is used to escape (treat literally) a single character (such as $ or *) that might otherwise be treated as a special character by the shell.

Now let's look at some examples that show when to use each method of quoting.

```
howdy='Good Morning $USER !'
echo $howdy
Good Morning $USER !

howdy="Good Morning $USER !"
echo $howdy
Good Morning hermie !
```

In the first case, the value of the **howdy** variable would probably not be what you wanted. The single quotes caused **bash** to not treat **$USER** as a variable. In the second case, the results look much better. The double quotes allowed **bash** to substitute the value of **$USER**, which is set automatically when you log in, in the string.

Here's another example that demonstrates a common error:

```
costmsg="Price is $5.00"
echo $costmsg
Actual Result: Price is .00
```

We thought enough to quote the string, but the dollar sign is going to tell **bash** to use the value in the **$5** variable, which is not what we wanted. We can easily solve the problem by prefixing the dollar sign with a backslash, as shown below.

```
$ costmsg="Price is \$5.00"
$ echo $costmsg
Actual result: Price is $5.00
```

PARAMETERS AND OTHER SPECIAL VARIABLES

Parameters are the values you pass to a shell script. Each value on the command line after the name of the script will be assigned to the special variables **$1, $2, $3,** and so on. The name of the currently running script is stored in the **$0** variable.

Here are some other special variables you will find useful in script writing:

$#   The number of parameters

$*   The entire parameter string

| $? | The return code from the last command issued |

So let's try some examples working with parameters and other special variables. Create an executable script called **testvars** containing these lines:

```
echo "My name is $0"
echo "First parm is: $1"
echo "Second parm is: $2"
echo "I got a total of $# parameters."
echo "The full parameter string was: $*"
```

Now if you run this script, here's what you'll see:

```
$ ./testvars birds have lips
My name is testvars
First parm is: birds
Second parm is: have
I got a total of 3 parameters.
The full parameter string was: birds have lips
```

FLOW CONTROL

So far all of our sample scripts have been just a sequence of commands executed one after the other. We haven't added any if-then-else logic or used looping constructs to control the flow of the program.

■ *NOTE: If you've never written or seen a computer program in your entire life, the rest of this chapter will probably seem a bit foreign. But try to follow the examples, then test and modify them on your own to get the hang of it.*

CONDITIONAL OPERATIONS   Let's look at the if-then-else construct in a **bash** shell script and see how to control the flow of a script with conditional logic. The general form of if-then-else is shown below, with the actual syntax shown in boldface and the parts you must supply in normal type.

```
if [ condition is true ]
then
      execute these commands
else
      execute those commands
fi
```

The **else** clause is optional, but you must end the construct with the **fi** command. You can also have nested **if** clauses by using the **elif** command like this:

```
if [ condition1 is true ]
then
    execute these commands
elif [ condition2 is true ]
then
    execute these commands
else
    execute those commands
fi
```

So what kind of conditions can we test for? If you're dealing with numbers, here are the conditional expressions you can use. In other words, any of these expressions can go inside the brackets on the **if** or **elif** statement.

num1 -eq *num2*	True if *num1* equals *num2*
num1 -ne *num2*	True if *num1* is not equal to *num2*
num1 -lt *num2*	True if *num1* is less than *num2*
num1 -gt *num2*	True if *num1* is greater than *num2*
num1 -le *num2*	True if *num1* is less than or equal to *num2*
num1 -ge *num2*	True if *num1* is greater than or equal to *num2*

If you're comparing character strings, these are the valid conditional expressions:

str1 = *str2*	True if *str1* and *str2* are identical.
str1 != *str2*	True if *str1* and *str2* are not identical.
-n *str1*	True if *str1* is not null (length is greater than zero).
-z *str1*	True if *str1* is null (length is zero).

You can also test certain file conditions, such as whether or not files exist, the type of file, and so on. Here are the conditional expressions for files:

-f *somefile*	True if *somefile* exists, and is an ordinary file.
-d *somefile*	True if *somefile* exists, and is a directory.
-s *somefile*	True if *somefile* contains data (size is not zero).
-r *somefile*	True if *somefile* is readable.
-w *somefile*	True if *somefile* is writable.
-x *somefile*	True if *somefile* is executable.

And finally, here are the logical operators, for performing tests that involve **and, or,** and **not** conditions.

cond1 -a *cond2*	True if both *cond1* and *cond2* are true.
cond1 -o *cond2*	True if either *cond1* or *cond2* is true.
! *cond1*	True if *cond1* is false.

SOME IF-THEN-ELSE EXAMPLES   Here are some examples using the conditional expressions just listed. Note that the spaces on either side of the square brackets are not optional!

```
if [ $carprice -gt 20000 ]
then
    echo 'Too rich for my blood.'
else
    echo 'Can you get that model in blue?'
fi


if [ $maker = 'Buick' ]
then
    echo 'Have you driven a Ford lately?'
fi
```

```
if [ -r $1    -a    -s $2 ]
then
    echo "The $1 file is readable and contains data."
fi
```

THE CASE STATEMENT   The **bash** shell provides a **case** statement that lets you compare a string with several possible values and execute a block of code when it finds a match. Here's an example of the **case** command, with the syntax shown in boldface and the parts you would supply in normal type:

```
case $1 in
 -a)
        commands;;
 -f)
        commands;;
  *)
        commands;;
esac
```

In this example, if the value of **$1** was **-a**, the first block of commands would execute. If the value of **$1** was **-f**, the second block of commands would execute. Otherwise, the third block of commands following the asterisk clause would execute. (Think of the asterisk as meaning *match anything*.)

You can put as many commands as you need in place of the word *commands* in the sample above, but be sure to end the block with a double semicolon. Only the first matching block of commands will execute in a **case** statement, and you must signal the end of the construct with the **esac** command.

LOOPING

Shell scripts written in **bash** can implement **looping** or iteration with the **while, until,** and **for** constructs. In each case, a block of code is executed repeatedly until a loop exit condition is satisfied. The script then continues on from that point.

THE WHILE STATEMENT   In a **while** loop, the block of code between the **do** and the **done** statements is executed as long as the conditional expression is true. Think of it as saying, "Execute *while* this condition remains true." Here's an example:

```
while [ "$*" != "" ]
do
 echo "Parameter value is: $1"
 shift
done
```

This trivial example prints out the value of each parameter passed to the shell script. Translated to English, the **while** condition says to continue as long as the input parameter string is not null. You could also code the **while** statement as

```
while [ -n "$*" ]
```

but I think the first method is much easier to read and understand.

You might think that this loop would continue to print the first parameter (**$1**) forever and ever, since you don't expect the value of the **$*** variable (the list of parameters from the command line) to change during the course of running the script. You'd be right, except that I slipped the **shift** command into the body of the loop.

What **shift** does is discard the first parameter and reassign all the **$n** variables. So the new **$1** gets the value that used to be in **$2**, and so on. Accordingly, the value in **$*** gets shorter and shorter each time through the loop, and when it finally becomes *null*, the loop is done.

THE UNTIL STATEMENT The **until** construct works almost exactly the same as **while**. The only difference is that **until** executes the body of the loop as long as the conditional expression is false, whereas **while** executes the body of the loop as long as the conditional expression is true. Think of it as saying, "Execute *until* this condition becomes true."

Let's code the previous example using an until loop this time, and make it a little fancier by adding a *counter variable*:

```
count=1
until [ "$*" = "" ]
do
   echo "Parameter number $count : $1 "
   shift
   count=`expr $count + 1`
done
```

Again, you could have coded the **until** statement as

```
until [ -z "$*" ]
```

but I recommend not using the **-n** and **-z** operators because it's harder to remember what they do. The only new concept here is the strange-looking line that increments the counter:

```
count=`expr $count + 1`
```

The **expr** command signals the shell that we're about to do a mathematical calculation instead of a string operation. And the doodads that look kind of like single quotes are not—they're the backtick (`) character, found to the left of the number 1 key on most keyboards. By enclosing an expression in backticks, you tell the shell to assign the result of a Linux command to a variable, instead of printing it to the screen.

■ *NOTE: The spaces on either side of the plus sign are required.*

THE FOR STATEMENT   The **for** statement is yet another way to implement a loop in a shell script. The general form of the **for** construct is shown below:

```
for item in list
do
   something useful with $item
done
```

Each time through the loop, the value of the **item** variable is assigned to the *n*th item in the list. When you've processed all the items in the list, the loop is done. Here's an example similar to the **until** and **while** loops you saw earlier in this chapter:

```
for $item in "$*"
do
   echo "Parameter value is: $item"
done
```

DEBUGGING SHELL SCRIPTS

Sometimes shell scripts just don't work the way you think they should, or you get strange error messages when running your script. Just remember, the computer is always right. It's easy to omit a significant blank, quote, or bracket, or to mistakenly use a single quote when you should have used double quotes or a backtick.

When you get unexpected behavior from a shell script and you're thinking "I just *know* this is coded right . . . the computer is wrong!"—remember, the computer is always right. But fortunately there is help. By prefixing your shell invocation with **bash -x** you can turn on tracing to see what's really happening. Let's say we have the following **listparm** script:

```
count=1
until [ "$*" = "" ]
do
  echo "Parm $count : $1 "
  shift
  count=$count+1
done
```

At first glance it looks golden, but for some reason the counter is not incrementing properly. Try running it with the command

```
% bash -x listparm abc def
```

and look at the trace output as the shell executes. The lines prefixed with a plus sign show the progress of the running script, and the lines without the plus sign are the script's normal output.

```
+ count=1
+ [ abc def =  ]
+ echo Parm 1 : abc
Parm 1 : abc
+ shift
+ count=1+1                          Hmmm . . .
+ [ def =  ]
+ echo Parm 1+1 : def
Parm 1+1 : def                       Not Good!
+ shift
+ count=1+1+1
+ [  =  ]
```

Instead of printing `Parm 2 : def` we got `Parm 1+1 : def`. But the trace output line reading `count=1+1` nails the problem. You forgot to use the **expr** command, so the shell is treating this as a string concatenate instead of a mathematical calculation.

■ **NOTE:** *You can always press* **CTRL-C** *to stop a running shell script. This is handy if you accidentally create a script with an infinite loop (one that will never end by itself).*

OTHER LINUX PROGRAMMING LANGUAGES

Shell scripts are fine for many tasks; but if you need to do lots of number-crunching, string manipulation, or complicated logic flow, look into one of the other languages briefly mentioned in this section.

PERL

Perl is an interpreted language that is very popular in the Unix community because it has a rich and powerful feature set, but is still easy to use. Perl borrows heavily from other languages such as C and **awk** and is especially useful for text processing, generating reports, and handling CGI (Common Gateway Interface) requests submitted via Web browsers.

Perl has been ported to many non-Unix environments, including DOS, OS/2, Macintosh, VMS, and Windows NT. The fact that a Perl program can run without modifications on many different platforms is another reason for its popularity. Try the **man perl** command to get info on Perl, or read *Programming Perl* by Larry Wall (O'Reilly & Associates), the inventor of the Perl language.

C AND C++

C is a general-purpose programming language originally written to help in the development of Unix. Most of the Linux operating system is written in C.

C is one of the most widely used programming languages (in spite of its awkward syntax) and is available on just about any computing platform you can imagine. Since it was designed for portability to other environments (it has source code compatibility), it is very popular with software developers.

The C compiler that comes with Linux is the GNU C compiler, created by the Free Software Foundation. To invoke the GNU C compiler, use the **gcc** command. Here's a very simple C program that will print "Hello, World!" on your screen:

```
#include <stdio.h>
main ()

{

  printf  ("Hello,World! \n");

}
```

Type those lines into a file named **hello.c** and then compile it like this:

```
gcc -o hello hello.c
```

This tells the compiler to compile **hello.c** and create an executable output file named **hello**. To run the program, enter the command **hello** at the prompt.

THE C++ LANGUAGE

C++ is an object-oriented programming language based on C that is fast becoming the language of choice for large software development projects. C++ compilers are available on a great many platforms, and of course on Linux as well. To invoke the GNU C++ compiler, use the **g++** command.

It is far beyond the scope of this book to delve into the syntax of the C and C++ languages. You can find stacks of C and C++ language reference books in any computer bookstore, or online at the Linux Mall (*http://www.linuxmall.com*). For more information on using C and C++ with Linux, visit the Linux Documentation Project at *http://sunsite.unc.edu/mdw/linux.html* and look for the Linux Programmer's Guide and the **GCC HOWTO** file.

MANAGING YOUR E-MAIL

E-Mail Addresses

Netiquette

Sending E-Mail with Linux

You've Got Mail!

The Pine Mail System

GUI E-Mail Programs for Linux

There's a lot of hype about the multimedia aspects of the Internet, but the true killer app in the online world has always been e-mail. More than anything else, people get online to communicate with other human beings—not other computers. In this chapter, you'll get a brief introduction to Internet e-mail and learn about the tools you can use on a Linux system to send and receive e-mail.

E-MAIL ADDRESSES

In order to send e-mail, you have to know the e-mail address of the person who is to receive your message. An e-mail address consists of two parts: a *user* and a *domain name*, separated by the at (**@**) sign. And unlike most everything else in the Unix world, e-mail addresses are NOT case sensitive.

For example, if your e-mail address is **hermie@fritz.com**, then **hermie** is the user name and **fritz.com** is the domain name. Most domain names end in a three-letter code, such as **com, edu,** or **gov,** which indicates something about the user's location (whether they're at a company, university, government office, and so on):

`com`	A company or business
`edu`	A college or university
`gov`	A government office
`mil`	A military institution
`net`	A network node (usually an Internet service provider)
`org`	An organization (i.e., professional societies, nonprofit groups)

As this book goes to press, there are proposals for adding new top-level domains, such as **biz, web, info,** and others. Here are some examples of e-mail addresses using the various domain names:

`XKUTV@hq.bigcorp.COM`	A user at a large company (headquarters)
`JaneDoe@CS.harvard.edu`	A computer science student at Harvard University

`Hacker7@WhiteHouse.Gov`	Hackers at the White House?
`Dbanger@ftriley.army.mil`	A user at a military site
`BobRankin@MHV.net`	Yours truly :-)
`elmo@IEEE.org`	A member of the IEEE society

The exceptions to this rule are non-U.S. addresses that end in a two-digit country code and are usually (but not always) preceded by "ac" (for a university) or "co" (for a company). For example:

`Peter@nms.ac.uk`	A student at a British university
`aldeana@business.ntu.edu.au`	A student at an Australian university
`rkoltz@audg.gov.ab.ca`	A goverment employee in Alberta Canada
`takemori@bs.mcts.co.jp`	A user at a Japanese company
`christoph.wolfe@metronet.de`	A user at a German company

NETIQUETTE

It's sometimes so simple to communicate electronically that you forget that users on the other end of the wire can't necessarily pick up on your message's emotions and nuances the way they might in a hand-written letter or in spoken conversation. They may even misinterpret a joke as an insult, and many people do. It's especially important to keep this danger in mind when you're participating in group discussions like Internet mailing lists.

The moral? Be extra careful to make your e-mail messages clear. If you're telling a joke that could be construed as a fact or a harsh, personal comment, say so! Don't use the excuse of being able to hide behind your terminal as a license to be rude. And be extra sensitive to the fact that the Internet is a *global* audience where not all users have a strong command of English.

emoticons

Smileys (sometimes called *emoticons*), or textual representations of emotions that people commonly use in their e-mail, are one way to express feelings in the otherwise emotionless world of e-mail. When you see a collection of dashes, parentheses, and other punctuation marks (like `:-)` or `:-(` for example) that don't seem to make sense, try turning your head sideways and the meaning should come into focus right away.

One final point on netiquette, DON'T SHOUT! Even though e-mail addresses are not case sensitive, the people who read e-mail often are. And the use of ALL CAPITAL LETTERS in e-mail is considered shouting. It'll also brand you (deservedly or not) as a clueless newbie who can't find the right key to turn off the caps.

SENDING E-MAIL WITH LINUX

The most basic way to send e-mail on a Linux system is with the **mail** command. The **mail** program is a command-line interface to sending and receiving electronic mail. It works, but it's not pretty. Later on in this chapter you'll learn about Pine, a much friendlier e-mail interface, but you should know how to use mail since it's guaranteed to be available on any Unix system.

Let's say you're logged in as **root** and you want to send a message to **hermie**. Start the process by typing

```
mail hermie
```

The system will respond with a `Subject:` prompt. Type in the subject for your note, press **ENTER,** and then write your message, line by line. When you've finished with your missive, press **CTRL-D** to send it. Here's a sample **mail** session. (The stuff you type is shown in bold, and the system prompts are normal intensity.)

```
# mail hermie
Subject: Gone Fishing
I've decided to kick back this afternoon and go fishing.
So if this crazy Linux system rolls over and dies,
I suggest you do likewise.
^D
EOT
```

After you press **CTRL-D** the system responds with the cryptic EOT message, which could mean "End of Text," or "Eat Only Twinkies," or whatever you like.

You may notice an apparent contradiction in the example above, since the e-mail address of the recipient does not have an **@** sign and a domain name in it. If the sender and recipient are on the same system, it's alright to give just the user name as the e-mail address. You could just as well have addressed your mail to **hermie@fritz.com** since they are equivalent in this case.

YOU'VE GOT MAIL!

If you log in as **hermie** now (pressing **ALT-F2** to access another virtual console would be convenient) you'll be greeted with the following cheery little message:

```
You have new mail.
```

You can receive and read your incoming e-mail by using the **mail** command again. Here's a sample **mail** session (text in bold is what you would enter):

```
$ mail
Mail version 5.6 6/1/95.   Type ? for help.
"/var/spool/mail/hermie":  1 message 1 new
>N  1 root@fritz.com      Mon Feb 10 14:58   "Gone Fishing"
>N  2 D.Rhodes@spam.net   Mon Feb 10 15:37   "Make Money Fast!"
 N  3 Chris@qwerty.com    Mon Feb 10 15:37   "Tennis, Anyone?"
& 1
Message 1:
Date: Mon, 10 Feb 1997 14:58:12 -0500
From: root@fritz.com
To: hermie@fritz.com
Subject: Gone Fishing
I've decided to kick back this afternoon and go fishing.
```

```
So if this crazy Linux system rolls over and dies,
I suggest you do likewise.
& q
Saved 1 message in /home/hermie/mbox
Held 2 messages in /var/mail/spool/hermie
```

Let's look at what just happened. After you entered the **mail** command, the system informed you of the version of the **mail** program that is running and told you how to get help for it.

The next line tells you that there is one new message in your mailbox, and that your incoming mail is stored in the file **/var/spool/mail/hermie**. (Each user on the system will have a mail file in the **/var/spool/mail** directory.) When new mail arrives, Linux tacks it on to the end of the recipient's mail file.

■ *NOTE: You should never directly edit your mail file—always use **mail** or another e-mail program to handle your mail. (If you're editing your mail file when a new message arrives, it will be lost.) But it's quite alright to scan your mail file with **grep** or some other utility that doesn't try to modify it. (You might want to **grep** your mail to find a particular string, such as the e-mail address of a person who has corresponded wih you.)*

The next line

```
>N  1 root@fritz.com     Mon Feb 10 14:58   "Gone Fishing"
```

is referred to as a "header line," and it tells you a number of things. The > tells you which message is the "current" one—the one you're working with.

The N 1 indicates that you're dealing with message 1 and that it's flagged as a New message. (Later on the flag could be "U" for Unread or "O" for an Old message.) The rest of the line tells you who the message is from, when it was sent, and the subject line.

The ampersand (&) on the following line is the mail prompt. In this example, we entered a **1** to display the first message, and the message text is shown on the lines that follow. Unfortunately, we can't tell from the context whether to roll over and die or just go fishing.

EXITING THE MAIL PROGRAM

The **q** command entered at the next **mail** prompt ends the session and returns you to the shell prompt. But take note of the messages that were printed on your way out, namely `Saved 1 message in /home/hermie/mbox` and `Held 2 messages in /var/mail/spool/hemie`. For some odd reason, **mail** does not think it's a good idea to keep the mail you've already read in the **/var/spool/mail/hermie** file, so it moves them to a separate file called **mbox** in your own home directory.

To access the messages in the **mbox** file, you have to use the command

```
mail -f
```

Kind of annoying, ain't it? But at least the **mail** program looks and acts the same regardless of which mail file you're working with.

OTHER MAIL COMMANDS

Let's get back into the **mail** program and have some fun with the two messages that we didn't read before with this scenario (again, bold type represents your input).

```
$ mail
Mail version 5.6 6/1/95.  Type ? for help.
"/var/spool/mail/hermie":  1 message 1 new
>U  1 D.Rhodes@spam.net  Mon Feb 10 15:37   "Make Money Fast!"
 U  2 Chris@qwerty.com   Mon Feb 10 15:37   "Tennis, Anyone?"
& 2
Message 2:
Date: Mon, 10 Feb 1997 15:37:52 -0500
From: Chris@qwerty.com
To: hermie@fritz.com
Subject: Tennis, Anyone?
Wanna whack a few a 4:30 today?  -Chris
& reply
Subject: Re: Tennis, Anyone?
Sure, I'll see you on the lower courts at 4:30.
^D
EOT
& header
 U  1 D.Rhodes@spam.net  Mon Feb 10 15:37   "Make Money Fast!"
>O  2 Chris@qwerty.com   Mon Feb 10 15:37   "Tennis, Anyone?"
& delete 1
& q
Saved 1 message in /home/hermie/mbox
```

We've introduced several new commands here, so let's take a closer look at the five operations that were performed in this mail session.

- As soon as I start the **mail** program the mail headers are displayed, and you can see that both messages are marked U for unread. I displayed message 2 by entering **2** at the prompt.

- The **reply** command responded with an appropriate Subject line for message 2, `Subject: Re: Tennis, Anyone?`, and waited for me to enter the text of my message to Chris. Pressing **CTRL-D** makes EOT appear and sends my reply.

- The **header** command displays the message headers. I've used it here to show the difference in the status flags. The > indicates message 2 is "current," and it's marked as "O" for Old.

- I deleted the first message with **delete 1** without even reading it, since the Subject line was rather dubious.

- And as a parting gesture, the **q** command told me that another message was squirreled away in that **mbox** file. At this point, if I issued the **mail** command again, the system would respond

```
No mail for hermie
```

Poor hermie. He needn't drink Drano, though—he can always send himself some more mail. ;-)

THE PINE MAIL SYSTEM

Pine is an e-mail handler that is much friendlier than the plain old mail command. Pine sports a full-screen interface and a context-sensitive list of commands on each screen. Even though it's text based (no GUI) it's very easy to use and has enough features to satisfy most any user. I personally use Pine in a Unix environment even though I access the Internet from a Windows machine.

In case you're wondering why an e-mail system would be named after a tree, here's the scoop. Pine was originally based on another e-mail program called Elm (short for ELectronic Mail), written by

Internet pioneer Dave Taylor. The name "Pine" was first an acronym for "Pine Is Not Elm," but today the official title is "Program for Internet News and E-Mail," (Revisionists:1, Geeks:0—Film at 11)

STARTING PINE

To fire up the Pine program, use the command below and you'll see the Pine MAIN MENU screen.

```
% Pine
PINE 3.91   MAIN MENU                    Folder: INBOX   3 Messages

    ?     HELP              -  Get help using Pine
    C     COMPOSE MESSAGE   -  Compose and send/post a message
    I     FOLDER INDEX      -  View messages in current folder
    L     FOLDER LIST       -  Select a folder OR news group to view
    A     ADDRESS BOOK      -  Update address book
    S     SETUP             -  Configure or update Pine
    Q     QUIT              -  Exit the Pine program
Copyright 1989-1996. PINE is a trademark of the U. of Washington
```

Typically I press I to jump right into my INBOX, but Pine also offers the options of pressing C to send a message, L to see a list of my saved mail folders, or A to manage my address book. (We'll touch on those options later.)

If you want to bypass this opening screen, you can add the -i flag to your **pine** command and go directly to the INBOX screen.

THE PINE INBOX

The INBOX folder is where you'll spend most of your time in Pine. Below is a sample screen showing three messages. Pine displays a message number, date sent, the real name of the sender (if available), the size (in bytes), and the subject line of each message in your INBOX.

The first message is flagged with an **A,** which indicates that I've already read and answered it. The other two are flagged with **N** because they are "new" messages. Messages that have been read but not answered will have a blank in the flag column.

So what about the "+" signs in front of certain messages? These tell me that these messages were addressed directly to me (your address appears in the **To:** field even though you don't see that field here). E-mail that comes from a mailing list manager, or "junk mail" that comes from a spammer will typically have a generic (or bogus) **To:** address.

Unlike **mail,** Pine doesn't keep your incoming and previously read messages in totally different places. All your messages show up on this screen, whether they are brand new or six months old.

```
PINE 3.91     FOLDER     INDEX                    Folder: INBOX  Message 1 of 3

+ A 1    Feb  8 Joe Kramer          (1,116) Let's do lunch
  N 2    Feb 10 Dave Rhodes         (7,264) MAKE MONEY FAST!!!
+ N 3    Feb 11 davey@surfer.com    (1,220) My new Toyota...
—
              [Folder "INBOX" opened with 3 messages]

? Help            M Main Menu      P PrevMsg     - PrevPage      D Delete      R Reply
O OTHER CMDS      V [ViewMsg]      N NextMsg    Spc NextPage     U Undelete    F Forward
```

MANAGING YOUR MAIL WITH PINE

You can display the current message (which is either underlined or in reverse video) by pressing **V** or the **ENTER** key while viewing the FOLDER INDEX screen. Here's an example of what you'll see when you view a message in Pine:

```
PINE 3.91    MESSAGE TEXT              Folder: INBOX   Message 1 of 3   ALL

    Date: Sat, 8 Feb 1997 13:57:22 -0800
    From: Joe Kramer <JoeK@asdf.com>
    To: hermie@fritz.com
    Subject: Let's do lunch
    Hey, howzabout we do a "power lunch" on Monday to work out the
    details of that Amorphous contract?  Call me at 555-0317...

? Help            M Main Menu      P PrevMsg     - PrevPage      D Delete      R Reply
O OTHER CMDS      V [ViewMsg]      N NextMsg    Spc NextPage     U Undelete    F Forward
```

From either this MESSAGE TEXT screen or the FOLDER INDEX, you can press one of these keys to act on the current message.

R   To reply to the current message.

D   To delete a message. (They don't actually go away when you ask to delete—they're just flagged with a **D** and expunged later when you exit Pine, just in case you change your mind and don't want the message deleted.)

U   To undelete a message (remove the **D** flag).

If you press **O** to display more Pine commands, the legend at the bottom of the screen changes to

? Help	**Q** Quit	**L** ListFldrs	**I** Index	**Y** prYnt	**S** Save
O OTHER CMDS	**C** Compose	**G** GotoFldr	**W** WhereIs	**T** TakeAddr	**E** Export

From here, you can do the following:

C   To compose a new message

I   To return to the FOLDER INDEX

W   To search for text in the current message

Y   To print the message

T   To add the sender to your address book

S   To save the message in a folder

PINE MAIL FOLDERS

Folders are a good way to organize your e-mail. When you press **S** to save a message in a folder, Pine asks you to choose a folder. If that folder already exists, Pine copies the message to that folder and marks it as `Deleted` in your INBOX. If the folder doesn't exist, Pine asks if you want to create it.

You might want to save all messages from a mailing list in a folder with the same name as the list, or have a folder called URGENT for high-priority items. I create folders for people with whom I communicate on a regular basis, so my INBOX stays uncluttered and I can still find an old message when I need it.

You can use the **L** command to display a list of all your folders, and then view the messages in a selected folder. The same FOLDER INDEX and MESSAGE TEXT screens are used whether you're dealing with the INBOX folder or another folder that you created.

PINE FOR POWER USERS

Pine is a great tool for managing your e-mail, because it's fast, easy to learn, and easily configurable. But it also has many advanced features for power users. Once you've become proficient at basic mail handling, try some of these features. (All are accessed from the FOLDER INDEX screen.)

SEARCHING   Use the **W** ("where is") command to search your FOLDER INDEX for messages with a certain word in the Subject line. You can also use the **W** command when you're viewing a message to search for text in the message body.

SORTING   Use the **$** command to sort your messages in a variety of ways, including subject, sender, size, and arrival time.

ADDRESS BOOK   Use the **T** command to "take" the sender's address and store it in your Pine address book. You can also assign a nickname to the address and use the nickname instead of the full address when composing a new message.

HEADERS   Use the **H** command to view the normally hidden message header lines. At first glance, it's a lot of gobbledygook, but the "Received" lines will tell you the path a message traveled to reach your system. This can be handy for identifying forged sender addresses. Press **H** again to turn off the display of the header lines.

FORWARD AND BOUNCE   The **F** command lets you forward messages to other users. The message composition screen appears like usual, with the forwarded message pasted into the message text area. You can add your own comments before sending.

The **B** command will "bounce" a message to another user with no opportunity to add comments. If the recipient's mail system complies with standards, it will appear as if the message came from the original sender—not from you. This is handy when you get mail that was obviously meant for someone else and you want to quietly redirect it.

EXPORT AND PIPE   The **E** command will export a message to a file in your home directory. This is useful if someone sends you a file that you want to save and edit, or if you receive a uuencoded or encrypted message. (See Chapter 10, "Compression, Encoding, and Encryption," for more on decoding and decryption.)

The | (vertical bar) command will "pipe" a message directly into any command or program. For example, you could use this feature to pipe a message to a program that strips off mail headers and formats notes for printing.

ATTACHMENTS Pine has excellent support for attached files. You can attach a binary file such as a program, image, or word procesor document to an outgoing message using the **CTRL-J** command while the cursor is on the "Attchmnt:" line in the message composition screen. Pine encodes the attached file using MIME (Multi-purpose Internet Mail Enhancements), which is a widely used standard understood by most modern e-mail programs.

Pine can also decode incoming MIME-attached files and either save them to disk or automatically launch the appropriate viewer tools. I used Pine to send Microsoft Word files back and forth to my publisher in the course of writing this book.

HELP The built-in help for Pine is excellent, so if you're interested in learning more, just press the **?** key from any screen.

GUI E-MAIL PROGRAMS FOR LINUX

If you prefer a graphical interface to send and receive e-mail, you have several options to select from while running the X Window GUI for Linux.

- The **exmh** program comes with Linux Pro, and has most of the features found in Pine.

- **ApplixWare** is a commercial office suite that includes a very nice e-mail client.

- **Netscape** for Linux has built-in e-mail capabilities, just like the Windows and Macintosh versions.

See Chapter 7, "The X Window System," for more information on X Window and how to launch these e-mail programs.

COMPRESSION, ENCODING, AND ENCRYPTION

Putting On the Squeeze—Compressing and Archiving

Decoder Rings Sold Here

Making Your Mail Top Secret

Compression, Encoding, and Encryption under DOS

T he Unix environment offers you several ways to transform your files. Depending on your needs, you can shrink files, smash them, or scramble them, and then return them to their original sizes and shapes.

This chapter will give you an understanding of the tools available for compressing, archiving, encoding, and encrypting your files, and show you when to use each.

PUTTING ON THE SQUEEZE— COMPRESSING AND ARCHIVING

When you *compress* a file you shrink it to a fraction of its original size in order to store it or transmit it to another person (compressed files travel faster and take up less space in file libraries). You can't open or execute a compressed file without first decompressing it.

When you smash a bunch of files together into a single file, you're creating an *archive*. (You don't necessarily compress them, though.) Archives are useful because they create a package of files that belong together, which makes it easier to distribute a group of related files— for example, the files that make up a program. Because archive files are not always smaller than the sum of their parts, you will sometimes use a compression tool on an archive, resulting in a compressed archive.

While **zip** is the most common compression format under DOS or Windows, Unix commonly uses files created with the **tar** and **gzip** commands. You'll certainly run into files with names like these:

`something.tar`	An archive file created with **tar**
`something.gz`	A compressed file created with **gzip**
`something.tar.gz`	A compressed archive file
`something.tgz`	Same as above

While the **gzip** program is built into all Linux systems, it may not be part of some Unix systems, in which case an older tool called **compress** is used. Files created by **compress** have names like this (note the capital "Z"):

`something.Z`	A compressed file
`something.tar.Z`	A compressed **tar** file

■ *TIP: If you find yourself on a Unix system that doesn't have **gzip**, you can download the source code (available free) and compile it yourself. See the GNU Project home page at http://www.gnu.ai.mit.edu/ to find out how to get the source code.)*

The sections that follow will show you how to create and undo compressed files and archives.

TAR

The **tar** (tape archive) command bundles a bunch of files together and creates an archive (commonly called a **tar** file) on tape, disk, or floppy. The original files are not deleted after being copied into the **tar** file.

To create an archive using **tar**, use a command like this, which bundles all the files in the current directory that end with .doc into the **alldocs.tar** file:

```
tar -cvf alldocs.tar *.doc
```

Here's a second example, which creates a **tar** file named **panda.tar** containing all the files from the **panda** directory (and any of its sub-directories):

```
tar -cvf panda.tar panda/
```

In these examples, the **c, v,** and **f** flags mean create a new archive, be verbose (list files being archived), and write the archive to a file. You can also create **tar** files on tape drives or floppy disks, like this:

`tar -cvfM /dev/fd0 panda`	Archive the files in the **panda** directory to floppy disk(s).
`tar -cvf /dev/rmt0 panda`	Archive the files in the **panda** directory to the tape drive.

The `/dev/fd0` above is Linux-ese for "floppy drive zero" (your A: drive under DOS), and `/dev/rmt0` means "removable media tape zero," or your primary tape drive. The **M** flag means use m̲ultiple floppy disks—when one disk is full, **tar** prompts you to insert another.

To automatically compress the **tar** file as it is being created, add the **z** flag, like this:

```
tar -cvzf alldocs.tar.gz *.doc
```

In this example, I added the **.gz** suffix to the archive file name, because the **z** flag tells **tar** to use the same compression as the **gzip** command.

To list the contents of a **tar** file, use the **t** (t̲ype) flag in a command, like this:

```
tar -tvf alldocs.tar
```
List all files in **alldocs.tar**

To extract the contents of a **tar** file, use the **x** (e̲x̲tract) flag in a command, like this:

```
tar -xvf panda.tar
```
Extract files from **panda.tar**

This will copy all the files from the **panda.tar** file into the current directory. When a **tar** file is created, it can bundle up all the files in a directory, as well as any subdirectories and the files in them. So when you're extracting a **tar** file, keep in mind that you might end up with some new subdirectories in the current directory.

We've used several different flags in the sample **tar** commands so far. Here's a list of the most common flags and what they mean:

-c	Create a new archive.
-t	List the contents of an archive.
-x	Extract the contents of an archive.
-f	Archive file name is given on the command line (required whenever the **tar** output is going to a file).
-M	Archive can span multiple floppies.
-v	Verbose (list file names as they are processed).
-u	Add file(s) to the archive if they are newer than the copy in the **tar** file.
-z	Compress or decompress automatically.

GZIP AND GUNZIP

The **gzip** program compresses a single file. One important thing to remember about **gzip** is that, unlike **tar**, it replaces your original file with a compressed version. (The amount of compression varies with the type of data, but a typical text file will be reduced by 70 to 80 percent.) Say you enter this command:

```
gzip cheap.suit
```

You'll end up with a compressed file named **cheap.suit.gz**, and **cheap.suit** will be deleted.

To decompress the **cheap.suit.gz** file, enter this:

```
gunzip cheap.suit.gz
```

You'll get the original **cheap.suit** back, and **cheap.suit.gz** will be deleted.

levels of compression

You can tell **gzip** to use different levels of compression with the **-n** flag, where **n** is a number from 1 to 9. The **-1** flag means "fast but less efficient" compression, while **-9** means "slow but most efficient" compression. Values of **n** between 1 and 9 will trade off speed and efficiency, and the default is **-6**. If you want to get the best possible compression and you don't mind waiting a little longer, use the **-9** flag, like this:

```
gzip -9 cheap.suit
```

One other useful option is the **-r** flag, which tells **gzip** and **gunzip** to recursively compress or decompress all files in the current directory and any subdirectories. (Even with the **-r** flag, **gzip** still compresses one file at a time.)

> `gzip -r somedir`   Zip all files in the *somedir* directory.
>
> `gunzip -r somedir`   Unzip all files in the *somedir* directory.

HANDLING COMPRESSED ARCHIVES   It's common to **gzip** a **tar** file, which is why you see files with names like ***something*.tar.gz** on Linux systems. When you want to extract the contents of a **gzip**'ed **tar** file, you have several choices. The first is to use **gunzip** followed by **tar,** like this:

```
gunzip something.tar.gz
tar -xvf something.tar
```

Or you could do it all in one command, like this:

```
gunzip -c something.tar.gz | tar -xvf -
```

The **-c** flag tells **gunzip** to decompress, but instead of creating a **something.tar** file it pipes the decompressed data directly to the **tar** command. The **tar** command on the right-hand side of the pipeline looks a little strange, too—instead of a file name after the **-xvf** there's just a dash. The dash tells **tar** that the input is not an actual file on disk, but rather a stream of data from the pipeline. (Note that the **gunzip** input file is not deleted when you use the **-c** flag.)

Here's a third method of extracting the contents of a compressed **tar** file that's even easier. Remember the **-z** flag with the **tar** command? You can use it to decompress and unbundle a **tar** file, like this:

```
tar -xvzf something.tar.gz
```

The end result is exactly the same (the files that were in the compressed **tar** are now in your current directory), but this is much easier than issuing multiple commands or writing a messy-looking **gunzip-tar** pipeline.

Note that this will work on all Linux systems, but the **-z** flag for **tar** is not always available on other flavors of Unix. (However, you can download and compile the source code for the GNU version of the **tar** command. See the note near the beginning of this chapter about getting the source code for the GNU utilities.)

COMPRESS, UNCOMPRESS, ZCAT

The **compress** and **uncompress** programs work just like **gzip** and **gunzip,** but they use an older and less efficient compression technique. If you're using Linux, you shouldn't have to bother with **compress** and **uncompress** at all. Even if you come across a file created with **compress** (something with a .Z suffix) you can decompress it with **gunzip,** because **gunzip** understands both formats.

Still, just for completeness, here's how to use the **compress** and and **uncompress** programs:

> **compress** *some.file*   Create compressed *some.file.Z*
>
> **uncompress** *some.file* Create decompressed *some.file*

The **zcat** program is another Linux antique. It does the same thing as uncompress with the **-c** flag (decompresses and writes output to the pipeline), so the following two commands would be equivalent:

```
uncompress -c something.tar.X | tar -xvf -
zcat something.tar.X | tar -xvf -
```

You should only have to use these commands if you're running some version of Unix besides Linux. (Even then, many Unix systems will have the GNU versions of **gzip, gunzip,** and **tar** available.)

ZIP AND UNZIP

The **zip** and **unzip** programs work almost exactly like their cousins PKZIP and PKUNZIP in the DOS environment. So you can squash a bunch of files together into a **zip** file like this:

```
zip squash.zip file1 file2 file3
```

Then you extract the original files like this:

```
unzip squash.zip
```

Most of the flags are the same as for PKZIP and PKUNZIP, but there are a few differences, so you might like to view the help with **zip -h** or **unzip -h** if you need to do anything fancier than the basic commands shown above.

If you use the **-k** flag when you **zip** a file under Linux, you can PKUN-ZIP it under DOS. This flag tells **zip** to translate the Unix file and directory names into something that fits the more restrictive DOS naming conventions.

For example, if you have Linux files named *another.longunix.filename* and *wontwork.withDOS*, the **-k** flag will cause these files to be stored in the **zip** as *another.lon* and *wontwork.wit*. If you don't use the **-k** flag, the PKUNZIP command under DOS will give you an error and refuse to create the files with the invalid names.

SHELL ARCHIVES

A shell archive is like a **tar** file, but it is used only for packaging source code and other plain-text files. It's a convenient way to smash together all the source files for a project into one file that can be distributed by e-mail. (The original files are not deleted.)

Shell archives (commonly called **shar** files, as in <u>sh</u>ell <u>ar</u>chive) get their name from the fact that they contain the Linux commands needed to extract the original files.

By convention, shell archives are named with a .shar extension. To create a **shar** file, use a command like this:

```
shar input_files > shar_file
```

So, to create a **panda.shar** file containing all the files from the **panda/source** directory, you'd issue a command like this (note the use of the asterisk as a wild card):

```
shar panda/source/* > panda.shar
```

If you look inside a **shar** file, you'll see the original files sandwiched between the commands to extract them. But you don't have to execute those commands directly to unpack a **shar** file. Just enter this command to extract the files to the current directory:

```
sh panda.shar
```

The **sh** command will run the Linux commands embedded in the **panda.shar** file, and re-create all the original files.

You might be wondering why you'd want to use **shar** files when **tar** files seem to serve the same purpose. The answer is that **shar** files are ready to send (because they're plain text), while a **tar** file must be encoded first. See the next section for more on encoding and decoding.

DECODER RINGS SOLD HERE

When you encode a file, you translate it into a format that other types of computers can understand. For example, if you want to send an executable program, compressed files, word processor file, or any other binary data by e-mail, you have to encode it in ASCII (plain text) format first, or it will most likely be unreadable on the receiving end.

Most modern e-mail programs can send and receive binary files, encoding them as MIME attachments and decoding them when they're received. (Almost any Windows-based e-mail program can handle attachments, as can Pine, Exmh, or Netscape Mail under Linux.) But if you're partial to a low-tech mailer like the Unix mail command, or you know the intended recipient cannot handle attachments, you'll have to **uuencode** your files before sending, or **uudecode** them after they arrive.

UUENCODE AND UUDECODE

The **uuencode** program creates an encoded ASCII copy of a binary file, suitable for e-mail transmission. The encoded file will be 35 percent larger than the original, and will look something like this (the word `begin`, a number, and the original file name on the first line, followed by a bunch of 61-character lines that all begin with "M"):

```
begin 644 panda.tar
M4$$L#!'H'!@'.'/6H?18.$Z$F@P'''@?''','''5$5,25@S,34N5%A480I[
M!P8;!KL,2P,!L!L.P%%..(!@4.!W@!@.6%WL*!@@.P4.%00.%W4*.`4.
. . . . . . (and so on)
```

By convention, **uuencoded** files are named with a .uue extension. To create a **uuencoded** file under Linux, enter a command like this:

```
uuencode panda.tar panda.tar > panda.uue
```

The first **panda.tar** on the line above is the name that appears on the `begin` line of the output file; the second `panda.tar` is the name of the file you want to encode. (You might want to put a name other than the actual input file name on the `begin` line if you're sending the encoded file to a DOS system where file names are more restricted.)

To decode a **uuencoded** file, enter a command like this:

```
uudecode panda.uue
```

The **uudecode** program will look for the `begin` line and create a decoded file with the name and file permissions specified there. In the example above, the **panda.tar** file will be created in the current directory with permissions set to 644 (shorthand notation for **rw-r--r--,** which equates to the following: owner: read/write, group: read, others: read).

■ *NOTE:* *To calculate the numeric equivalent of a file permissions string, look at each "triplet" in the permissions. Read gets four points, write gets two, and execute gets one. See Chapter 3, "The Linux File System," for more on file permissions.*

Files that are created with the **tar, gzip, compress,** or **zip** commands in Linux must be uuencoded before they can be sent by e-mail.

ENCODED FILES AND E-MAIL   If you want to **uuencode** a file and e-mail it in one step, try a command like this:

```
uuencode panda.tar | mail whoever@whatever.com
```

This tells **uuencode** to pipe the output directly into the **mail** program instead of creating a .uue file. If you want to take it one step further, you could even archive, encode, and mail in one command, like this:

```
tar -cvf - panda | uuencode | mail whoever@whatever.com
```

That should all make sense if you read about pipelines in Chapter 2, "Living in a Shell," and understand that the dash in the **tar** command means "send the file to a pipeline" instead of creating a **tar** file on disk. Of course you could also do this:

```
tar -cvf panda.tar panda
uuencode panda.tar > panda.uue
mail whoever@whatever.com < panda.uue
rm panda.uue
rm panda.tar
```

But that's a lot more work!

MAKING YOUR MAIL TOP SECRET

Internet e-mail is about as secure as sending a postcard—any postal clerk along the delivery path could read your message if they wanted to, since there's no envelope to protect it. So if you're concerned about your private e-mail falling into the wrong hands, encryption is the solution.

Encryption will scramble your message so that only the holder of the secret decryption key will be able to read it. The de facto standard for encryption is the PGP (Pretty Good Privacy) program, written by Phil Zimmerman.

Actually *pretty good* privacy is a pretty serious understatement. Nobody has ever been able to crack the code that PGP uses. It's such a good program that the United States government has classified it as a "munition" and made it illegal for export. It is also illegal to use PGP in a few countries (it's legal in the United States), so check with your local authorities to see if cryptography usage qualifies you as a terrorist.

GETTING PGP

If you're interested in learning more about PGP, see the PGP FAQ by Andre Bacard, which is at *http://ftp.eff.org/pub/Net_info/Tools/Crypto/PGP/pgp.faq* on the Web.

To get a copy of the PGP software, visit *http://web.mit.edu/network/pgp-form.html* to see the PGP Distribution Authorization Form. If you are a citizen of the United States or Canada, promise to use it for non-commercial purposes, and never export it to any other countries, you can download the Unix source code for PGP, which you will have to compile yourself.

COMPRESSION, ENCODING, AND ENCRYPTION UNDER DOS

If you're working on a DOS system and you come across a **tar** file, a **gzip** file, or one that has been **uuencoded**, all is not lost. Fortunately, you can find DOS tools for dealing with compressed and encoded files at a variety of sites on the Internet, and most of them are free.

Visit *http://www.shareware.com* or *http://www.download.com* and use the search engines there to find DOS or Windows versions of **tar**, **gzip, uuencode,** or PGP. The Wincode and WinZip shareware programs are very popular, so you might want to try them first.

CONNECTING TO THE INTERNET

SETTING UP YOUR SERIAL PORT TO WORK WITH YOUR MODEM

MAKING A SLIP OR PPP CONNECTION

TEXT-BASED INTERNET TOOLS

GRAPHICAL INTERNET TOOLS FOR X

OPERATING AN INTERNET SITE

UPGRADING YOUR LINUX KERNEL

HELP WITH LINUX NETWORKING

Linux is an excellent platform for exploring the online world and for providing Internet services of your own. As a personal "surfboard" Linux Pro comes with everything you need to connect to an Internet service provider (ISP), including TCP/IP software; client programs such as FTP, Telnet, Finger, Mail, Ping; and Lynx, a text-based Web browser; and arena, a graphical browser. (If you prefer Netscape, you can download a Linux version at *http://home.netscape.com*.)

Linux also makes it easy to set up your own servers so you can operate FTP or Web sites, and even provide Telnet or dial-up access to your system. If you have dreams of becoming an ISP, the Linux Pro product is an excellent platform to build on. The really nice thing is that TCP/IP and all the popular network services are installed and pre-configured for you.

If you've ever tried to configure a Unix network, set up e-mail delivery, or get a Web server running, you will really appreciate this feature. (In technical terms, it means that local loopback, sendmail, inetd, httpd, and several other network daemons are configured and running when you boot up Linux Pro.)

In this chapter, you'll learn

- How to connect your Linux system to the Internet with SLIP or PPP.

- What tools are available for Internet access (text and graphical).

- How to operate your own Internet site.

- Where to get more information on Linux networking.

SETTING UP YOUR SERIAL PORT TO WORK WITH YOUR MODEM

By default, Linux Pro is configured to run your serial (modem) port at a speed of 9600 bps. But faster modems such as 14.4, 28.8, and 33.6 Kbps are quite common now. It would be a shame to spend money on a fast modem and not use it to the fullest, so in order to get the best performance you'll have to tweak your serial port settings.

Unless you have a very slow modem (9600 bps or less), you should use the **setserial** command to enable Linux to make a high-speed connection. Depending on your modem speed, at the command prompt enter one of the commands shown below. It would also be a good idea to log in as **root** and put the same command in your **/etc/profile** file so you don't have to enter it each time you boot up Linux.

```
setserial /dev/modem spd_hi
```
for a 14.4-Kbps modem

```
setserial /dev/modem spd_vhi
```
for a 28.8-Kbps or faster modem

Since modems have built-in compression capabilities, you can transfer data at speeds up to 57.6 Kbps with a 14.4-Kbps modem or 115.2 Kbps with a 28.8-Kbps modem. (Compression enables a theoretical data rate of four times the speed of your modem.) But if you don't issue the **setserial** command, your maximum data rate will be four times 9600 bps, or 38.4 Kbps.

IF YOU HAVE TROUBLE CONNECTING

Under certain uncommon circumstances (such as having nonstandard IRQs or multiple I/O cards in your computer), you may need to use some of the other options of the **setserial** command in order to use your modem with Linux.

If you haven't changed the default IRQ setting on your modem (by fiddling with the jumpers), and you haven't added a second I/O card, you should have no problem. But if you do have trouble dialing out with your modem, issue the **man setserial** command for information on how to set your serial port for nonstandard configurations.

MAKING A SLIP OR PPP CONNECTION

In order to connect your Linux system to the Internet with a modem, the first thing you will need is a SLIP or PPP account with a local ISP. If you're lucky, you might be able to get a free account through a local university or library. SLIP and PPP are protocols that allow you to use TCP/IP networking over a serial (dial-up) line. Given a choice, select a PPP account because it will be faster and more reliable than SLIP.

In any event, you will need the following pieces of information from your ISP to connect using Linux:

- Your ISP dial-up phone number

- Your log-in id

- Your password

- Your ISP's name-server addresses

With these four items, you can modify your network configuration and build the log-in script to connect to your ISP from Linux. If you have a SLIP account, you use a Linux program called **dip** to connect. With a PPP account, you use the **pppd** and **chat** programs, both of which I'll discuss later.

WHAT'S IN A NAMESERVER?

When you want to access a site on the Internet, your TCP/IP software must first translate the site name (for example, http://www.yahoo.com) into an IP address (205.216.146.102). A nameserver performs this translation.

Typically the nameserver software runs on a separate computer accessible via your network; but since your connection to the Internet is through your ISP, you can use your ISP's nameservers. (That's good, because nameservers require lots of memory and CPU power.) To tell your computer's TCP/IP software to use your ISP's name servers, you have to edit the **/etc/resolv.conf** file. Your ISP will supply you with one or more nameserver addresses, which must be added to this configuration file. For example, here's the **resolv.conf** file that I use on my own Linux machine:

```
domain mhv.net
nameserver 199.0.0.2
nameserver 199.0.0.7
nameserver 204.97.212.10
```

If the **resolv.conf** file already contains some lines, you should delete them. Make sure the first line in the file is the `domain` record (your ISP's domain name) and follow that with one or more `nameserver` records as shown above. (Be sure to use *your* ISP's domain and name-server addresses, not the ones in this example!)

CONNECTING WITH A SLIP ACCOUNT

The **dip** utility is a smart little communications program that can dial a remote system, log you in, and configure your serial port for SLIP communications. It's similar to the Trumpet Winsock dialer popular with Windows users.

When you dial your ISP, the remote terminal server prompts you for your log-in and password, and may ask you to enter a command to choose SLIP or PPP. But since the order in which these prompts appear can differ from one ISP to another, you will need to create a "dip script" customized for your ISP (**dip** has a powerful scripting language to help you connect to your ISP no matter what the order of the prompts).

Here's an example of a **dip** log-in script, divided into stages (the line numbers are not part of the file):

```
1  main:
2  port modem
3  speed 38400
4  reset

5  # You may need to modify the modem set-up string
6  send ATE1V1Q0\r
7  wait OK 2
8  if $errlvl != 0 goto error

9  # Modify the line below - use YOUR dialup number
10 dial 555-1234
11 wait CONNECT 45
12 if $errlvl != 0 goto error

13 login:
14 # Modify the line below to match the log-in prompt.
15 wait login: 10
16 if $errlvl != 0 goto error

17 # Modify the line below—use your log-in.
18 send MYLOGIN\n
19 if $errlvl != 0 goto error
20 # Modify the line below to match the log-in prompt.
21 wait password: 10
22 if $errlvl != 0 goto error

23 # Modify the line below—use your password.
24 send MYPASSWD\n
25 if $errlvl != 0 goto error
```

```
26 # Modify the line below to match the command prompt.
27 wait command: 30
28 if $errlvl != 0 goto error
29 # Send SLIP command and wait for connection
30 send SLIP\n
31 wait SLIP 30
32 if $errlvl != 0 goto error

33 # Read the dynamic IP addresses from the remote server.
34 get $rmtip remote 30
35 get $locip remote 30
36 if $errlvl != 0 goto error

37 done:
38 default
39 mode SLIP
40 print CONNECTED to $rmtip with local address: $locip
41 exit

42 error:
43 print Connection failed.
```

This is a simple computer program, but you don't have to be a programmer to modify it for your own use. Boldface items are things you might have to change. Bold underlined items are ones you will definitely have to change. And you might have to move the lines shown in italics to a different spot in the script. Here's a bit more explanation, with references to lines in the sample shown above:

Line 3	Set the speed of your modem—19200, 38400, 57600, and so on.
Line 6	Your modem may need a special init string—consult the manual.
Line 10	You *must* provide the dial-up number for your ISP here.
Line 15	Your server might say username instead of login.
Line 18	You *must* provide your actual log-in name here.
Line 21	Your server might say Password instead of password.

Line 24	You *must* provide your actual log-in password here.
Lines 26 to 30	You might need to move, modify, or remove these lines.

Your terminal server may present a dialog like this (many do):

```
Welcome to Ed's Garage Internet Services

Please enter your login: <your login here>
Please enter your password: <your password here>
Enter command: <SLIP or PPP>

Starting SLIP ...
```

The script above will work without any changes, as long as you substitute the correct phone number, log-in, and password. But say its dialog looks like this instead:

```
Welcome to the CyberSurf Domain, Dude!

Enter SLIP or PPP command: <SLIP or PPP>

Please enter your login: <your login here>
Please enter your password: <your password here>

Starting SLIP ...
```

You will need to move lines 26 to 30 right after line 12, so that the order of the dial-in script will match the order of the terminal server's prompts. Some terminal servers don't show the `Enter command` prompt at all—they just ask for the log-in and password, then start either a SLIP or a PPP connection immediately.

Use a text editor to create your script and save it in your home directory with **myslip.dip** as the file name. (Use the sample script in **/etc/dip-script** as a starting point to save yourself some typing.) Once your script is ready, you can make the SLIP connection with this command:

```
dip -v myslip
```

This will start **dip** and then execute your script. The **-v** flag enables you to see the terminal server prompts and the script commands as they run. If something goes wrong, you should be able to modify your script to correct the problem by following the interplay of commands and prompts on your screen and identifying any glitches.

CONNECTING WITH A PPP ACCOUNT

If you have a PPP account, getting connected will be a bit easier than it is with **dip**. You'll use the **pppd** and **chat** utilities, and all you need to do is create two short executable scripts.

Use a text editor to create the file shown below and save it in your home directory with **ppp** as the file name. You may need to change the modem speed (38400) to a different setting. After creating the file, make it executable with the **chmod +x ppp** command.

```
#!/bin/sh
/usr/sbin/pppd connect $HOME/ppp_chat \
    /dev/modem 38400 crtscts modem noipdefault defaultroute
```

Now use a text editor to create the file shown below (the **ppp_chat** script) and save it in your home directory with **ppp_chat** as its file name. Be sure to substitute the correct phone number, log-in, and password. And just as in the SLIP discussion, you may need to modify or switch the order of the prompts on the last line of the script.

```
#!/bin/sh
/usr/sbin/chat -v ABORT BUSY "" ATZ OK ATDT5551234 \
    'login:' MYLOGIN 'password:' MYPASSWD 'command:' PPP
```

The final line of the **ppp_chat** script above consists of a set of expected prompts (in quotes) followed by the responses to those prompts. Just make sure you put the prompts in the same order in which your terminal server presents them, and the script should work fine.

After creating the file, make it executable and nonreadable by other users (since it will contain your log-in password) with these commands:

```
chmod +x ppp_chat
chmod go-r ppp_chat
```

Once your script is ready, you can make a PPP connection with this command:

```
ppp
```

This will start **pppd** and then execute your **ppp_chat** script. Unfortunately, nothing appears on the screen as you connect, so if something goes wrong it may not be obvious at first. If you hear the modem hang up unexpectedly, look in the **/var/syslog/messages** file for any message that might tell you if your **ppp_chat** script needs a tweak to run properly.

DID IT WORK?

To find out if your Internet connection was successful, examine the output of the **ifconfig** command (issue it with your connection up and running), which might look like this:

```
lo0        Link encap: Local Loopback
           inet addr:127.0.0.1  Bcast:127.255.255.255
           UP BROADCAST LOOPBACK RUNNING  MTU:2000  Metric:1

ppp0       Link encap: Point-Point Protocol
           inet addr:205.161.119.112  P-t-P:205.161.119.3
           UP POINTOPOINT RUNNING  MTU:1500  Metric:1
```

The first few lines show the status of **lo0**, your "local loopback" interface. The local loopback is like your *intranet*—a local network that allows you to exchange e-mail with other users on your system, access files on the local Web server, and so on. The **lo0** device will always have an IP address of 127.0.0.1 and it should say UP and RUNNING in the status line.

If you see an **sl0** or **ppp0** device listed in the **ifconfig** output, you've got an active SLIP or PPP connection to the Internet. Your computer is now a peer to all the other computers on the Internet, with its very own IP address (205.161.119.112 in this example). In fact, anyone on the Internet could connect to this address via Telnet, FTP, or a Web browser! But be aware that this IP address is dynamically assigned from a pool of addresses that your ISP makes available for dial-up users. Next time you connect, you will likely get a different IP address.

Your ISP can probably assign you a permanent IP address (for a fee) if you like, but that would require some changes to your PPP connection setup. Refer to the **PPP-HOWTO** file for information on how to specify a permanent IP address for use with **pppd**. (Visit the "Linux Documentation Project Home Page" on the Web at *http://sunsite.unc. edu/mdw/linux.html* to find all the **HOWTO** files.)

TEXT-BASED INTERNET TOOLS

Believe it or not, the Internet existed prior to the advent of the graphical Web browser. Before the invention of Mosaic in 1990, netizens were e-mailing, transferring files, logging into remote machines, and even surfing the Web using text-based tools from a Unix command line.

Many users actually prefer to use *text-based clients* (tools that enable end users to connect to various types of Internet servers) because the graphical environment adds a lot of overhead, slowing things down. And some people just prefer the keyboard to a mouse.

■ *NOTE: It's important to know the basics of using the Net from a command line, since you might not want (or have the hardware) to run X Windows on your system. These same techniques will come in handy if you have a Unix shell account through your ISP.*

FTP

FTP (which stands for *file transfer program* or *file transfer protocol*, depending on how many pencils you wear in your pocket protector) is the Internet file mover. You use it to transfer files from one computer to another. Most often you'll be using it to download software to your computer, so try that now. To start a text-based FTP client from your Linux command line, enter the **ftp** command followed by a site name, like this:

```
ftp ftp.netscape.com
```

When prompted, specify **anonymous** for the log-in and your e-mail address for the password. You'll be connected to Netscape's FTP site, where you can download the latest Netscape Navigator Web browser for Linux. After getting logged in to the server, you can enter these commands to download the compressed binary file for Navigator:

```
bin
cd /pub/navigator/3.01/unix
get netscape-v301-export.x86-unknown-linux-elf.tar.gz
quit
```

Use the **help** command if you're not familiar with FTP. After the **get** command is finished, **quit** will return you to the Linux command prompt and you'll have a file named **netscape-v301-export.x86-unknown-linux-elf.tar.gz** in the current directory. To uncompress the file and create the netscape executable on your system, do this:

```
tar xvfz netscape-v301-export.x86-unknown-linux-elf.tar.gz
mv netscape /usr/local/bin
```

Refer to Chapter 10, "Compression, Encoding, and Encryption," for more information on dealing with compressed files. How ironic, we just downloaded a graphical browser with a text-based client!

■ *NOTE: When you're downloading software for Linux, sometimes you will have a choice between an **a.out** or **ELF** executable. Your system will execute either type, but given a choice, opt for **ELF** since it's a newer format.*

TELNET

Telnet is a tool that lets you log in to other computers on the Internet. Why would you want to do that? Simple—to access the interesting stuff on those other computers, like databases, games, card catalogs, and information services.

Telnet is strictly text based—you can't point or click on anything. Whether you Telnet from a command line or from a GUI, your Telnet session will look pretty much the same, and all your navigation in a Telnet session is via the keyboard. To start a text based Telnet client from your Linux command line, enter the **telnet** command followed by a site name (and sometimes a port number), like this:

```
telnet cybersurf.com
```

This is a fictitious example that shows how you might log in to a shell account on your ISP's system. Here's a real example that will connect you to the "Ham Radio Call Book" database at the University of Buffalo (commands you enter are shown in boldface):

```
telnet electra.cs.buffalo.edu 2000

Connected to electra.cs.buffalo.edu.
Callbook v1.3 — Type 'help' for help
>> help
Available commands:
    call [filters] callsign    - lookup callsign
    city [filters] city        - lookup city
    name [filters] surname     - lookup last name
    quit                       - exit the server
    zip [filters] zipcode      - lookup zip code
>> city Tillson
Call-Sign: WA2TNV                  Class: GENERAL
Real Name: DONALD G WOOD           Birthday: OCT 31, 1919
Mailing Address: BOX 873 ROSE AVE, TILLSON, NY  12486
Valid From: DEC 29, 1987           To: DEC 29, 1997
>> quit
```

FINGER

Finger is a nifty little tool that can tell you who owns a particular e-mail address, or sometimes display other interesting data. As the name implies, when you use Finger you are "pointing" at someone. When you finger an address, you send a request to another system asking it to tell you everything it knows (or is willing to tell) about that address. The results of fingering vary widely from system to system, and some systems will not even honor Finger requests at all for privacy reasons. Still, most Finger requests will return some limited information about the user, like their real name or the last time they logged in to their system. To use the Finger client from your Linux command line, enter the **finger** command followed by an e-mail address, like this:

```
finger jsmith@hotdog.edu

Home: /user/jsmith      In real life: Janet Smith
Shell: /bin/csh
New mail received Thu May 16 13:33:18 1996;
    unread since Tue May 14 07:50:31 1996
Janet Smith (jsmith) is not presently logged in.
```

And as you'll see in this example, sometimes people connect strange things to the Net and allow you to query them via Finger . . .

```
finger coke@cs.cmu.edu

  M & M                       Coke Buttons
 /-----\               C: CCCCCCCCCCCCCCCCCCCCCCCCC
 |?????|        C: ...........    D: ...........
 |?????|        C: ...........    D: ...........
 |?????|        C: ...........    D: ...........
 |?????|                          C: CCCCCCCCCCCC
 \-----/                          S: CCCCCCCCCCCC
    |          Key:
    |            0 = warm;  9 = 90% cold;  C = cold;  . = empty
    |            Beverages: C = Coke, D = Diet Coke, S = Sprite
    |            Leftmost soda/pop will be dispensed next
 ---^---         M&M status guessed.
```

This example shows how to get the status of a Coke machine, which has been connected to a minicomputer and wired into the Internet at Carnegie-Mellon University!

E-MAIL

In Chapter 9, "Managing Your E-Mail," you learned about the **mail** and **pine** programs, which are text-based e-mail handlers on your Linux system. With a SLIP or PPP connection, you can send e-mail to Internet addresses, but you can't receive Internet mail directly on your system without a permanent connection and a registered domain name. (You could also use UUCP instead of a permanent connection—see below.)

When you installed Linux you assigned yourself a host name (for example, **fritz.com**). So mail that you send from your system will show up with root@fritz.com in the From: line, but it's not possible for the recipient to respond to you because none of the name servers on the Internet know about **fritz.com**.

If you want to be able to receive mail on your Linux system, you'll have to work with your ISP to register a domain name and get either a permanent or UUCP connection to the Internet. You can create a permanent connection (up to 56 Kbps) with a modem and a dedicated phone line, or you can install some expensive equipment and special phone connections to forge a high-speed link.

A UUCP connection is one where you occasionally dial up your ISP to send outgoing and receive incoming e-mail messages. Any mail destined for your domain will queue up at your ISP until you dial in to receive it. Running UUCP is much less expensive than a dedicated phone connection to your ISP, and is quite common on BBS systems in rural areas of the United States and in other countries, where long-distance telephone costs are much higher.

Refer to the **UUCP-HOWTO** file on the CD-ROM and the "Help with Linux Networking" section later in this chapter for more details on UUCP connections. (Visit the "Linux Documentation Project Home Page" on the Web at *http://sunsite.unc.edu/mdw/linux.html* to find all the **HOWTO** files.)

PING

Ping is a simple utility that can tell you the status of another computer on the Internet, and the quality of the connection between your computer and the remote host. Ping works by throwing electronic pebbles at other computers. Every computer on the Internet has a little daemon just waiting for other computers to "ping" it, and when this happens it tries to catch the pebbles and throw them back. If the network connection is sluggish, some of the pebbles might never hit their target, and if the other computer is slow or busy the little daemon might miss or drop some pebbles.

To use the Ping client from your Linux command line, enter the **ping** command followed by a domain name or IP address, like this (press **CTRL-C** to stop after a few lines of output):

```
ping cqu.edu.au
PING cqu.edu.au: 56 data bytes
64 bytes from cqu.EDU.AU (138.77.1.23): icmp_seq=1 time=8100 ms
64 bytes from cqu.EDU.AU (138.77.1.23): icmp_seq=2 time=7354 ms
64 bytes from cqu.EDU.AU (138.77.1.23): icmp_seq=3 time=6281 ms
^C
----cqu.edu.au PING Statistics----
13 packets transmitted, 3 packets received, 77% packet loss
round-trip (ms)  min/avg/max = 6281/7245/8100
```

This output tells you three things:

1. The other computer (located at a university in Australia, represented by the `au` in its address) is running and connected to the Internet. We know this because we didn't get a `no such host` or `host is not responding` message.

2. It has an IP address of `138.77.1.23`. This is the value in parentheses on the second line of the output.

3. The connection is lousy. We can tell this because of the `Statistics` section at the end of the output. We sent out 13 pebbles, er, packets and only 3 were acknowledged. The `77%` `packet loss` and the average response time of `7245` milliseconds (7.245 seconds) is terrible. A more reasonable Ping response time would be under 750 milliseconds.

You can use Ping to test the speed of a connection before trying to connect via Telnet or FTP. Especially with FTP, you often have a choice of servers that all mirror the same set of files, so pick the quickest one.

USENET

Tin is a text-based program you can use to read and post to Usenet newsgroups. From the initial menu, you can select a newsgroup to read, and Tin displays the current postings in that group, as shown here:

```
Group Selection (news.mhv.net 5)

     1    884   alt.internet.services
     2    167   news.announce.newusers
     3    343   news.newusers.questions
     4     49   news.answers
     5    183   comp.internet.net-happenings

<n>=set current to n, TAB=next unread, /=search pattern, c)atchup,
g)oto, j=line down, k=line up, h)elp, m)ove, q)uit, r=toggle unread,
s)ubscribe, S)ub pattern, u)nsubscribe, U)nsub pattern, y)ank in/out
```

You do all your navigating with the cursor keys.

To start Tin, you must first set the **NNTPSERVER** (Network News Transport Protocol Server) environment variable to the name of your ISP's news server (usually, **news** will work fine). Issue the command below from the prompt, and also add it to the **/etc/profile** file (you must log in as **root**) so it will be set automatically next time you boot up.

```
NNTPSERVER=news
```

After setting the environment variable, enter one of the Tin startup commands shown below:

`rtin -rq`	The first time only
`rtin -rqn`	Thereafter

The first time you use Tin it will download a huge list of all available newsgroups from your ISP's server, so don't be surprised if it takes several minutes for the first screen to appear.

For more information on using Tin, use the **man tin** command to read the excellent online help for this program.

LYNX

Lynx is a text-based Web browser. You don't get to see the graphics on a Web page, but for some people that's a plus. Many Web pages are loaded with gratuitous images that take forever to load and add little or no real value. So Lynx can usually get you to the information you're after a lot faster than a graphical browser. Here's what a Lynx screen might look like:

```
Yahoo!
    [ Reuters News Headlines | What's New | Cool Sites ]
    [ Write Us | Add URL | Random Link | Info ]

    _____ Search Options

       * Arts — Humanities, Photography, Architecture ...
       * Business and Economy [Xtra!] — Directory, Investments ...
       * Computers and Internet [Xtra!] — Internet, WWW, Software
       * Education — Universities, K-12, Courses ...
       * Entertainment [Xtra!] — TV, Movies, Music, Magazines ...
       * Government — Politics [Xtra!], Agencies, Law, Military ...
       * Health [Xtra!] — Medicine, Drugs, Diseases, Fitness ...
       * News [Xtra!] — World [Xtra!], Daily, Current Events ...
       * Recreation and Sports [Xtra!] — Sports, Games, Travel ...

Arrow keys: Up/Down to move. Right to follow link; Left to go back.
H)elp  O)ptions  P)rint  G)o  M)ain screen  Q)uit  /=search
```

In addition to displaying Web pages, Lynx can navigate FTP sites and download files for you. It can also send e-mail, read or post Usenet newsgroups, and display information stored on gopher servers. To start the Lynx client from your Linux command line, enter the **lynx** command, optionally followed by a Web address (URL), like this:

`lynx`	Show the default Web page.
`lynx http://www.yahoo.com`	Show a specified Web page.
`lynx ftp://ftp.netscape.com`	Show files at an FTP site.
`lynx gopher://cwis.usc.edu`	Show files at a gopher site.
`lynx mailto:user@site.com`	Prepare to send e-mail.
`lynx news:rec.humor.funny`	Show postings in a newsgroup.

Use the **help** command in Lynx to learn more about navigating the Web without a mouse.

WHOIS

The **whois** command will search the central domain registry at InterNIC and give you information about a domain, such as who owns it, where it is located, and how to contact the owners. Here's an example of **whois** output:

```
whois aol.com
    America Online (AOL-DOM)
    12100 Sunrise Valley Drive
    Reston, Virginia 22091 USA

    Administrative Contact:
        O'Donnell, David B  (DBO3)  PMDAtropos@AOL.COM
        703/453-4255 (FAX) 703/453-4102
    Technical Contact, Zone Contact:
        America Online  (AOL-NOC)  trouble@aol.net
        703-453-5862
```

NSLOOKUP

The **nslookup** command will tell you the IP address associated with an Internet domain name, or vice versa.

```
nslookup well.com
```

Server: csbh.mhv.net	Your ISP's name server
Address: 199.0.0.2	Your ISP's IP address
Name: well.com	
Address: 206.15.64.10	The IP address of well.com

TRACEROUTE

The **traceroute** command will show you the path your network connection would take to reach a remote host. You might find it interesting to learn the actual geographic location of the routers that sit between you and a remote destination on the Internet. Here's an example:

```
$ traceroute cqu.edu.au
traceroute to cqu.edu.au (138.77.1.23), 30 hops max, 40 byte packets
 1  router.mhv.net (199.0.0.1)  8 ms   103 ms   3 ms
 2  sl-pen-10-S3/4-T1.sprintlink.net (144.228.160.41) 560 ms 34 ms   33 ms
 3  sl-pen-1-F0/0.sprintlink.net (144.228.60.1)  136 ms   200 ms   217 ms
 4  core4-hssi5-0.WestOrange.mci.net (206.157.77.105)  23 ms   22 ms   22 ms
 5  core2-hssi-3.LosAngeles.mci.net (204.70.1.237)  141 ms   159 ms   140 ms
 6  border7-fddi-0.LosAngeles.mci.net (204.70.170.51)  111 ms   146 ms   92 ms
 7  qld-new.gw.au (139.130.247.227)   315 ms   311 ms   368 ms
 8  qldrno.gw.au (139.130.5.2)   322 ms   319 ms   321 ms
 9  hub.questnet.net.au (203.22.86.241)   328 ms   386 ms   331 ms
10  cqu-gw.questnet.net.au (203.22.86.146)   349 ms   331 ms   338 ms
11  centaurus.cqu.EDU.AU (138.77.5.1)   410 ms   360 ms   336 ms
12  janus.cqu.EDU.AU (138.77.1.23)   327 ms   346 ms   331 ms
```

If you look at the router names carefully, you can see that the route from my ISP in southeastern New York to Columbia Queens University in Australia passes through a local SprintLink router to MCI routers in West Orange (New Jersey) and Los Angeles before hopping Down Under.

MINICOM

Minicom is a communications program, similar to Telix or Procomm. It's not really an Internet tool, but you could use it to dial in to your shell account or access a bulletin board system. Use the **minicom** command to start this program.

GRAPHICAL INTERNET TOOLS FOR X

For those who prefer point and click to hunt and peck, Linux Pro provides you with graphical tools to handle your e-mail and explore the Web. This section will introduce you to **Exmh** for e-mail, and **Arena** for Web browsing.

Both of these are free and already installed on your system, but I suggest that you also download and check out Netscape for Linux—an excellent browser with a built-in e-mail handler.

EXMH

The **exmh** program (shown in Figure 11-1) is a full-featured e-mail client for the X environment, similar to the popular Eudora mail program. It will send, receive, and store mail in folders. Just as with the text-based mail clients, you can't receive Internet mail directly on your system without a permanent (or UUCP) connection and a registered domain name.

For more information on using **exmh**, use its help facility, available via the **Help** button.

FIGURE 11-1: *The exmh program is similar to the Eudora mail program*

ARENA

Arena is a graphical Web browser that lacks some of the advanced features found in Netscape, such as support for frames and Java. Nonetheless, it's free, loads pretty quickly, and is already installed on your system. (You can see a screen shot of the Arena browser on page 136 in Chapter 7, "The X Window System.")

Netscape

NETSCAPE

You've undoubtedly heard of Netscape—by far the most popular Web browser. Netscape works well with FTP sites and also comes with a built-in e-mail client and Usenet newsgroup reader, making it the Swiss army knife of Internet tools.

Netscape is not free, but you can download a free trial copy using the instructions given earlier in this chapter on page 196. You can also download it by visiting the Netscape home page at *http://home.netscape.com* with Lynx or Arena.

OPERATING AN INTERNET SITE

If you plan to run a public Web site from a Linux system, you will have to register a domain name and make arrangements to connect your computer permanently (24 hours a day) to the Internet.

REGISTERING YOUR DOMAIN NAME

To register a domain name, contact InterNIC (keepers of the central name registry for the Internet) at *http://rs.internic.net*. Complete details and online registration forms are available at this site. If you choose a name other than **fritz.com** (a good idea), you will have to update the **/etc/hosts** and **/etc/HOSTNAME** files to reflect the new domain name.

You'll have to work with your ISP to get the domain registered and operational. The InterNIC fee for domain name registration is currently $100 for the first two years, and $50 per year thereafter. Your ISP will probably charge an additional $50 to $100 to set things up locally.

GETTING YOURSELF CONNECTED

You have a number of options for full-time connectivity, depending on the expected traffic to your site and the amount of money in your budget. You'll have to pay the telephone company for installation and monthly usage, and your ISP will charge a monthly connection fee, too.

Depending on the type of connection you choose and the local telephone company rates, your monthly connectivity bill could range from several hundred to several thousand dollars. Here's a summary of the types of possible connections.

DIAL-UP MODEM LINE   This is the least expensive option, because it uses a regular phone line and a standard modem. But you're limited to a maximum speed of 33.6 Kbps, which would only service 3 or 4 visitors at once. Recommended for hobby usage only.

56K LEASED LINE   As the name implies, this is a line you lease from the phone company with a maximum speed of 56 Kbps. It will handle 7 or 8 concurrent users. It requires the installation of a *router* (about $1000) and it's upgradable to T1 speeds.

ISDN   A digital phone service available in many areas, with a top speed of 128 Kbps, ISDN will handle about 15 concurrent users. It requires an ISDN adapter, which costs about $500. ISDN is a good choice for many start-ups but is not upgradable to higher speeds.

T1 CONNECTION   A high-speed (1544 Kbps) and expensive digital connection that can handle 300 or more concurrent users—sufficient for all but the busiest sites. You can also get **fractional T1** service, which provides either 256 or 512 Kbps for less than the cost of a full T1. T1 connections typically require the installation of a *router* (a piece of hardware that the T1 line plugs into).

One alternative to a router is the RISCom/N2 adapter card from SDL Communications (*http://www.sdlcomm.com*), which allows you to plug a full or fractional T1 line directly into a Linux box. This card is much cheaper than other alternatives and has great performance.

ONSITE ISP CONNECTION   This option requires no phone line, because your computer resides at your ISP's place of business. In this case, your Linux system is cabled directly into the ISP's ethernet network, and you have T1 access. The downside is that you don't have physical access to your computer, so you have to log in via Telnet.

The book *How to Build an Internet Service Company*, by Charles Burke (see *http://www.index.mis.net/kanti*), offers a wealth of information on this subject. You should also get a copy of *Boardwatch Magazine*'s "Directory of Internet Service Providers" (see *http://www.boardwatch.com*) to help you find a quality Internet service provider in your area. In addition, the Unix BBS FAQ at

http://www.dsnet.com/unixbbsfaq may provide some helpful information. You'll also find lots of helpful books and products at the Linux
Mall (*http://www.linuxmall.com*).

SETTING UP YOUR WEB SITE

Linux Pro comes with the very popular Apache Web (**httpd**) server. All
you have to do to get it working is edit the file **/etc/httpd/conf/
httpd.conf** and change the **ServerName** line to read like this:

```
ServerName <your domain name>
```

To test it out, start the Lynx browser and display the default Web page,
which is stored as **index.html** in the **/home/httpd/html** directory. Of
course, you'll want to create your own home page, so edit the
index.html file to suit your needs, and you're in business.

The default Apache configuration files in the **/etc/httpd/conf**
directory will work fine for most people; but if you're curious about
ways to change the behavior of the server, have a look at the other
files in this directory. Refer to the Apache home page at *http://www.
apache.org* for help.

UPGRADING YOUR LINUX KERNEL

The version of Linux Pro that you've installed from the CD-ROM in this
book uses the Linux 1.2 kernel as the core of the operating system. A
newer Linux 2.0 kernel, also available on the CD-ROM, offers many
improvements in the areas of networking speed and security.

You can upgrade your system to use the 2.0 kernel by following the
instructions in the **README.TXT** file on the CD.

HELP WITH LINUX NETWORKING

If you run into trouble establishing your dial-up connection, or if you have
questions about Linux networking, visit the "Linux Documentation
Project Home Page" on the Web at *http://sunsite.unc.edu/mdw/linux.html*
to find the **Net-2-HOWTO, PPP-HOWTO,** and **Serial-HOWTO** files.

This site is also home to a very comprehensive document called *The Linux Network Administrator's Guide,* which goes into great detail on SLIP and PPP connections, setting up your system to allow others to dial in, and security-related procedures you should follow.

These documents will be useful in answering any questions you may have about Linux networking, and I highly recommend them if you plan to allow others to make SLIP or PPP connections to your Linux machine.

LINUX DOES DOS AND WINDOWS

Accessing DOS Floppies with MTOOLS

Accessing DOS Partitions with Mount

Running DOS Programs with DOSemu

Running Windows Programs with Wine

More Linux Compatibility Tools

Even though Linux is a very complete operating system, you will probably have occasion to access the programs and files you left behind in the DOS world. Fortunately, there are several ways to do so without shutting down Linux and booting up DOS.

This chapter will show you how to use the MTOOLS package to read and write DOS floppy disks under Linux, and how to mount your DOS hard drive partition to access a DOS file system while running Linux. You'll also learn about DOSemu, a DOS emulator that runs under Linux, as well as WINE and WABI—two Windows emulators that allow you to run MS Windows applications in Linux's X Window environment.

ACCESSING DOS FLOPPIES WITH MTOOLS

Do you need to list the files on a DOS-formatted floppy disk while running Linux? Copy a file from a DOS diskette to your Linux file system, or vice versa? You can use the MTOOLS commands to do these and lots of other DOS-like things with Linux.

The MTOOLS package is a set of Linux commands that mimic the DOS commands **DIR, COPY, TYPE, DEL, RENAME,** and a few others. They're called the MTOOLS because they all start with the letter "m," and they work much like their DOS counterparts.

Here's a list of the MTOOLS commands and what they do:

`matttrib`	Modify the attributes of a file
`mcd`	Change current directory
`mcopy`	Copy a file
`mdel`	Delete a file
`mdir`	List the directory
`mformat`	Format a diskette
`mlabel`	Change the disk label
`mmd`	Make a new directory
`mrd`	Remove a directory
`mren`	Rename a file
`mtype`	Display contents of a file

Okay, pop a DOS diskette in the machine and let's try some examples. Here we see the **mdir** command in action, listing the files on a diskette:

```
$ mdir A:
Volume in drive A has no label
Volume Serial Number is 1205-1049
Directory of A:\

COMMAND   COM        54,645 05-31-94    6:22a
FORMAT    COM        22,974 05-31-94    6:22a
SYS       COM         9,432 05-31-94    6:22a
MOUSE     COM        28,949 04-02-93    4:39p
EDIT      COM           413 05-31-94    6:22a
FDISK     EXE        29,336 01-01-97   12:39a
        6 file(s)         145,749 bytes
                        1,311,915 bytes free
```

Now let's copy a file from Linux to the diskette, and vice versa:

```
$ mcopy /tmp/kornmeal.txt A:
$ mcopy A:pandavu.tgz /tmp
```

The **mcopy** command figures out which direction to do the file transfer by looking for the **A:** in either the source or target file name. If you have two floppy drives, you can use **B:** when referring to the second floppy drive.

Here's an example showing the use of the **mdel** command to delete a file on the diskette:

```
$ mdel mouse.com
```

Note that we didn't prefix the name of the file to be deleted with A: this time. All of the MTOOLS commands (except **mcopy**) will assume you're working with the A drive, so you can omit the A: if you like; but I recommend that you don't, just for safety's sake.

ACCESSING DOS PARTITIONS WITH MOUNT

Most people running Linux have a DOS partition on their hard drive, and if you followed the instructions in Chapter 1, "Installing Linux on Your PC," you should, too. You can read, write, and manipulate your DOS files just as if they were native Linux files by *mounting* the DOS partition.

When you mount the DOS partition, it becomes just another directory under the root of your Linux file system, and you can treat it just like any other Linux directory. When you move a Linux file to the DOS partition (or vice versa), Linux figures out whether the file is plain text or binary data and does any appropriate conversions behind the scenes. And it's pretty cool to use **find, grep,** and other Linux commands on your DOS files!

Before you do the mount, you have to create a new directory in the root of your Linux file system. You can call this directory whatever you like, but I recommend **/dos** for simplicity. Create the directory with this command (you must be logged in as **root**):

```
$ mkdir /dos
```

mount

Now we're ready to mount the DOS partition on top of the **/dos** directory. Here's the command to use:

```
$ mount -t msdos /dev/hda1 /dos
```

Translated into English, this tells Linux to mount the file system of type MSDOS (-t msdos) found on the first partition of the first hard drive (/dev/hda1) on top of the /dos directory.

If you've got a SCSI hard drive, you should use **/dev/sda1** instead of **/dev/hda1** in the example above. If you have a second hard drive on your system with a DOS partition, reference it as **/dev/hdb1**. (See Chapter 1 for more information on hard drives, devices, and partitions.)

Okay, your DOS partition is mounted—now have a look around. If you issue the **ls /dos** command you'll see the same list of files that would result from a **dir C:** command under DOS. You can **cd** to other directories under **/dos** and use any Linux command to slice and dice your DOS files.

sharing files

It's great to have the ability to copy files back and forth between Linux and DOS, but you can do some clever things if you think creatively. I find it particularly useful to use the **ln** command ("link") to share my Netscape bookmark file between Linux and DOS like this:

```
ln -s /dos/netscape/bookmark.htm $HOME/.netscape/bookmarks
```

/etc/fstab

By linking these files together I need to manage only one bookmark file. Of course this trick only works if both the DOS and Linux versions of a product use the same format for the file(s) being shared. If you

want your DOS partition to mount each time you boot Linux, add the
line shown below to the **/etc/fstab** file to make it so.

```
/dev/hda1   /dos  msdos   umask=022
```

When Linux boots up, it looks in the **/etc/fstab** file and mounts all the
file systems specified there, so you won't have to manually issue the
mount command to access your DOS partition. The line you just added
to **/etc/fstab** has the same effect as the **mount -t msdos /dev/
hda1 /dos** command shown earlier.

RUNNING DOS PROGRAMS WITH DOSEMU

virtual machine

DOSemu (DOS Emulator) is a program that lets you run many of your
favorite DOS applications under Linux. The name is a little bit mislead-
ing—it doesn't actually emulate DOS, it boots DOS into a *virtual machine*
using the special hardware features in Intel 80386 and higher CPUs.

A DOSemu session looks and acts like a real DOS session, with a
few limitations on what it can do. Not all video and sound cards are
supported under DOSemu, and some programs that require DPMI
(DOS Protected Mode Interface) will not run. The most notable example of this is Windows 3.1, although some people do report being able
to run it under DOSemu.

SETTING UP DOSEMU

Setting up DOSemu is not hard but it does require quite a few steps to
get a fully functioning DOS session up and running. The first thing
you'll need to do is boot up the "real" MS-DOS and then create a
bootable DOS diskette using this command:

```
format a: /s
```

Make sure you have a diskette in the floppy drive (here's where those
pesky AOL disks come in handy) when you issue this command. Next,
copy the files **format.com, sys.com, edit.com,** and **fdisk.exe** from your
DOS directory to the floppy. When you've completed these steps,
remove the floppy disk from the drive and restart Linux.

After logging in, reinsert the floppy and issue the **dos** command from your Linux command prompt. In a few seconds you should see a DOS session start up and the familiar A:> prompt will appear. Voila— you're running DOS under Linux!

If all you want to do is run DOS programs from the floppy disk, you've completed the DOSemu configuration. You can copy additional DOS programs to the floppy (from the mounted DOS partition or from "real" DOS) and run them under DOSemu, but to make good use of DOSemu, you should configure it to recognize the DOS partition on your hard drive.

Exit the DOSemu session by pressing CTRL-ALT-PGDN. Or, if that doesn't work, log in from another virtual console, then use the **ps** and **kill** commands to find and terminate the DOSemu task. (See Chapter 2, "Living in a Shell," for details on killing an active task.)

STARTING DOSEMU WITHOUT A FLOPPY

Keeping a floppy disk around for those times when you want to use DOSemu is a nuisance. Here's how to run DOSemu without it. Edit the **/etc/DOSemu.conf** file and uncomment (remove the # in column one) the line reading:

```
disk { image "/var/lib/DOSemu/hdimage" }
```

hard disk image

The file **/var/lib/DOSemu/hdimage** is a "hard disk image"—a special Linux file that contains a miniature DOS file system. The line you just uncommented tells DOSemu to treat the **hdimage** file as the C: drive next time we start DOSemu. This C: drive is not your DOS partition, it's a simulated hard disk that makes it possible to start DOSemu without having to use a floppy disk. But keep that floppy in the A: drive for just a while longer . . .

Now start DOSemu again with the **dos** command and issue the **dir C:** command. Don't panic if the listing of files is unfamiliar. Remember, what you've got here is a special C: directory that DOSemu will use to boot up instead of using the floppy disk.

However, at this point, the C: drive is functional, but not bootable. To prepare this C: drive for DOSemu booting, issue these two commands from the A:> prompt:

```
fdisk /mbr
sys c:
```

This will transfer the MS-DOS system files from the floppy disk to the C: drive, which is the hard disk image. Be very careful to NOT issue those two commands while running "real" MS-DOS. If you do, it will remove LILO from your boot partition and you'll have to boot up Linux from your emergency diskette. (See Chapter 1 for details on how to handle this situation.)

GETTING DOSEMU TO RECOGNIZE THE DOS PARTITION

emufs.sys

The next step is to tweak the **CONFIG.SYS** file on that funny C: drive. Use the command **EDIT C:\CONFIG.SYS** and insert the line shown below as the first line of the file:

```
device = emufs.sys /dos
```

This tells DOSemu to mount your DOS partition when DOSemu is started and assign it to the next drive letter, which would be D: in our case. Now exit DOSemu and edit the **/etc/DOSemu.conf** file again. This time change the line that reads **bootA** to **bootC** and then restart DOSemu with the **dos** command after removing the diskette from the floppy drive. Instead of getting the A:› prompt, you should see a C:› prompt. At this point, you can switch to the D: drive and you should see all your DOS files.

If any of your DOS programs don't run correctly as a result of finding themselves on a D: drive instead of a C: drive, you can skip the instructions in the "Starting DOSemu Without a Floppy" section and add the **device = emufs.sys /dos** command to the **CONFIG.SYS** on your floppy disk instead. You will have to start DOSemu with a floppy, but your DOS partition will be assigned to the C: drive.

FURTHER DOSEMU CONFIGURATION

By default, DOSemu starts up with text-only video support, and no support for serial or parallel ports. So if you want to run any graphics programs, or use the mouse, modem or printer, exit DOSemu and continue on.

To enable support for graphics, the mouse, modem, or printer, edit the **/etc/DOSemu.conf** file as described in the instructions that follow. I recommend that you configure only the features you really need. Take these steps one at a time and test out each new feature separately by starting DOSemu. That way if a problem arises, you'll know which feature caused it and you can go back to the **/etc/DOSemu.conf** file and disable it or try an alternative.

SETTING UP VIDEO GRAPHICS Look for the line that reads `video{vga}` and comment it out by placing a **#** in column one. Then uncomment the lines reading `allowvideoportaccess on` and `video {vga consolegraphics}`. Start DOSemu and test your graphics program. If it doesn't work, see the copious comments in the **/etc/DOSemu.conf** file for other ideas to try.

SETTING UP MOUSE SUPPORT Look for the line that reads `serial { mouse com 1 device /dev/mouse }` and uncomment it. (If your mouse is not on COM1, select the line corresponding to your mouse port.) Then uncomment one of the `mouse { ... }` lines depending on what type of mouse you have. The most common case is `mouse{ microsoft }`. Start DOSemu and test your mouse.

SETTING UP MODEM SUPPORT Look for the line that reads `serial { com 2 device /dev/modem }` and uncomment it. (If your modem is not on COM2, select the line corresponding to your modem port.) Start DOSemu and test your modem.

SETTING UP PRINTER SUPPORT Look for the line that reads `printer { options "%s" command "lpr" timeout 20 }` and uncomment it. Start DOSemu and test your printer.

RUNNING DOSEMU UNDER X WINDOW

You can run a DOSemu session under X Window by issuing the **xdos** command from an **xterm** window. A new window titled "DOS in a Box" should appear on the screen. The **xdos** session should behave the same as any other DOSemu session, except that graphics are not supported.

GETTING MORE INFORMATION ON DOSEMU

The volunteer developers of DOSemu are working hard to fix bugs and resolve existing compatibility problems. You can visit James Maclean's DOSemu Home Page at *http://www.ednet.ns.ca/~macleajb/ dosemu.html* to get the latest news on DOSemu.

You can find additional help and information on DOSemu in the **DOSEMU-HOWTO** file, found in the **/doc/HOWTO** directory on the CD-ROM. There is also a DOSemu information file at **/usr/doc/dosemu-0.60.4-3/QuickStart** on your hard disk.

RUNNING WINDOWS PROGRAMS WITH WINE

Wine (Windows Emulator) is a program that allows you to run some MS Windows applications under Linux. Wine works by intercepting the internal Windows program calls and translating them into equivalent X Window functions.

Although work on Wine has come a long way, it is still considered to be Alpha (experimental) code. Many people have reported varying degrees of success running some of the larger shareware and commercial programs under Wine, but a lot of programs still run poorly or not at all.

The newsgroup *comp.emulators.ms-windows.wine* is the best place to look for the latest news on Wine, and will occasionally have postings that tell of successes and failures to run various MS Windows programs under Wine. There are also a few websites that maintain lists of programs that have been tested under Wine. (See *http://www.linpro.no/wine/working-apps.html* or *http://www.prog soc.uts.edu.au/~wildfire*)

HOW DO I GET A TASTE OF WINE?

The Wine source code is not included on the CD-ROM that comes with this book because a new version of Wine is distributed about twice a month. If you want to try out Wine, you'll have to download the source code and compile it on your Linux system. You can find Wine stored at one of these locations:

> *ftp://sunsite.unc.edu/pub/Linux/ALPHA/wine/development/ Wine-YYMMDD.tar.gz*

> *ftp://tsx-11.mit.edu/pub/linux/ALPHA/Wine/development/ Wine-YYMMDD.tar.gz*

The *YYMMDD* in the filename will be replaced by an actual release date, so be sure to pick the latest version. For instance, the distribution released on February 15, 1997, was called Wine-970215.tar.gz. After you download the file, store it in the **/usr/src** directory.

HOW DO I COMPILE AND RUN WINE?

You'll need about 50 megabytes of hard drive space to store and compile the Wine source code, and it's recommended that you have at least 16 megabytes of RAM and a 16-megabyte swap partition to run Wine. You'll also need to have a mounted DOS partition with MS Windows installed in it.

To compile the Wine source code, first expand the **gzip**'d **tar** file you just downloaded with commands like these:

```
cd /usr/src
tar -zxvf Wine-YYMMDD.tar.gz
```

then follow the simple instructions contained in the README file that will be located in the **/usr/src/WineYYMMDD** directory. Depending on the speed of your processor, it can take anywhere from 10 to 30 minutes for the compilation to complete.

When the compilation is finished, you have just one more setup step to perform. Copy the **/usr/src/WineYYMMDD/wine.ini** file to your **/usr/local/wine.conf** directory and edit the **Path=** line in the **[Drive C]** section so that it reads **Path=/dos**, then save the file.

```
[Drive C]
Path=/dos
Type=hd
Label=MS-DOS
Filesystem=msdos
```

To run a MS Windows program under Wine, you must first enter X Window with the **startx** command. From an **xterm** window, enter a command like

```
wine /path/program
```

For example, if you want to run the MS Windows Solitaire program, and you've mounted the DOS partition as **/dos** then you would type

```
wine /dos/windows/sol.exe
```

A new window for the Solitaire game should appear on the screen in a few seconds. All of the applets that come with MS Windows–like File Manager, Clock, Calculator, Notepad, and Paintbrush–will work fine, as will most of the games in the Microsoft Entertainment pack. However, larger and more complex programs like Netscape and Microsoft Word for Windows will probably run poorly or not at all.

If you're intoxicated by the mere thought of learning more about Wine, the best source of up-to-date information is the *comp. emulators.ms-windows.wine* newsgroup. You can also find the Wine FAQ online at *http://www.asgardpro.com/wine*.

WABI—AN ALTERNATIVE TO WINE

There's also a commercial product from Caldera called WABI that provides very good MS Windows support under Linux. WABI is a more mature product and supports popular Windows packages like MS Word, but it's not free. WABI also runs Windows programs faster than if they were running natively under MS Windows!

If you have a serious need to run nontrivial Windows applications under Linux, you can find more information on WABI at *http://www. caldera.com* or purchase a copy online at *http://www.linuxmall.com*. (See also the catalog pages in the back of this book.)

MORE LINUX COMPATIBILITY TOOLS

executor 2

If you're a Mac user, you might want to check out the **Executor 2** product from ARDI, which is a Mac emulator for Linux. Not only does it read and write Macintosh format files on floppies and hard drives, but it also runs many Macintosh applications flawlessly.

samba

And if you have multiple computers running a mixture of Windows and Linux, you should have **Samba**. Samba gives you an easy way to share disks and printers between the two systems and, best of all, it's free. You can learn more about Samba on the Web at *http://lake.canberra.edu.au/pub/samba*

LEARNING MORE ABOUT LINUX

Finding Software for Linux

Linux FTP Sites

Linux-Specific Search Engines

Linux Bulletin Board Systems

Linux Newsgroups

Linux Mailing Lists

Linux Web Sites

This book was not intended to be the final word on Linux. Rather, it's meant to provide enough Linux knowledge to get you up and running, without being too terribly overwhelming or geeky. I wanted to call this book *Just Enough Linux to Be Dangerous,* but my publisher wouldn't go for it.

By now, you've learned how to install Linux and use it productively. You know what shells are, and how to move around in the Linux file system. You can use a text editor or one of many Linux commands to manipulate the contents of a file.

Running your favorite DOS and Windows programs under X Window is no problem, and hey—you're a programmer now! You can even connect your Linux system to the Internet, explore the online world, and operate your own Web site.

But still, there's a lot more to learn about Linux. And since Linux is constantly under development by a small army of volunteers all around the world, you should be aware of how to get the latest information. This chapter will tell you how to find Linux software, Web sites, FTP sites, bulletin board systems, Usenet newsgroups, mailing lists, and search engines.

FINDING SOFTWARE FOR LINUX

If you're looking for a program for a specific task, check out the **Linux Software Map** (LSM) on the Web at *http://www.boutell.com/lsm*. The LSM is a searchable database of over 2,500 noncommercial software packages available for Linux. You can search by keyword or title, or just browse through all the titles to see what's available. Whether you're looking for a Galaga game or a GIF manipulator for Linux, this is a good place to start.

The **Commercial-HOWTO** file in the **doc/HOWTO** directory on the CD-ROM is a good place to look next. This file contains information on commercial software packages that you can buy for Linux. The categories covered include databases, CAD, application development, finance, mathematics, networking, and text processing. Pricing and contact information is supplied.

LINUX FTP SITES

You can find the source code for Linux distributions and applications on many FTP sites. Here are some of the best places to find Linux files via FTP. Try to use a site that's geographically close to get faster downloads.

Site Address	Directory	Location
tsx-11.mit.edu	/pub/linux	Massachusetts, U.S.
sunsite.unc.edu	/pub/Linux	North Carolina, U.S.
ftp.funet.fi	/pub/Linux	Finland
wuarchive.wustl.edu	/mirrors/linux	Missouri, U.S.
ftp.nether.net	/Linux	Michigan, U.S.
ftp.mcc.ac.uk	/pub/linux	United Kingdom
ftp.win.tue.nl	/pub/linux	United Kingdom
ftp.sun.ac.za	/pub/linux	South Africa
ftp.ibp.fr	/pub/linux	France
nic.switch.ch	/mirror/linux	Switzerland
ftp.lysator.liu.se	/pub/linux	Sweden
ftp.cs.tu-berlin.de	/pub/linux	Germany
nwg.nectec.or.th	/pub/mirrors/linux	Thailand
swdsrv.edvz.univie.ac.at	/unix/systems/linux	Austria
ftp.dstc.edu.au	/pub/linux	Australia
ftp.cdrom.com	/pub/linux	California, U.S.
ftp.wgs.com	/pub/linux	Colorado, U.S.

LINUX-SPECIFIC SEARCH ENGINES

Several search engines are available to help you find Linux-related information. Here's a list of some Web-based search tools you might find useful.

Linux search	*http://theory.uwinnipeg.ca/search/* *linux-search.html* Search for files in Linux FTP libraries.
Linux man pages	*http://www.ctyme.com/linuxdoc.htm* Online search of Linux man pages.
LDP search	*http://amelia.db.erau.edu/Harvest/* *brokers/LDP/query.html* Search the Linux Documentation Project files.
LSM search	*http://www.boutell.com/lsm* Search the Linux Software Map.
InterBoard	*http://www.theforge.com:8090/* A discussion board with searchable question- and-answer area for both newbies and pros.

LINUX BULLETIN BOARD SYSTEMS

If you don't have convenient access to the Internet, many BBSs around the world have Linux file libraries. Here's a list with some of the best Linux BBSs.

UNITED STATES

Acquired Knowledge BBS	305/720-3669	Fort Lauderdale, Florida
Information Overload	770/471-1549	Riverdale, Georgia
WayStar BBS	508/481-7147	Marlborough, Massachusetts
Programmer's Corner	301/596-7693	Columbia, Maryland
WaterDeep BBS	410/614-2190	Baltimore, Maryland

The Wizzard's Cave	516/483-5841	East Meadow, New York
Intermittent Connection	503/344-9838	Eugene, Oregon
Sevenex PubAcc. Linux	414/843-4169	Paddock Lake, Wisconsin

CANADA

WorldGate/VALIS	403/444-7685	Edmonton, Canada
Serendipity	604/599-3820	Richmond, Canada
Mark's Linux BBS	613/829-1941	Ottawa, Canada
The UnderGround Palace	418/622-9583	Charlesbourg, Canada
Petrel Systems	506/455-1963	Fredericton, Canada
Research and Development	416/691-4150	Toronto, Canada

FRANCE

Modula BBS	+33-1-4043-0124	Paris, France
Libernet BBS	+33-1-402-290-93	Paris, France
Stdin	+33-72345437	Lyon, France
BBS Viking	+33-76-93-13-48	Grenoble, France

SWITZERLAND

| Baboon BBS | +41-62-7528441 | Strengelback, Switzerland |

Baerengraben	+41-31-9340131	Stettlen, Switzerland
Alphanet	+41-328-41-40-81	Colombier, Switzerland
Eulen BBS	+41-1-4319649	Zurich, Switzerland
Zuerich Live BBS	+41-1-4312321	Zurich, Switzerland

GERMANY

umibox	+49-4152-824-93	Geesthacht, Germany
troehl	+49-40-791-43-025	Hamburg, Germany
Formel-Box	+49-4191-2846	Kaltenkirchen, Germany
Zaphods BBS	+49-228-264-146	Bonn, Germany
Mitropa	+49-203-482-319	Duisburg, Germany
Bigcomm Linux-Box	+49-211-398-52-58	Düsseldorf, Germany
Interworld	+49-30-251-37-71	Berlin, Germany
Crystal BBS	+49-7152-240-86	Leonberg, Germany
Echoblaster BBS #2	+49-7142-212-35	Bietigheim, Germany
LinuxServer	+49-711-975-49-21	Stuttgart, Germany

NETHERLANDS

Openworld Intl	+31-1720-42580	Alphen a/d Rijn, Netherlands
Filosoft/Programmers BBS	+31-50-412288	Groningen, Netherlands
Columbus BBS	+31-23-547-0578	Hoofddorp, Netherlands

BELGIUM

In Limbo	+32-2-582-66-50	Lennik, Belgium
MicroTEch res. dept.	+32-19-567337	Borlez Faimes, Belgium
Bad WaZOO BBS	+32-4-3445020	Liege, Belgium

ITALY

nonsolopoint	+39-51-432904	Bologna, Italy
Nixnet	+39-862-316-950	L'Aquila, Italy
Pappaconda On-Line	+39-51-6233671	Bologna, Italy

ENGLAND

The Linux BBS	+44-1705-814613	Portsmouth, England
TiggerBBS	+44-1753-672520	Berkshire, England
Dream Machine II	+44-1222-689812	Cardiff, England

NEW ZEALAND

mserve.kiwi.gen.nz	+64-9-366-44-62	Auckland, New Zealand
BugBoard	+64-4-526-4840	Wellington, New Zealand

VARIOUS

Nemesis's Dungeon	+353-1-324755	Dublin, Ireland
Dream World BBS	+358 -1-4389 843	Raisio, Finland
Super 7	+42-2421-8007	Prague, Czechoslovakia
sci	+7-831-234-3045	Nizhny Novgorod, Russia
Pats System	+27-12-333-2049	Pretoria, South Africa
Galaktische Archive	+43-222-830-38-04	Wien, Austria
Gunship BBS	+46-31-693306	Gothenburg, Sweden
Wintech BBS	+55-011-5238883	Sao Paulo, Brazil
500cc Formula 1 BBS	+61-2-550-4317	Sydney, Australia
Olisc Unix BBS	+852-429-6157	Hong Kong, Hong Kong
Don't Panic	+91-11-6426681	New Delhi, India

LINUX NEWSGROUPS

Usenet is another great place to ask questions and share Linux information. Here's a listing of Usenet newsgroups where Linux is spoken.

comp.os.linux.advocacy	Benefits of Linux compared to other operating systems.
comp.os.linux.announce	Announcements important to the Linux community (moderated).
comp.os.linux.answers	FAQs, HOWTOs, READMEs, and so on, about Linux (moderated).
comp.os.linux.development.apps	Writing Linux applications, porting to Linux.
comp.os.linux.development.system	Linux kernels, device drivers, modules.
comp.os.linux.hardware	Hardware compatibility with the Linux operating system.
comp.os.linux.m68k	Linux operating system on 680X0 Amiga, Atari, VME.
comp.os.linux.misc	Linux-specific topics not covered by other groups.
comp.os.linux.networking	Networking and communications under Linux.
comp.os.linux.setup	Linux installation and system administration.
comp.os.linux.x	Linux X Window servers, clients, libraries, and fonts.

LINUX MAILING LISTS

If you don't have Usenet access, mailing lists are a good alternative to the newsgroups. To get a long list of Linux-related mailing lists, visit *http://www.liszt.com* and search for *linux,* or send e-mail to *liszter@ bluemarble.net* with *search linux* in the message body.

There are several dozen Linux mailing lists hosted by the Majordomo server at Rutgers University. For information, send e-mail to *majordomo@vger.rutgers.edu* with *lists* in the message body.

A Web page at *http://summer.snu.ac.kr/~djshin/linux/mail-list/ index.shtml* offers push button subscribe and unsubscribe to many Linux mailing lists.

THE LINUX NEWSLETTER

The Linux Newsletter from WGS is a free monthly e-mail publication for those who want to know more about Linux. For a subscription, write to *wgsnews@wgs.com* with *SUBSCRIBE* in the subject line.

Back issues of the Linux Newsletter can also be found at *http: //www.all-linux.com/announce.html* in case you want to have a look before you subscribe.

LINUX WEB SITES

There are many excellent sites on the Web where you can get information on Linux. One of the best is the **Linux Documentation Project** (LDP) at *http://sunsite.unc.edu/mdw/linux.html*, which is an effort to develop reliable and freely available documents for the Linux operating system.

You can find several introductory and tutorial documents, as well as the complete set of Linux **HOWTO** files. If you're interested in learning about Linux versions for Atari, Amiga, Mac, or DEC Alpha systems, or Linux information in languages other than English, this is the place to look. The LDP also has dozens of pointers to other Web sites with Linux information. Here's a sampling:

Linux Hardware Survey at *http://www.cris.com/~cwhoover/hardware. htm* is a running survey of what hardware people are using to run

Linux on. This is a good way to find out if others are using Linux with the same hardware you have.

Reptile's Linux Security Page at *http://207.237.120.45/linux/* is a great place to learn about Linux security (and security holes).

The **Linux Forum** at *http://www.pssltd.co.uk/kontagx/linux/* is a place for new and intermediate Linux users to pick up Linux tips and tricks.

Links to Linux Users Groups at *http://sunsite.unc.edu/mdw/lugs.html* is a list of Linux user groups, sorted by location. Find out if there are any Linux fanatics in your neighborhood!

The **Linux Programmer's Guide** at *http://linuxwww.db.erau.edu/LPG* is well, what you think it is.

The **All-Linux Shopping Mall** at *http://www.LinuxMall.com* was created by WorkGroup Solutions in order to make all commercial software for Linux easily available in one location. It also offers Linux-friendly hardware.

The **Linux Journal** is also an important resource. This printed publication's mission is to serve the Linux community and to promote the use of Linux worldwide. It helps both in getting started and in staying on the cutting edge. For subscription information, see *http://www.ssc.com/lj*.

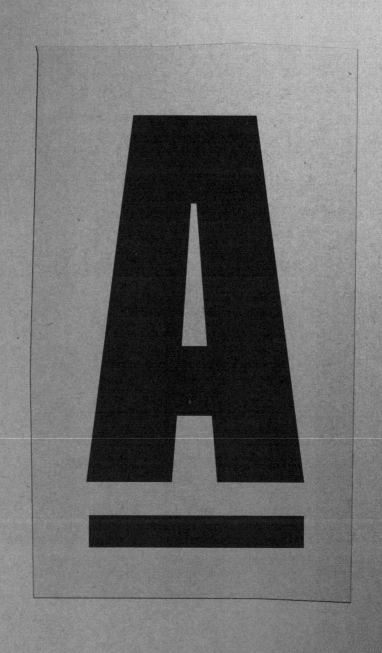

WHAT'S ON THE CD-ROM?

WHAT'S ON THE CD-ROM?

T he Linux Pro CD-ROM that comes with this book contains over 300 software packages. If you install all of them, you will have a very complete and robust Unix system at your disposal. Use this appendix as a handy guide for finding a tool to suit the task at hand. To learn more about any of the commands listed here, use the **man** command to display the online help.

To install packages from the CD-ROM or remove packages from your hard disk, use the **glint** command under X Window. It's a very friendly point-and-click application that guides you through the process.

APPLICATIONS

COMMUNICATIONS

efax	Sends and receives faxes, modems.
ircii	Popular Unix IRC client.
ircii-help	Help files and documentation for ircii.
lrzsz	Zmodem utilitieslz, sz, rz and friends.
minicom	TTY mode communications package à la Telix.

DATABASES

mb	MetalBase relational database.

EDITORS

ed	GNU line editor.

jed	Editor with multiple key bindings, a C-like extension language, colors, and many other features.
jed-xjed	X binary of JED.
joe	Easy-to-use editor.
nvi	New Berkeley Vi editor (experimental).
vim	Visual editor improved.
emacs	GNU emacs.
emacs-el	.el source files not necessary to run emacs.
emacs-nox	No X libraries required.

EMULATORS

dosemu	DOS emulator.

ENGINEERING

spice	SPICE circuit simulator.
units	Units conversion program.

GRAPHICS

ghostscript	PostScript interpreter and renderer.
ghostscript-fonts	Fonts for GhostScript.
giftrans	Converts and manipulates GIFs.
libgr-progs	Graphics utility programs.
netpbm	Loads of image conversion and manipulation tools (hpcd support is missing due to a very restrictive redistribution clause).

xfig	X11 drawing tool.
zgv	Console viewer for many graphics formats.

MAIL

elm	ELM mail user agent.
exmh	EXMH mail program.
mailx	Enhanced mail program.
metamail	Collection of MIME-handling utilities.
mh	Mail-handling system (with POP support).
pine	MIME-compliant mail reader with news support.
popclient	Retrieve mail from a mail server using Post Office Protocol.

MATH

bc	GNU base calculator.
gnuplot	Plotting package.

NETWORKING

lynx	World Wide Web tty browser.
ncftp	FTP client with a nice interface.
tcpdump	Dumps packets that are sent or received over a network interface.

NEWS

slrn	Small NNTP newsreader.

| tin | Tin newsreader. |
| trn | Threaded newsreader. |

PRODUCTIVITY

| ical | Calender application made with Tcl7.4:Tk4.0. |

PUBLISHING

groff	GNU groff text formatting package.
groff-gxditview	GNU groff X previewer.
linuxdoc-sgml	Text formatting system used by the Linux Documentation Project.
lout	Lout text formatting system.
lout-doc	Full lout documentation.
texinfo	Texinfo formatter and info reader.

PUBLISHING — TEX

| tetex-xtexsh | X11 shell for TeX work. |

SOUND

aumix	Text-based audio mixer.
cdp	Full-screen text mode program for playing audio CDs.
playmidi	Play midi files on FM, GUS, and MIDI devices.

| sox | General-purpose sound-file conversion tool. |
| tracker | Plays Amiga MOD sound files via :dev:dsp. |

SPREADSHEETS

| slsc | Spreadsheet based on sc, but with many enhancements. |

BASE & KERNEL

crontabs	Root crontab file.
etcskel	Skelton user dot files.
initscripts	Inittab and :etc:rc.d scripts.
logrotate	Log rotator.
mailcap	Red Hat mailcap package.
redhat-release	Release file.
rootfiles	Root dot files.
setup	Simple setup files.
termcap	Termcap file.
iBCS	IBCS module.
kernel-modules	Loadable kernel modules.
kernel-source	Linux kernel sources.
umsdos_progs	Utilities for doing UMSDOS FS operations.

SysVinit	Sys V init.
at	at job spooler.
bdflush	System Cache flusher.
gpm	General-purpose mouse support for Linux.
pcmcia-cs	PCMCIA card services.
procmail	Procmail mail delivery agent.
sendmail	Sendmail mail transport agent.
sendmail-cf	Sendmail configuration files and m4 macros.
sendmail-doc	Sendmail documentation.
sysklogd	Linux system and kernel logger.
uucp	GNU uucp.
vixie-cron	Vixie cron daemon.

DEVELOPMENT

BUILDING

autoconf	GNU autoconf-source configuration tools.
make	GNU make.
pmake	Berkeley's Parallel Make.

DEBUGGERS

ElectricFence	Electric Fence C memory debugging library.

gdb	Symbolic debugger for C and other languages.
strace	Prints system call strace of a running process.
xxgdb	X interface to the gdb debugger.

LANGUAGES

bin86	Real-mode 80X86 compiler and linker.
gcc	GNU C compiler.
gcc-c++	C++ support for gcc.
gcc-objc	Objective C support for gcc.
p2c-basic	BASIC interpreter.
p2c-devel	Programs and header for Pascal-to-C translator.
python	Very high-level scripting language with X interface.
umb-scheme	Scheme interpreter from University of Massachusetts at Boston.
xlispstat	Xlist by David Betz with statistics extensions.

LANGUAGES — FORTRAN

f2c	f2c program and static libraries.
fort77	Driver for f2c.

LANGUAGES — TCL

blt	More widgets for the tk widget set.

blt-devel	Development libraries and header files for the BLT widgets.
expect	Tcl extension that allows easy interaction between programs and scripts.
expect-demos	A set of demo programs from Expect.
tcl	Tool Command Language version 7.4, with shared libraries.
tclx	Extensions to tcl and tk for POSIX systems.
tix	Many metawidgets (such as notepads) for tk.
tk	Tk toolkit for Tcl, version 4.0, with shared libraries.

LIBRARIES

e2fsprogs-devel	E2fs static libraries and headers.
gpm-devel	Development libraries and headers for writing mouse-driven programs.
pythonlib	Library of python code used by various Red Hat programs.
rpm-devel	Header files and libraries for programs that manipulate rpm packages.
slang-devel	Static library and header files for slang C-like language.
typhoon	Library and utilities for relational databases.
zlib-devel	Header files and libraries for zlib development.

LIBRARIES — LIBC

libc-debug	Libc with debugging information.
libc-devel	Additional libraries required to compile.

libc-include	Include files for libc and related libraries.
libc-profile	Libc with profiling support.
libc-static	Libraries for static linking.

TOOLS

binutils	GNU binary utility development utilities.
bison	GNU parser generator.
byacc	Public-domain yacc parser generator.
cproto	C Prototype Utility.
flex	GNU fast lexical analyzer generator.
gencat	Gencat message catalog program (from NetBSD).
indent	GNU C indenting program.
xwpe	X Window Programming Environment.

VERSION CONTROL

| cvs | Concurrent Versioning System. |
| rcs | RCS—version control system. |

JAPANESE

| kterm | Kterm (Kanji Terminal Emulator). |

aout-libs	Compatability libraries for old a.out applications.
bind-lib	DNS revolver library and headers.
db	BSD database library for C.
db-devel	Development libraries and header files for Berkeley database library.
f2c-libs	Shared libraries for running dynamically linked Fortran programs.
faces-devel	Face-saver library and header.
gdbm	GNU database library for C.
gdbm-devel	Development libraries and header files for gdbm.
ld.so	Linux dynamic loader.
libc	Libc and related libraries.
libelf	ELF object file access library.
libg++	GNU g++ library.
libg++-devel	Header files and libraries for C++ development.
libgr	Graphics libraries, fbm, jpeg, pbm, pgm, png, pnm, ppm, rle, tiff.
libgr-devel	Headers and static libraries for building with the libraries.
libtermcap	Library for accessing the termcap database.
libtermcap-devel	Development libraries and header files for termcap library.
ncurses	Curses terminal control library.
ncurses-devel	Development libraries for ncurses.

p2c	Shared library for programs built with p2c Pascal-to-C converter.	
readline	Library for reading lines from a terminal.	
readline-devel	File for developing programs that use the readline library.	
slang	Shared library for C-like extension language.	
svgalib	Library for full-screen SVGA graphics.	
svgalib-devel	Development libraries that include files for SVGA graphics.	
zlib	Library for compression and decompression.	

NETWORKING

NetKit-A	Various network programs (part 1).	
NetKit-B	Various network programs (part 2).	
pidentd	Internet daemon authorization, user identification.	
samba	SMB client and server.	

ADMINISTRATION

anonftp	Enables anonymous ftp access.	
net-tools	Basic network tools.	
nfs-server-clients	Client apps for use with remote NFS servers.	
tcp_wrappers	Security wrapper for tcp daemons— maximum setting.	

DAEMONS

amd	NFS automount daemon.
apache	Http server daemon to provide World Wide Web services.
bind	BIND—DNS name server.
cmu-snmp	CMU SNMP agent.
gn	Gopher server.
imap	Provides support for IMAP and POP network mail protocols.
intimed	Time server for clock synchronization.
nfs-server	NFS server daemons.
ppp	Ppp daemon package for Linux.
wu-ftpd	Washington University FTP daemon.
ypserv	NIS:YP server.

NEWS

inews	Inews program (used for posting by inn and trn).
inn	InterNetNews news transport system.

UTILITIES

bind-utils	DNS utils—host, dig, dnsquery, nslookup.
bootpc	Bootpc, a client to get networking info from bootpd.
cmu-snmp-devel	CMU SNMP development libraries and headers.
cmu-snmp-utils	CMU SNMP utilities.

dip	Dip modem dialer.
fwhois	Finger-style whois.
pmirror	Pmirror, a perl script for mirroring an FTP site.
rdate	Remote clock reader (and local setter).
rdist	File distributor—maintain files on multiple machines.
statnet	Monitors network traffic in a terminal.
yp-clients	NIS (YP) clients.

SHELLS

bash	GNU Bourne Again Shell (bash).
csh	BSD c-shell.
pdksh	Public Domain Korn Shell.
tcsh	Enhanced C-shell.

UTILITIES

ARCHIVING

cpio	GNU cpio archiving program (used by rpm).
gzip	GNU gzip file compression.
lha	Creates and expands lharc format archives.
ncompress	A fast-compress utility.
tar	GNU Tape Archiver (tar).
unarj	Decompressor for .arj format archives.

	unzip	Unpacks .zip files such as those made by pkzip under DOS.
	zip	Creates .zip files.

AUDIO

	maplay	Plays MPEG-2 audio files in 16-bit stereo.

CONSOLE

	open	Tools for creating and switching between virtual consoles.
	vlock	Locks one or more virtual consoles.

FILE

	color-ls	Color ls—patched from GNU fileutils.
	file	File(1) command.
	fileutils	GNU file utilities.
	findutils	GNU find utilities (find, xargs, and locate).
	git	GIT—GNU interactive tools.
	macutils	Utilities for manipulating Macintosh file formats.
	mtools	Programs to access DOS disks without mounting them.
	sharutils	GNU shar utils—shar, unshar, uuencode, uudecode.
	stat	File information reporter.

symlinks	Symbolic link sanity checker.
which	Finds which executable would be run based on your PATH.

PRINTING

mpage	Places multiple pages of text onto a single PostScript page.

SYSTEM

MAKEDEV	Script to make and update /dev entries.
adduser	User-creation program.
adjtimex	Kernel clock management.
control-panel	Red Hat control panel.
dump	Dump/Restore backup system.
e2fsprogs	Tools for the second extended (ext2) file system.
eject	Ejects ejectable media and controls auto ejection.
ext2ed	Ext2 file system editor for hackers *only*.
fstool	File system configuration tool.
gcal	Extended calendar with highlighting, holidays, and so on.
getty_ps	Getty and uugetty.
glint	Graphical Linux installation tool.
hdparm	Utility for setting IDE/EIDE performance parameters.
helptool	Simple Help file searching tool.
ipfwadm	IP firewall admin tool.

kbd	Linux key-map utilities.
lilo	Boot loader for Linux and other operating systems.
liloconfig	Text-based lilo configuration tools.
lpr	Printing daemon and client.
man	Manual page reader.
mkdosfs-ygg	Creates a DOS FAT file system on a device.
mkisofs	Creates a ISO9660 file system image.
modemtool	Configuration tool for /dev/modem.
modules	Module utilities.
mt-st	Tape controller (mt).
netcfg	Network configuration tool.
npasswd	Npasswd—passwd and friends.
npasswd-dicts	Auxiliary npasswd dictionaries.
printtool	Printer configuration tool.
procinfo	/proc file system information.
procps	Process-monitoring utilities.
psmisc	More ps type tools for :proc file system.
rpm	Red Hat packaging system.
sh-utils	GNU sh utilities.
sliplogin	Log-in program for SLIP.
statserial	Displays status of the serial lines in a terminal.
swatch	System log watcher and alarm.
taper	Backup system.
texinfo-info	Text-based stand-alone info reader.
time	GNU time utilities.
timetool	Time and date configuration tool.

tksysv	X:Tk-based SYSV run-level editor.
tunelp	Configures kernel parallel-port driver.
usercfg	User and group configuration tool.
util-linux	Rik Faith's utility collection for Linux.
zoneinfo	Time zone utilities and data.

TERMINAL

dialog	Tty dialog boxes.
screen	Manages multiple sessions on one tty.
tset-jv	Change terminal settings.

TEXT

diffutils	GNU diff utilities.
faces	Face-saver database tools.
faces-xface	Utilities to handle X-Face headers.
gawk	GNU gawk text processor.
grep	GNU grep utilities.
ispell	GNU ispell—interactive spelling checker.
less	Text file browser, less is more.
m4	GNU macro processor.
mawk	Mike's New:Posix AWK interpreter.
nenscript	Converts plain ascii to PostScript.
patch	GNU patch utilities.
perl	Practical extraction and report language.
perl4	Practical extraction and report language (old version).

sed	GNU stream editor.
textutils	GNU text utilities.
words	English dictionary for :usr:dict.

X11

AMUSEMENTS

multimedia	A CD player and audio mixer for X11.

APPLICATIONS

seyon	X communications program for modems.
xfm	X file manager.
xterm-color	Ansi color xterm.

APPLICATIONS — GRAPHICS

ImageMagick	Image display, conversion, and manipulation under X.
ghostview	X11 PostScript viewer (needs ghostscript).
mxp	X11 Mandelbrot set generator and explorer.
transfig	Converts .fig files (such as those from xfig) to other formats.
xanim	Viewer for various animated graphic formats, including quicktime and flic.
xloadimage	X-based image viewer.
xmorph	Morphing program with an X interface.
xmplay	X MPEG viewer.

xpaint	Paint program for X.
xv	X-based image viewer for almost all images.

APPLICATIONS — NETWORKING

arena	A World Wide Web HTML-3 browser.
x3270	X-based 3270 emulator.
xgopher	X-based gopher client.

LIBRARIES

ImageMagick-devel	Static libraries and header files for ImageMagick development.
Xaw3d	X athena widgets in 3d.
Xaw3d-devel	Files for developing programs that use Xaw3d.
nls	NLS files used by Motif, Netscape, and so on.
xpm	X11 Pixmap library.
xpm-devel	Development libraries and header files for X Pixmap library.
xview	XView library and open windows interface for X11.
xview-devel	Header files and static libraries for XView development.

UTILITIES

Xconfigurator	X configuration utility.
moonclock	Traditional clock with moon phase hacks.

rxvt	Rxvt—terminal emulator in an X window.
xdaliclock	Marc's favorite clock.
xlockmore	X terminal locking program with many screen savers.
xmailbox	X-based mail notification tool.
xosview	X11 util for viewing system resources.
xscreensaver	X screen savers.
xsysinfo	Display bar graphs of system load.
xwpick	Efficient X screen grabber.

WINDOW MANAGERS

fvwm	Feeble (Fine?) Virtual Window Manager.

XFREE86

X11R6-contrib	Programs for X11 from the contrib tapes.
XFree86	XFree86 Window System servers and basic programs.
XFree86-devel	X11R6 static libraries, headers, and programming man pages.
XFree86-fonts	X11R6 fonts—only needed on server side.
XFree86-SVGA	XFree86 server.

LINUX HARDWARE COMPATIBILITY HOW-TO

LINUX HARDWARE COMPATIBILITY HOW-TO

T his HOWTO document is reproduced here in its entirety. It is posted regularly to the *comp.os.linux.answers* newsgroup on Usenet.

If a piece of hardware is not listed here, that doesn't necessarily mean it's unsupported. Undoubtedly this guide needs some updating, since it was last modified in late 1995, but it's a good starting point. See also the **Linux Hardware Survey** at *http://www.cris.com/ ~cwhoover/hardware.htm* to find out if others have had success running Linux with the same hardware you have.

Author: FRiC, frac@pobox.com
Version: v6969, 14 November 1995

This document lists most of the hardware supported by Linux and helps you locate any necessary drivers.

TABLE OF CONTENTS

B

7. Controllers (SCSI)

7.1. Supported
7.2. Others
7.3. Unsupported

8. Controllers (I/O)

9. Controllers (multiport)

9.1. Nonintelligent cards

    9.1.1. Supported

9.2. Intelligent cards

    9.2.1. Supported
    9.2.2. Others

10. Network Adapters

10.1. Supported

    10.1.1. Ethernet
    10.1.2. Pocket and portable adapters
    10.1.3. Slotless
    10.1.4. ARCnet
    10.1.5. Token Ring
    10.1.6. Amateur radio (AX.25)

10.2. Others

    10.2.1. Ethernet
    10.2.2. ISDN
    10.2.3. PCMCIA cards
    10.2.4. ATM
    10.2.5. Frame Relay

10.3. Unsupported

11. SOUND CARDS

11.1. Supported
11.2. Others
11.3. Unsupported

12. HARD DRIVES

13. TAPE DRIVES

13.1. Supported
13.2. Others
13.3. Unsupported

14. CD-ROM DRIVES

14.1. Supported
14.2. Others
14.3. Notes

15. REMOVABLE DRIVES

16. MICE

16.1. Supported
16.2. Others
16.3. Notes

17. MODEMS

18. PRINTERS/PLOTTERS

18.1. Ghostscript

18.1.1. *Ghostscript-supported printers*
18.1.2. *Others*

19. SCANNERS

20. Other Hardware

20.1. VESA Power Savings Protocol (DPMS) monitors
20.2. Joysticks
20.3. Video capture boards
20.4. UPS
20.5. Data acquisition
20.6. Miscellaneous

21. Related Sources of Information

22. Acknowledgments

23. Appendix A—S3 cards supported by XFree86 3.1.2

24. Appendix B—Supported PCMCIA cards

24.1. Ethernet cards
24.2. Modem cards
24.3. Memory cards
24.4. SCSI adapters
24.5. Unsupported

1. Introduction

1.1. Welcome

Welcome to the Linux Hardware Compatibility HOWTO. This document lists most of the hardware supported by Linux. Now if only people would read this first before posting their questions on Usenet.

Subsections titled "Others" list hardware with alpha or beta drivers in varying degrees of usability or other drivers that aren't included in standard kernels. Note that some drivers only exist in alpha kernels, so if you see something listed as supported that isn't in your version of the Linux kernel, upgrade.

The latest version of this document can be found on the Internet at the usual sites where the Linux HOWTOs are kept.

If you know of any Linux hardware compatibilities or incompatibilities not listed here, please let me know. Send mail or find me on IRC. Thanks.

1.2. Copyright

Standard LDP copyrights apply. If you use this or any other Linux HOWTOs in a commercial distribution, it would be nice to send the authors a complimentary copy of your product.

1.3. System Architectures

This document only deals with Linux for Intel platforms. For other platforms check the following:

ARM Linux
‹http://whirligig.ecs.soton.ac.uk/~rmk92/armlinux.html›

Linux/68k
‹http://www-users.informatik.rwth-aachen.de/~hn/linux68k.html›

Linux/8086
‹http://www.linux.org.uk/Linux8086.html›

Linux/Alpha
‹http://www.azstarnet.com/~axplinux/›

Linux/MIPS
‹http://www.waldorf-gmbh.de/linux-mips-faq.html›

Linux/PowerPC
‹http://liber.stanford.edu/linuxppc/›

Linux for Acorn
‹http://www.ph.kcl.ac.uk/~amb/linux.html›

MacLinux
‹http://www.ibg.uu.se/maclinux/›

2. COMPUTERS/MOTHERBOARDS/BIOS

ISA, VLB, EISA, and PCI buses are all supported. PS/2 and Microchannel (MCA) are not supported in the standard kernel. Alpha test PS/2 MCA kernels are available but not yet recommended for beginners or serious use.

2.1. SPECIFIC SYSTEMS

Compaq Deskpro XL
‹http://www-c724.uibk.ac.at/XL/›

IBM PS/2 MCA systems
‹ftp://invaders.dcrl.nd.edu/pub/misc/›

3. LAPTOPS

Linux Laptop Homepage
‹http://www.cs.utexas.edu/users/kharker/linux-laptop/›

APM
‹ftp://ftp.cs.unc.edu/pub/users/faith/linux/›

non-blinking cursor
‹ftp://sunsite.unc.edu/pub/Linux/kernel/patches/console/
    noblink-1.5.tar.gz›

power savings (WD7600 chipset)
‹ftp://sunsite.unc.edu/pub/Linux/system/Misc/low-level/
    pwrm-1.0.tar.Z›

other general info
‹ftp://tsx-11.mit.edu/pub/linux/packages/laptops/›

3.1. Specific Laptops

Compaq Concerto (pen driver)
<http://www.cs.nmsu.edu/~pfeiffer/>

Compaq Contura Aero
<http://domen.uninett.no/~hta/linux/aero-faq.html>

IBM ThinkPad
<http://peipa.essex.ac.uk/tp-linux/tp-linux.html>

Linux and X on notebook computers
<http://www.castle.net/~darin/>

NEC Versa M and P
<http://www.santafe.edu:80/~nelson/versa-linux/>

Tadpole P1000
<http://www.tadpole.com/Support/online/linux.html>

Tadpole P1000 (another one)
<http://peipa.essex.ac.uk/tadpole-linux/tadpole-linux.html>

TI TravelMate 4000M
<ftp://ftp.biomath.jussieu.fr/pub/linux/
   TM4000M-mini-HOWTO.txt.Z>

TI TravelMate 5100
<http://www.wri.com/~cwikla/ti5100.html>

Toshiba Satellite Pro 400CDT
<http://terra.mpikg-teltow.mpg.de/~burger/T400CDT-Linux.html>

3.2. PCMCIA

PCMCIA
<http://hyper.stanford.edu/~dhinds/pcmcia/>

PCMCIA drivers currently support all common PCMCIA controllers, including Databook TCIC/2, Intel i82365SL, Cirrus PD67xx, and Vadem VG-468 chipsets. Motorola 6AHC05GA controller used in some Hyundai laptops is not supported. See Appendix B of this document for a list of supported PCMCIA cards.

4. CPU/FPU

Intel/AMD/Cyrix 386SX/DX/SL/DXL/SLC, 486SX/DX/SL/SX2/ DX2/DX4, Pentium. Basically all 386 or better processors will work. Linux has built-in FPU emulation if you don't have a math coprocessor.

Experimental SMP (multiple CPU) support is included in kernel 1.3.31 and newer versions. Check the Linux/SMP Project page for details and updates.

Linux/SMP Project
‹http://www.linux.org.uk/SMP/title.html›

A few very early AMD 486DXs may hang in some special situations. All current chips should be okay and getting a chip swap for old CPUs should not be a problem.

ULSI Math*Co series has a bug in the FSAVE and FRSTOR instructions that causes problems with all protected-mode operating systems. Some older IIT and Cyrix chips may also have this problem.

There are problems with TLB flushing in UMC U5S chips in very old kernels (1.1.X).

enable cache on Cyrix processors
‹ftp://sunsite.unc.edu/pub/Linux/kernel/patches/ CxPatch030.tar.z›

Cyrix software cache control
‹ftp://sunsite.unc.edu/pub/Linux/kernel/patches/linux.cxpatch›

5. Video Cards

Linux will work with all video cards in text mode. VGA cards not listed below probably will still work with mono VGA and/or standard VGA drivers.

If you're looking into buying a cheap video card to run X, keep in mind that accelerated cards (ATI Mach, ET4000/W32p, S3) are much faster than unaccelerated or partially accelerated (Cirrus, WD) cards. S3 Trio64-based cards with 2 megs DRAM go for around US$160 and S3 868-based cards with 2 megs DRAM are around US$200.

"32 bpp" is actually 24-bit color aligned on 32-bit boundaries. It does NOT mean the cards are capable of 32-bit color, they still display 24-bit color (16,777,216 colors). 24-bit packed pixels modes are not supported in XFree86, so cards that can do 24-bit modes to get higher resolutions in other OSs are not able to do this in X using XFree86. These cards include Mach32, Cirrus 542x, S3 801/805/868/968, ET4000, and others.

5.1. DIAMOND VIDEO CARDS

Most currently available Diamond cards are supported by the current release of XFree86. Early Diamond cards may not be officially supported by XFree86, but there are ways of getting them to work. Diamond is now actively supporting the XFree86 Project.

Diamond support for XFree86
‹http://www.diamondmm.com/linux.html›

Diamond FAQ (for older cards)
‹ftp://sunsite.unc.edu/pub/Linux/X11/Diamond.FAQ›

Diamond Disgruntled Users Page (for older cards)
‹http://gladstone.uoregon.edu/~trenton/diamond/›

5.2. SVGALIB (GRAPHICS FOR CONSOLE)

VGA
EGA
ARK Logic ARK1000PV/2000PV
ATI VGA Wonder
ATI Mach32
Cirrus 542x, 543x
OAK OTI-037/67/77/87
S3 (limited support)
Trident TVGA8900/9000
Tseng ET3000/ET4000/W32

5.3. XFREE86 3.1.2

5.3.1. ACCELERATED

ATI Mach8
ATI Mach32 (16 bpp (does not work with all Mach32 cards))
ATI Mach64 (16/32 bpp (support depends on RAMDAC))
Cirrus Logic 5420, 542x/5430 (16 bpp), 5434 (16/32 bpp), 62x5
IBM 8514/A
IBM XGA, XGA-II

IIT AGX-010/014/015/016 (16 bpp)
Oak OTI-087
S3 911, 924, 801, 805, 928, 864, 964, Trio32, Trio64, 868, 968
  (see Appendix A for a list of supported S3 cards)
Tseng ET4000/W32/W32i/W32p
Weitek P9000 (16/32 bpp)
Diamond Viper VLB/PCI
Orchid P9000
Western Digital WD90C31/33

5.3.2. UNACCELERATED

ARK Logic ARK1000PV/VL, ARK2000PV
ATI VGA Wonder series
Avance Logic AL2101/2228/2301/2302/2308/2401
Chips & Technologies 65520/65530/65540/65545
Cirrus Logic 6420/6440
Compaq AVGA
Genoa GVGA
MCGA (320x200)
MX MX68000/MX68010
NCR 77C22, 77C22E, 77C22E+
Oak OTI-067, OTI-077
RealTek RTG3106
Trident TVGA8800, TVGA8900, TVGA9xxx (no support for
  TGUI chipsets)
Tseng ET3000, ET4000AX
VGA (standard VGA, 4 bit, slow)
Video 7 / Headland Technologies HT216-32
Western Digital/Paradise PVGA1, WD90C00/10/11/24/30/31/33

5.3.3. MONOCHROME

Hercules mono
Hyundai HGC-1280
Sigma LaserView PLUS

VGA mono

5.3.4. OTHERS

EGA (ancient, from c. 1992)
<ftp://ftp.funet.fi/pub/OS/Linux/BETA/Xega/>

ET4000/W32 and X-ICS5341 GenDAC
‹ftp://sunsite.unc.edu/pub/Linux/X11/servers/›

Trident TGUI9440
‹ftp://sunsite.unc.edu/pub/Linux/X11/X-servers/›

5.3.5. WORKS IN PROGRESS

Compaq QVision
Number Nine Imagine 128

No, I do not know when support for these cards will be finished, please don't ask me. If you want support for these cards now get Accelerated-X.

5.4. COMMERCIAL X SERVERS

Commercial X servers provide support for cards not supported by XFree86, and might give better performances for cards that are supported by XFree86. In general, they support many more cards than XFree86, so I'll only list cards that aren't supported by XFree86 here. Contact the vendors directly or check the Commercial HOWTO for more info.

5.4.1. ACCELERATED-X 1.2

Chips & Technologies 82C45x, 82C48x, F655xx
Compaq QVision 2000
Matrox MGA, Millenium
Number Nine I-128 / I-128 Pro
Weitek P9100

$199, X Inside, Inc.
‹info@xinside.com›

Accel-X supports most cards in 16- and 32-bpp modes and it also supports 24-bit packed pixel modes for cards that have these modes, including ATI Mach32, Mach64 (1280x1024@24bpp), ET4000/W32p, S3-866/868/968, and more. Accel-X also supports other input hardware like graphics tablets and touchscreens.

Accel-X also supports XVideo (Xv) extensions (on Matrox Comet, Marvel-II, and SPEA ShowTime Plus), PEX, and XIE.

5.4.2. Metro-X 2.3

$199, Metro Link

<sales@metrolink.com>

Metro-X supports more boards than XFree but less than Accel-X. However, I don't have much more information as I can't seem to view the PostScript files they sent me. Mail them directly for more info.

6. Controllers (hard drive)

Linux will work with standard IDE, MFM, and RLL controllers. When using MFM/RLL controllers it is important to use ext2fs and the bad block checking options when formatting the disk.

Enhanced IDE (EIDE) interfaces are supported. With up to two IDE interfaces and up to four hard drives and/or CD-ROM drives. Linux will detect these EIDE interfaces.

CMD-640

DTC 2278D

FGI/Holtek HT-6560B

RZ1000

Triton (82371FB) IDE (with busmaster DMA)

ESDI controllers that emulate the ST-506 (MFM/RLL/IDE) interface will also work. The bad block checking comment also applies to these controllers. Generic 8-bit XT controllers also work.

7. Controllers (SCSI)

It is important to pick a SCSI controller carefully. Many cheap ISA SCSI controllers are designed to drive CD-ROMs rather than anything else. Such low-end SCSI controllers are no better than IDE. See the SCSI HOWTO and look at performance figures before buying a SCSI card.

7.1. Supported

AMI Fast Disk VLB/EISA (BusLogic compatible)

Adaptec AVA-1505/1515 (ISA) (Adaptec 152x compatible)

Adaptec AHA-1510/152x (ISA) (AIC-6260/6360)

Adaptec AHA-154x (ISA) (all models)

Adaptec AHA-174x (EISA) (in enhanced mode)
Adaptec AHA-274x (EISA) / 284x (VLB) (AIC-7770)
Adaptec AHA-2940/3940 (PCI) (AIC-7870) (since 1.3.6)
Always IN2000
BusLogic (ISA/EISA/VLB/PCI) (all models)
DPT PM2001, PM2012A (EATA-PIO)
DPT Smartcache (EATA-DMA) (ISA/EISA/PCI) (all models)
DTC 329x (EISA) (Adaptec 154x compatible)
Future Domain TMC-16x0, TMC-3260 (PCI)
Future Domain TMC-8xx, TMC-950
Media Vision Pro Audio Spectrum 16 SCSI (ISA)
NCR 5380 generic cards
NCR 53c400 (Trantor T130B) (use generic NCR 5380 SCSI support)
NCR 53c406a (Acculogic ISApport / Media Vision Premium 3D SCSI)
NCR 53c7x0, 53c8x0 (PCI)
Qlogic / Control Concepts SCSI/IDE (FAS408) (ISA/VLB)
Seagate ST-01/ST-02 (ISA)
SoundBlaster 16 SCSI-2 (Adaptec 152x compatible) (ISA)
Trantor T128/T128F/T228 (ISA)
UltraStor 14F (ISA), 24F (EISA), 34F (VLB)
Western Digital WD7000 SCSI

7.2. Others

AMD AM53C974, AM79C974 (PCI)
(Compaq, HP, Zeos onboard SCSI)
‹ftp://sunsite.unc.edu/pub/Linux/kernel/patches/scsi/
AM53C974-0.3.tgz›

Adaptec ACB-40xx SCSI-MFM/RLL bridgeboard
‹ftp://sunsite.unc.edu/pub/Linux/kernel/patches/scsi/
adaptec-40XX.tar.gz›

Always Technologies AL-500
‹ftp://sunsite.unc.edu/pub/Linux/kernel/patches/scsi/
al500-0.2.tar.gz›

BusLogic (ISA/EISA/VLB/PCI)
(new beta driver)
‹ftp://ftp.dandelion.com/BusLogic-1.0-beta.tar.gz›

Iomega PC2/2B
‹ftp://sunsite.unc.edu/pub/Linux/kernel/patches/scsi/
iomega_pc2-1.1.x.tar.gz›

Qlogic (ISP1020) (PCI)
‹ftp://sunsite.unc.edu/pub/Linux/kernel/patches/scsi/
isp1020-0.5.gz›

Ricoh GSI-8
‹ftp://tsx-11.mit.edu/pub/linux/ALPHA/scsi/gsi8.tar.gz›

7.3. UNSUPPORTED

Parallel port SCSI adapters
Non Adaptec compatible DTC boards (327x, 328x)

8. CONTROLLERS (I/O)

Any standard serial/parallel/joystick/combo cards. Linux supports
8250, 16450, 16550, and 16550A UARTs. Cards that support nonstandard IRQs (IRQ greater than 9) can be used.

See National Semiconductor's "Application Note AN-493" by Martin
S. Michael. Section 5.0 describes in detail the differences between the
NS16550 and NS16550A. Briefly, the NS16550 had bugs in the FIFO circuits, but the NS16550A (and later) chips fixed those. However, there
were very few NS16550s produced by National, long ago, so these
should be very rare. And many of the 16550 parts in actual modern
boards are from the many manufacturers of compatible parts, which
may not use the National "A" suffix. Also, some multiport boards will
use 16552 or 16554 or various other multiport or multifunction chips
from National or other suppliers (generally in a dense package soldered to the board, not a 40-pin DIP). Mostly, don't worry about it
unless you encounter a very old 40-pin DIP National NS16550 (no A)
chip loose or in an old board, in which case treat it as a 16450 (no
FIFO) rather than a 16550A. – Zhahai Stewart ‹zstewart@hisys.com›

9. CONTROLLERS (MULTIPORT)

9.1. NONINTELLIGENT CARDS

9.1.1. SUPPORTED

AST FourPort and clones (4 port)
Accent Async-4 (4 port)
Arnet Multiport-8 (8 port)
Bell Technologies HUB6 (6 port)
Boca BB-1004, 1008 (4, 8 port) - no DTR, DSR, and CD
Boca BB-2016 (16 port)
Boca IO/AT66 (6 port)
Boca IO 2by4 (4 serial / 2 parallel, uses 5 IRQs)
Computone ValuePort (4, 6, 8 port) (AST FourPort compatible)
DigiBoard PC/X (4, 8, 16 port)
Comtrol Hostess 550 (4, 8 port)
PC-COMM 4-port (4 port)
SIIG I/O Expander 4S (4 port, uses 4 IRQs)
STB 4-COM (4 port)
Twincom ACI/550
Usenet Serial Board II (4 port)

Non-intelligent cards usually come in two varieties, one using standard com port addresses and 4 IRQs, and another that's AST FourPort compatible and uses a selectable block of addresses and a single IRQ. (Addresses and IRQs are set using **setserial**.) If you're getting one of these cards, be sure to check which standard it conforms to; prices are no indication.

9.2. INTELLIGENT CARDS

9.2.1. SUPPORTED

Cyclades Cyclom-8Y/16Y (8, 16 port) (ISA/PCI)
Stallion EasyIO (ISA) / EasyConnection 8/32 (ISA/MCA)
Stallion EasyConnection 8/64 / ONboard (ISA/EISA/MCA) /
    Brumby / Stallion (ISA)

9.2.2. OTHERS

Comtrol RocketPort (8/16/32 port)
‹ftp://tsx-11.mit.edu/pub/linux/packages/comtrol/›

Computone IntelliPort II (4/8/16 port)
contact Michael H. Warfield ‹mhw@wittsend.atl.ga.us›

DigiBoard COM/Xi
contact Simon Park ‹si@wimpol.demon.co.uk›

DigiBoard PC/Xe (ISA) and PC/Xi (EISA)
‹ftp://ftp.digibd.com/drivers/linux/›

Hayes ESP8
contact Dennis Boylan ‹dennis@lan.com›

Moxa C218 (8 port) / C320 (8/16/24/32 expandable)
‹ftp://ftp.moxa.com.tw/drivers/c-218-320/linux/›

Specialix SIO/XIO (modular, 4 to 32 ports)
‹ftp://sunsite.unc.edu/pub/Linux/kernel/patches/serial/
    sidrvo_5.taz›

10. NETWORK ADAPTERS

Ethernet adapters vary greatly in performance. In general, the newer
the design, the better. Some very old cards like the 3Com 3C501 are
only useful because they can be found in junk heaps for $5 a time. Be
careful with clones, not all are good clones and bad clones often cause
erratic lockups under Linux. Read the Ethernet HOWTO for detailed
descriptions of various cards.

10.1. SUPPORTED

10.1.1. ETHERNET

3Com 3C501—"avoid like the plague"
3Com 3C503, 3C505, 3C507, 3C509/3C509B (ISA) / 3C579 (EISA)
AMD LANCE (79C960) / PCnet-ISA/PCI (AT1500, HP J2405A,
    NE1500/NE2100)
AT&T GIS WaveLAN
Allied Telesis AT1700
Ansel Communications AC3200 EISA
Apricot Xen-II
Cabletron E21xx
DEC DE425 (EISA) / DE434/DE435 (PCI)
DEC DEPCA and EtherWORKS

HP PCLAN (27245 and 27xxx series)
HP PCLAN PLUS (27247B and 27252A)
HP 10/100VG PCLAN (ISA/EISA/PCI)
Intel EtherExpress
Intel EtherExpress Pro
NE2000/NE1000 (be careful with clones)
New Media Ethernet
Racal-Interlan NI5210 (i82586 Ethernet chip)
Racal-Interlan NI6510 (am7990 lance chip)—doesn't work with
    more than 16 megs RAM
PureData PDUC8028, PDI8023
SEEQ 8005
SMC Ultra
Schneider & Koch G16
Western Digital WD80x3
Zenith Z-Note / IBM ThinkPad 300 built-in adapter

10.1.2. POCKET AND PORTABLE ADAPTERS

AT-Lan-Tec/RealTek parallel port adapter
D-Link DE600/DE620 parallel port adapter

10.1.3. SLOTLESS

SLIP/CSLIP/PPP (serial port)
EQL (serial IP load balancing)
PLIP (parallel port)—using "LapLink cable" or bidirectional cable

10.1.4. ARCNET

Works with all ARCnet cards.

10.1.5. TOKEN RING

IBM Tropic chipset cards

10.1.6. AMATEUR RADIO (AX.25)

Ottawa PI/PI2
Most generic 8530-based HDLC boards

10.2. Others

10.2.1. Ethernet

3Com Demon Ethercards (3C592, 3C597 (100 mbps)) (EISA)
<http://cesdis.gsfc.nasa.gov/linux/drivers/vortex.html>

3Com Vortex Ethercards (3C590, 3C595 (100 mbps)) (PCI)
<http://cesdis.gsfc.nasa.gov/linux/drivers/vortex.html>

DEC 21040/21140 "Tulip" / SMC PCI EtherPower 10/100
<http://cesdis.gsfc.nasa.gov/linux/drivers/tulip.html>

HP J2585 (PCI) / HP J2573 (ISA) (ATT2MDx1 / 100VG)
<http://cesdis1.gsfc.nasa.gov:80/linux/drivers/100vg.html>

10.2.2. ISDN

Linux ISDN WWW page
<http://www.ix.de/ix/linux/linux-isdn.html>

3Com Sonix Arpeggio
<ftp://sunsite.unc.edu/pub/Linux/kernel/patches/network/
sonix.tgz>

Combinet EVERYWARE 1000 ISDN
<ftp://sunsite.unc.edu/pub/Linux/patches/network/
combinet1000isdn-1.02.tar.gz>

Diehl SCOM card
<ftp://sunsite.unc.edu/pub/Linux/kernel/patches/network/
isdndrv-0.1.1.tar.gz>

ICN ISDN / Teles ISDN / Creatix AVM ISDN cards
<ftp://ftp.franken.de/pub/isdn4linux/>

ISDN cards that emulate standard modems or common Ethernet
adapters don't need any special drivers to work.

10.2.3. PCMCIA cards

See Appendix B of this document for a complete list.

10.2.4. ATM

Efficient Networks ENI155P-MF 155 Mbps ATM adapter (PCI)
<http://lrcwww.epfl.ch/linux-atm/>

10.2.5. Frame Relay

Sangoma S502 56K Frame Relay card
‹ftp://ftp.sovereign.org/pub/wan/fr/›

10.3. Unsupported

Xircom adapters (PCMCIA and parallel port) are not supported.

11. Sound Cards

11.1. Supported

6850 UART MIDI
Adlib (OPL2)
Audio Excell DSP16
Aztech Sound Galaxy NX Pro
Crystal CS4232 (PnP)–based cards
ECHO-PSS cards (Orchid SoundWave32, Cardinal DSP16)
Ensoniq SoundScape
Gravis Ultrasound
Gravis Ultrasound 16-bit sampling daughterboard
Gravis Ultrasound MAX
Logitech SoundMan Games (SBPro, 44kHz stereo support)
Logitech SoundMan Wave (Jazz16/OPL4)
Logitech SoundMan 16 (PAS-16 compatible)
MPU-401 MIDI
MediaTriX AudioTriX Pro
Media Vision Premium 3D (Jazz16)
Media Vision Pro Sonic 16 (Jazz)
Media Vision Pro Audio Spectrum 16
Microsoft Sound System (AD1848)
OAK OTI-601D cards (Mozart)
OPTi 82C928/82C929 cards (MAD16/MAD16 Pro)
Sound Blaster
Sound Blaster Pro
Sound Blaster 16
Turtle Beach Wavefront cards (Maui, Tropez)
Wave Blaster (and other daughterboards)

B

11.2. OTHERS

MPU-401 MIDI (intelligent mode)
‹ftp://sunsite.unc.edu/pub/Linux/kernel/sound/
   mpu401-0.2.tar.gz›

PC speaker / Parallel port DAC
‹ftp://ftp.informatik.hu-berlin.de/pub/os/linux/hu-sound/›

Turtle Beach MultiSound/Tahiti/Monterey
‹ftp://ftp.cs.colorado.edu/users/mccreary/archive/tbeach/
   multisound/›

11.3. UNSUPPORTED

The ASP chip on Sound Blaster 16 series and AWE32 is not supported. AWE32's onboard Emu MIDI synthesizer is not supported. Nathan Laredo *laredo@gnu.ai.mit.edu* is willing to write AWE32 drivers if you send him a complimentary card. He is also willing to write drivers for almost any hardware if you send him free samples of your hardware.

Sound Blaster 16's with DSP 4.11 and 4.12 have a hardware bug that causes hung/stuck notes when playing MIDI and digital audio at the same time. The problem can happen with either Wave Blaster daughterboards or MIDI devices attached to the MIDI port. There is no known fix.

12. HARD DRIVES

All hard drives should work if the controller is supported. (From the SCSI HOWTO.) All direct access SCSI devices with a block size of 256, 512, or 1024 bytes should work. Other block sizes will not work. (Note that this can often be fixed by changing the block and/or sector sizes using the MODE SELECT SCSI command.)

Large IDE (EIDE) drives work fine with newer kernels. The boot partition must lie in the first 1024 cylinders due to PC BIOS limitations. Some Conner CFP1060S drives may have problems with Linux and ext2fs.

The symptoms are inode errors during e2fsck and corrupt file systems. Conner has released a firmware upgrade to fix this problem. Contact Conner at 1-800-4CONNER (United States) or +44-1294-315333 (Europe). Have the microcode version (found on the drive label, 9WA1.6x) handy when you call.

Certain Micropolis drives have problems with Adaptec and BusLogic cards. Contact the drive manufacturers for firmware upgrades if you suspect problems.

Multiple device driver (RAID-0, RAID-1)
‹ftp://sweet-smoke.ufr-info-p7.ibp.fr/public/Linux/›

13. TAPE DRIVES

13.1. SUPPORTED

13.1.1. SCSI TAPE DRIVES

(From the SCSI HOWTO.) Drives using both fixed and variable-length blocks smaller than the driver buffer length (set to 32K in the distribution sources) are supported. Virtually all drives should work. (Send mail if you know of any incompatible drives.)

13.1.2. QIC-02 DRIVES

13.2. OTHERS

QIC-117, QIC-40/80, QIC-3010/3020 (QIC-WIDE) drives. Most tape drives using the floppy controller should work. Various dedicated controllers (Colorado FC-10/FC-20, Mountain Mach-2, Iomega Tape Controller II) are also supported.

‹ftp://sunsite.unc.edu/pub/Linux/kernel/tapes›

13.3. UNSUPPORTED

Emerald and Tecmar QIC-02 tape controller cards—Chris Ulrich
‹insom@math.ucr.edu›

Drives that connect to the parallel port (e.g., Colorado Trakker)
Some high-speed tape controllers (Colorado TC-15)
Irwin AX250L/Accutrak 250 (not QIC-80)
IBM Internal Tape Backup Unit (not QIC-80)
COREtape Light

14. CD-ROM Drives

14.1. Supported

14.1.1. SCSI CD-ROM drives

(From the CD-ROM HOWTO) Any SCSI CD-ROM drive with a block size of 512 or 2048 bytes should work under Linux; this includes the vast majority of CD-ROM drives on the market.

14.1.2. EIDE (ATAPI) CD-ROM drives

Aztech CDA268, Orchid CDS-3110, Okano/Wearnes CDD-110, Conrad TXC
GoldStar R420
LMS Philips CM 206
Matsushita/Panasonic, Creative Labs, Longshine, Kotobuki (SBPCD)
Mitsumi
Optics Storage Dolphin 8000AT
Sanyo H94A
Sony CDU31A/CDU33A
Sony CDU-535/CDU-531
Teac CD-55A SuperQuad

14.2. Others

LMS/Philips CM 205/225/202
‹ftp://sunsite.unc.edu/pub/Linux/kernel/patches/cdrom/ lmscdo.3d.tar.gz›

Mitsumi FX001D/F (alternative drivers)
‹ftp://ftp.gwdg.de//pub/linux/cdrom/drivers/mitsumi/ mcdx-1.0a.tar.gz›

NEC CDR-35D (old)
‹ftp://sunsite.unc.edu/pub/Linux/kernel/patches/cdrom/ linux-neccdr35d.patch›

Sony SCSI multisession CD-XA
‹ftp://tsx-11.mit.edu/pub/linux/patches/sony-multi-0.00.tar.gz›

14.3. Notes

PhotoCD (XA) is supported. All CD-ROM drives should work similarly for reading data. There are various compatibility problems with audio CD playing utilities (especially with newer low-end NEC drives). Some alpha drivers may not have audio support yet.

Early (single speed) NEC CD-ROM drives may have trouble with currently available SCSI controllers.

15. Removable Drives

All SCSI drives should work if the controller is supported, including optical (MO), WORM, floptical, Bernoulli, Zip, SyQuest, PD, and others.

Parallel port Zip drives
‹ftp://gear.torque.net/pub/›

Removable drives work like floppies: just **fdisk**/**mkfs** and mount the disks. Linux provides drive locking if your drives support it. Mtools can also be used if the disks are in MS-DOS format.

CD-R drives require special software to work. Read the CD-R Mini-HOWTO.

Linux supports both 512 and 1024 bytes/sector disks.

16. Mice

16.1. Supported

Microsoft serial mouse
Mouse Systems serial mouse
Logitech Mouseman serial mouse
Logitech serial mouse
ATI XL Inport busmouse
C&T 82C710 (QuickPort) (Toshiba, TI Travelmate)
Microsoft busmouse
Logitech busmouse
PS/2 (auxiliary device) mouse

16.2. Others

Sejin J-mouse
‹ftp://sunsite.unc.edu/pub/Linux/kernel/patches/console/
jmouse.1.1.70-jmouse.tar.gz›

MultiMouse—use multiple mouse devices as single mouse
‹ftp://sunsite.unc.edu/pub/Linux/system/Misc/
MultiMouse-1.0.tgz›

16.3. Notes

Touchpad devices like Alps Glidepoint also work, as long as they're compatible with another mouse protocol.

Newer Logitech mice (except the Mouseman) use the Microsoft protocol, and all three buttons do work. Even though Microsoft's mice have only two buttons, the protocol allows three buttons.

The mouse port on the ATI Graphics Ultra and Ultra Pro use the Logitech busmouse protocol. (See the Busmouse HOWTO for details.)

17. Modems

All internal modems or external modems connected to the serial port. A small number of modems come with DOS software that downloads the control program at runtime. These can normally be used by loading the program under DOS and doing a warm boot. Such modems are probably best avoided because you won't be able to use them with non-PC hardware in the future.

All PCMCIA modems should work with the PCMCIA drivers. Fax modems need appropriate fax software to operate.

Digicom Connection 96+/14.4+—DSP code downloading program
‹ftp://sunsite.unc.edu/pub/Linux/system/Serial/
smdl-linux.1.02.tar.gz›

ZyXEL U-1496 series—ZyXEL 1.4, modem/fax/voice control program
‹ftp://sunsite.unc.edu/pub/Linux/system/Serial/
ZyXEL-1.4.tar.gz›

18. PRINTERS/PLOTTERS

All printers and plotters connected to the parallel or serial port should work.

HP LaserJet 4 series – free-lj4, printing modes control program
‹ftp://sunsite.unc.edu/pub/Linux/system/Printing/
free-lj4-1.1p1.tar.gz›

BiTronics parallel port interface
‹ftp://sunsite.unc.edu/pub/Linux/kernel/misc/
bt-ALPHA-0.0.1.tar.gz›

18.1. GHOSTSCRIPT

Many Linux programs output PostScript files. Non-PostScript printers can emulate PostScript Level 2 using Ghostscript.

Ghostscript
‹ftp://ftp.cs.wisc.edu/pub/ghost/aladdin/›

18.1.1. GHOSTSCRIPT-SUPPORTED PRINTERS

Apple Imagewriter
C. Itoh M8510
Canon BubbleJet BJ10e, BJ200
Canon LBP-8II, LIPS III
DEC LA50/70/75/75plus
DEC LN03, LJ250
Epson 9 pin, 24 pin, LQ series, Stylus, AP3250
HP 2563B
HP DesignJet 650C
HP DeskJet/Plus/500
HP DeskJet 500C/520C/550C/1200C color
HP LaserJet/Plus/II/III/4
HP PaintJet/XL/XL300 color
IBM Jetprinter color
IBM Proprinter
Imagen ImPress
Mitsubishi CP50 color
NEC P6/P6+/P60
Okidata MicroLine 182
Ricoh 4081

SPARCprinter
StarJet 48 inkjet printer
Tektronix 4693d color 2/4/8 bit
Tektronix 4695/4696 inkjet plotterXerox XES printers (2700, 3700, 4045, etc.)

18.1.2. OTHERS

Canon BJC600 and Epson ESC/P color printers
‹ftp://petole.imag.fr/pub/postscript/›

19. SCANNERS

A4 Tech AC 4096
‹ftp://ftp.informatik.hu-berlin.de/pub/local/linux/ac4096.tgz›

Epson GT6000
‹ftp://sunsite.unc.edu/pub/Linux/apps/graphics/scanners/ ppico.5.tar.gz›

Fujitsu SCSI-2 scanners
contact Dr. G.W. Wettstein at
‹greg%wind.UUCP@plains.nodak.edu›

Genius GS-B105G
‹ftp://tsx-11.mit.edu/pub/linux/ALPHA/scanner/ gs105-0.0.1.tar.gz›

Genius GeniScan GS4500 handheld scanner
‹ftp://tsx-11.mit.edu/pub/linux/ALPHA/scanner/ gs4500-1.3.tar.gz›

HP ScanJet, ScanJet Plus
‹ftp://ftp.ctrl-c.liu.se/unix/linux/wingel/›

HP ScanJet II series SCSI
‹ftp://sunsite.unc.edu/pub/Linux/apps/graphics/scanners/ hpscanpbm-0.3a.tar.gz›

HP ScanJet family (including ScanJet 3c)
‹http://www.tummy.com/xvscan/›

Logitech Scanman 32 / 256
‹ftp://tsx11.mit.edu/pub/linux/ALPHA/scanner/
logiscan-0.0.2.tar.gz›

Mustek M105 handheld scanner with GI1904 interface
‹ftp://tsx-11.mit.edu/pub/linux/ALPHA/scanner/
scan-driver-0.1.8.tar.gz›

Mustek Paragon 6000CX
‹ftp://sunsite.unc.edu/pub/Linux/apps/graphics/scanners/
muscan-1.1.5.taz›

Nikon Coolscan SCSI 35mm film scanner
‹ftp://sunsite.unc.edu/pub/Linux/apps/graphics/scanners/›

UMAX SCSI scanners
contact Craig Johnston at ‹*mkshenk@u.washington.edu*›

20. OTHER HARDWARE

20.1. VESA POWER SAVINGS PROTOCOL (DPMS) MONITORS

Support for power savings is included in the Linux kernel. Just use
setterm to enable support.

20.2. JOYSTICKS

Joystick driver
‹ftp://sunsite.unc.edu/pub/Linux/kernel/patches/console/
joystick-0.7.3.tgz›

Joystick driver (module)
‹ftp://sunsite.unc.edu/pub/Linux/kernel/patches/console/
joyfixed.tgz›

20.3. VIDEO CAPTURE BOARDS

FAST Screen Machine II
‹ftp://sunsite.unc.edu/pub/Linux/apps/video/
ScreenMachineII.1.2.tgz›

ImageNation Cortex I
‹ftp://sunsite.unc.edu/pub/Linux/apps/video/cortex.drv.0.1.tgz›

ImageNation CX100
‹ftp://sunsite.unc.edu/pub/Linux/apps/video/
    cxdrv-0.1beta.tar.gz›

Pro Movie Studio
‹ftp://sunsite.unc.edu/pub/Linux/apps/video/
    PMS-grabber.2.0.tgz›

Quanta WinVision video capture card
‹ftp://sunsite.unc.edu/pub/Linux/apps/video/fgrabber-1.0.tgz›

Video Blaster, Rombo Media Pro+
‹ftp://sunsite.unc.edu/pub/Linux/apps/video/vid_src.gz›

VT1500 TV cards
‹ftp://sunsite.unc.edu/pub/Linux/apps/video/
    vt1500-1.0.5.tar.gz›

20.4. UPS

APC SmartUPS
‹ftp://sunsite.unc.edu/pub/Linux/system/UPS/apcd-0.1.tar.gz›

UPSs with RS-232 monitoring port (unipower package)
‹ftp://sunsite.unc.edu/pub/Linux/system/UPS/
    unipower-1.0.0.tgz›

Various other UPSs are supported, read the UPS HOWTO.

20.5. DATA ACQUISITION

The Linux Lab Project site collects drivers for hardware dealing
with data acquisition, they also maintain some mailing lists dealing with the subject. I have no experience with data acquisition so
please check the site for more details.

Linux Lab Project
‹ftp://koala.chemie.fu-berlin.de/pub/linux/LINUX-LAB/›
    CED 1401
    DBCC CAMAC
    IEEE-488 (GPIB, HPIB) boards
    Keithley DAS-1200
    National Instruments AT-MIO-16F / Lab-PC+

Analog Devices RTI-800/815 ADC/DAC board
contact Paul Gortmaker at ‹*gpg109@anu.edu.au*›

20.6. Miscellaneous

Maralu chip-card reader/writer
‹ftp://ftp.thp.uni-koeln.de/pub/linux/chip/›

Mattel Powerglove
‹ftp://sunsite.unc.edu/pub/Linux/apps/linux-powerglove.tgz›

AIMS Labs RadioTrack FM radio card
‹ftp://sunsite.unc.edu/pub/Linux/apps/sound/radiotrack-1.1.tgz›

Reveal FM Radio card
‹ftp://magoo.uwsuper.edu/pub/fm-radio/›

Videotext cards
‹ftp://sunsite.unc.edu/pub/Linux/apps/video/
    videoteXt-0.5.tar.gz›

21. Related sources of information

Cameron Spitzer's hardware FAQ archive
‹ftp://rahul.net/pub/cameron/PC-info/›

Computer Hardware and Software Vendor Phone Numbers
‹http://mtmis1.mis.semi.harris.com/comp_ph1.html›

Guide to Computer Vendors
‹http://www.ronin.com/SBA/›

System Optimization Information
‹http://www.dfw.net/~sdw/›

22. Acknowledgments

Thanks to all the authors and contributors of other HOWTOs—many things here are shamelessly stolen from their works; to Zane Healy and Ed Carp, the original authors of this list; and to everyone else who sent in updates and feedbacks. Special thanks to Eric Boerner and lilo (the person, not the program) for the sanity checks. And thanks to Dan Quinlan for the original SGML conversion.

23. APPENDIX A—S3 CARDS SUPPORTED BY XFREE86 3.1.2.

CHIPSET	RAMDAC	CLOCKCHIP	BPP	CARD
801/805	AT&T	20C490	16	Actix GE 32 Orchid Fahrenheit 1280+
801/805	AT&T 20C490	ICD2061A	16	STB PowerGraph X.24
805		S3 GENDAC	16	Miro 10SD VLB/PCI SPEA Mirage VLB
805	SS2410	ICD2061A	8	Diamond Stealth 24 VLB
801/805	AT&T 20C490	Ch8391	16	JAX 8231, SPEA Mirage
928	AT&T 20C490		16	Actix Ultra
928	Sierra SC15025	ICD2061A	32	ELSA Winner 1000 ISA/VLB/EISA
928	Bt485	ICD2061A	32	STB Pegasus VL
928	Bt485	SC11412	16	SPEA Mercury VLB
928	Bt485	ICD2061A	32	#9 GXE Level 10/11/12
928	Ti3020	ICD2061A	32	#9 GXE Level 14/16
864	AT&T 20C498	ICS2494	32	Miro 20SD (BIOS 1.x)
864	AT&T 20C498/ STG1700	ICD2061A/ ICS9161	32	ELSA Winner 1000 PRO VLB/PCI MIRO 20SD (BIOS 2.x)
864	STG1700	ICD2061A	32	Actix GE 64 VLB
864	AT&T 20C498/ AT&T 21C498	ICS2595	16	SPEA Mirage P64 DRAM (BIOS 3.x)
864	S3 86C716	SDAC	32	ELSA Winner 1000 PRO Miro 20SD (BIOS 3.x) SPEA Mirage P64 DRAM (BIOS 4.x) Diamond Stealth 64 DRAM
864	ICS5342	ICS5342	32	Diamond Stealth 64 DRAM (some)
864	AT&T 20C498-13	ICD2061A	32	#9 GXE64 PCI
964	AT&T 20C505	ICD2061A	32	Miro Crystal 20SV PCI
964	Bt485	ICD2061A	32	Diamond Stealth 64
964	Bt9485	ICS9161A	32	SPEA Mercury 64
964	Ti3020	ICD2061A	8	ELSA Winner 2000 PRO PCI
964	Ti3025	Ti3025	32	#9 GXE64 Pro VLB/PCI Miro Crystal 40SV
964	IBM RGB		32	Hercules Terminator 64
868	S3 86C716	SDAC	32	ELSA Winner 1000AVI

CHIPSET	RAMDAC	CLOCKCHIP	BPP	CARD
968	TVP3026		32	ELSA Winner 2000PRO/X Diamond Stealth 64 Video VRAM
968	IBM RGB		32	Genoa VideoBlitz III AVI Hercules Terminator Pro 64 STB Velocity 64V #9 FX Motion 771
732	(Trio32)		32	Diamond Stealth 64 DRAM SE (all Trio32-based cards)
764	(Trio64)		32	SPEA Mirage P64 (BIOS 5.x) Diamond Stealth 64 DRAM #9 FX Vision 330 STB PowerGraph 64 (all Trio64-based cards)

B

24. APPENDIX B—SUPPORTED PCMCIA CARDS

These cards are supported by David Hinds' PCMCIA package and this list is taken from his Web page.

24.1. ETHERNET CARDS

3Com 3c589, 3c589B
Accton EN2212 EtherCard
CNet CN30BC Ethernet
D-Link DE-650
EFA InfoExpress SPT EFA 205 10baseT
EP-210 Ethernet
Farallon Etherwave
GVC NIC-2000P Ethernet Combo
HYPERTEC HyperEnet
IBM CreditCard Ethernet Adapter
IC-Card Ethernet
Katron PE-520 Ethernet
Kingston KNE-PCM/M
LANEED Ethernet
Linksys EtherCard
Maxtech PCN2000 Ethernet
Network General "Sniffer"
New Media Ethernet
Novell/National NE4100 InfoMover
Proteon Ethernet
PreMax PE-200 Ethernet
RPTI EP400 Ethernet
Socket Communications Socket EA LAN Adapter
Thomas-Conrad Ethernet
Volktek Ethernet

24.2. MODEM CARDS

All modem cards should work.

24.3. MEMORY CARDS

New Media SRAM
Epson 2MB SRAM
Intel Series 2 and Series 2+ Flash

24.4. SCSI ADAPTERS

Qlogic FastSCSI PCMCIA
New Media Bus Toaster SCSI
Adaptec APA-1460 SlimSCSI

24.5. UNSUPPORTED

Xircom ethernet and ethernet/modem cards
Canon/Compaq PCMCIA floppy drive

B

THE GNU GENERAL PUBLIC LICENSE

THE GNU GENERAL PUBLIC LICENSE

L inux is not shareware, freeware or public domain software. It is licensed and distributed under the terms of the GNU General Public License (sometimes called the copyleft or GPL) and is copyrighted by Linus Torvalds and others who have contributed to its development.

The GPL is a document that was created by the Free Software Foundation (the group responsible for the GNU project) as a means of allowing people to create "free software". In the context of the GPL, "free" refers to freedom, and not price.

The FSF believes that traditional copyrights and patents stifle innovation and slow the advance of software technology. They created the GPL as a way to give people the freedom to run, copy, distribute, study, change and improve software without fear of being sued. You can even sell software covered under GPL at a profit, but you must provide the source code for your derivative product and a copy of the GPL when you redistribute it.

The Linux kernel and many of the utilities that collectively make up the Linux operating system are covered under the GPL. This means all the Linux source code is available for you to study, improve, give away or sell, so long as you abide by the terms of the GPL, which follows.

GNU GENERAL PUBLIC LICENSE

Version 2, June 1991

Copyright © 1989, 1991 Free Software Foundation, Inc.
675 Mass Ave., Cambridge, MA 02139, USA

Everyone is permitted to copy and distribute verbatim copies of this license document, but changing it is not allowed.

PREAMBLE

The licenses for most software are designed to take away your freedom to share and change it. By contrast, the GNU General Public License is intended to guarantee your freedom to share and change free software—to make sure the software is free for all its users. This General Public License applies to most of the Free Software Foundation's software and to any other program whose authors commit to using it. (Some other Free Software Foundation software is covered by the GNU Library General Public License instead.)

You can apply it to your programs, too.

When we speak of free software, we are referring to freedom, not price. Our General Public Licenses are designed to make sure that you have the freedom to distribute copies of free software (and charge for this service if you wish), that you receive source code or can get it if you want it, that you can change the software or use pieces of it in new free programs; and that you know you can do these things.

To protect your rights, we need to make restrictions that forbid anyone to deny you these rights or to ask you to surrender the rights.

These restrictions translate to certain responsibilities for you if you distribute copies of the software, or if you modify it.

For example, if you distribute copies of such a program, whether gratis or for a fee, you must give the recipients all the rights that you have. You must make sure that they, too, receive or can get the source code. And you must show them these terms so they know their rights.

We protect your rights with two steps: (1) copyright the software, and (2) offer you this license which gives you legal permission to copy, distribute and/or modify the software.

Also, for each author's protection and ours, we want to make certain that everyone understands that there is no warranty for this free software. If the software is modified by someone else and passed on, we want its recipients to know that what they have is not the original, so that any problems introduced by others will not reflect on the original authors' reputations.

Finally, any free program is threatened constantly by software patents. We wish to avoid the danger that redistributors of a free program will individually obtain patent licenses, in effect making the program proprietary. To prevent this, we have made it clear that any patent must be licensed for everyone's free use or not licensed at all.

The precise terms and conditions for copying, distribution and modification follow.

GNU GENERAL PUBLIC LICENSE— TERMS AND CONDITIONS FOR COPYING, DISTRIBUTION AND MODIFICATION

0. This License applies to any program or other work which contains a notice placed by the copyright holder saying it may be distributed under the terms of this General Public License. The "Program", below, refers to any such program or work, and a "work based on the Program" means either the Program or any derivative work under copyright law: that is to say, a work containing the Program or a portion of it, either verbatim or with modifications and/or translated into another language. (Hereinafter, translation is included without limitation in the term "modification".) Each licensee is addressed as "you".

    Activities other than copying, distribution and modification are not covered by this License; they are outside its scope. The act of running the Program is not restricted, and the output from the Program is covered only if its contents constitute a work based on the Program (independent of having been made by running the Program). Whether that is true depends on what the Program does.

1. You may copy and distribute verbatim copies of the Program's source code as you receive it, in any medium, provided that you conspicuously and appropriately publish on each copy an appropriate copyright notice and disclaimer of warranty; keep intact all the notices that refer to this License and to the absence of any warranty; and give any other recipients of the Program a copy of this License along with the Program.

    You may charge a fee for the physical act of transferring a copy, and you may at your option offer warranty protection in exchange for a fee.

2. You may modify your copy or copies of the Program or any portion of it, thus forming a work based on the Program, and copy and distribute such modifications or work under the terms of

Section 1 above, provided that you also meet all of these conditions:

a) You must cause the modified files to carry prominent notices stating that you changed the files and the date of any change.

b) You must cause any work that you distribute or publish, that in whole or in part contains or is derived from the Program or any part thereof, to be licensed as a whole at no charge to all third parties under the terms of this License.

c) If the modified program normally reads commands interactively when run, you must cause it, when started running for such interactive use in the most ordinary way, to print or display an announcement including an appropriate copyright notice and a notice that there is no warranty (or else, saying that you provide a warranty) and that users may redistribute the program under these conditions, and telling the user how to view a copy of this License. (Exception: if the Program itself is interactive but does not normally print such an announcement, your work based on the Program is not required to print an announcement.)

These requirements apply to the modified work as a whole. If identifiable sections of that work are not derived from the Program, and can be reasonably considered independent and separate works in themselves, then this License, and its terms, do not apply to those sections when you distribute them as separate works. But when you distribute the same sections as part of a whole which is a work based on the Program, the distribution of the whole must be on the terms of this License, whose permissions for other licensees extend to the entire whole, and thus to each and every part regardless of who wrote it.

Thus, it is not the intent of this section to claim rights or contest your rights to work written entirely by you; rather, the intent is to exercise the right to control the distribution of derivative or collective works based on the Program.

In addition, mere aggregation of another work not based on the Program with the Program (or with a work based on the Program) on a volume of a storage or distribution medium does not bring the other work under the scope of this License.

3. You may copy and distribute the Program (or a work based on it, under Section 2) in object code or executable form under the terms of Sections 1 and 2 above provided that you also do one of the following:

    a) Accompany it with the complete corresponding machine-readable source code, which must be distributed under the terms of Sections 1 and 2 above on a medium customarily used for software interchange; or,

    b) Accompany it with a written offer, valid for at least three years, to give any third party, for a charge no more than your cost of physically performing source distribution, a complete machine-readable copy of the corresponding source code, to be distributed under the terms of Sections 1 and 2 above on a medium customarily used for software interchange; or,

    c) Accompany it with the information you received as to the offer to distribute corresponding source code. (This alternative is allowed only for noncommercial distribution and only if you received the program in object code or executable form with such an offer, in accord with Subsection b above.)

    The source code for a work means the preferred form of the work for making modifications to it. For an executable work, complete source code means all the source code for all modules it contains, plus any associated interface definition files, plus the scripts used to control compilation and installation of the executable. However, as a special exception, the source code distributed need not include anything that is normally distributed (in either source or binary form) with the major components (compiler, kernel, and so on) of the operating system on which the executable runs, unless that component itself accompanies the executable.

If distribution of executable or object code is made by offering access to copy from a designated place, then offering equivalent access to copy the source code from the same place counts as distribution of the source code, even though third parties are not compelled to copy the source along with the object code.

4. You may not copy, modify, sublicense, or distribute the Program except as expressly provided under this License. Any attempt otherwise to copy, modify, sublicense or distribute the Program is void, and will automatically terminate your rights under this License. However, parties who have received copies, or rights, from you under this License will not have their licenses terminated so long as such parties remain in full compliance.

5. You are not required to accept this License, since you have not signed it. However, nothing else grants you permission to modify or distribute the Program or its derivative works. These actions are prohibited by law if you do not accept this License. Therefore, by modifying or distributing the Program (or any work based on the Program), you indicate your acceptance of this License to do so, and all its terms and conditions for copying, distributing or modifying the Program or works based on it.

6. Each time you redistribute the Program (or any work based on the Program), the recipient automatically receives a license from the original licensor to copy, distribute or modify the Program subject to these terms and conditions. You may not impose any further restrictions on the recipients' exercise of the rights granted herein. You are not responsible for enforcing compliance by third parties to this License.

7. If, as a consequence of a court judgment or allegation of patent infringement or for any other reason (not limited to patent issues), conditions are imposed on you (whether by court order, agreement or otherwise) that contradict the conditions of this License, they do not excuse you from the conditions of this License. If you cannot distribute so as to satisfy simultaneously your obligations under this License and any other pertinent obligations, then as a consequence you may not distribute the Program at all. For example, if a patent license would not permit royalty-free redistribution of the Program by all those who

receive copies directly or indirectly through you, then the only way you could satisfy both it and this License would be to refrain entirely from distribution of the Program.

If any portion of this section is held invalid or unenforceable under any particular circumstance, the balance of the section is intended to apply and the section as a whole is intended to apply in other circumstances.

It is not the purpose of this section to induce you to infringe any patents or other property right claims or to contest validity of any such claims; this section has the sole purpose of protecting the integrity of the free software distribution system, which is implemented by public license practices. Many people have made generous contributions to the wide range of software distributed through that system in reliance on consistent application of that system; it is up to the author/donor to decide if he or she is willing to distribute software through any other system and a licensee cannot impose that choice.

This section is intended to make thoroughly clear what is believed to be a consequence of the rest of this License.

8. If the distribution and/or use of the Program is restricted in certain countries either by patents or by copyrighted interfaces, the original copyright holder who places the Program under this License may add an explicit geographical distribution limitation excluding those countries, so that distribution is permitted only in or among countries not thus excluded. In such case, this License incorporates the limitation as if written in the body of this License.

9. The Free Software Foundation may publish revised and/or new versions of the General Public License from time to time. Such new versions will be similar in spirit to the present version, but may differ in detail to address new problems or concerns.

Each version is given a distinguishing version number. If the Program specifies a version number of this License which applies to it and "any later version", you have the option of following the terms and conditions either of that version or of any later version published by the Free Software Foundation.

If the Program does not specify a version number of this License, you may choose any version ever published by the Free Software Foundation.

10. If you wish to incorporate parts of the Program into other free programs whose distribution conditions are different, write to the author to ask for permission. For software which is copyrighted by the Free Software Foundation, write to the Free Software Foundation; we sometimes make exceptions for this. Our decision will be guided by the two goals of preserving the free status of all derivatives of our free software and of promoting the sharing and reuse of software generally.

NO WARRANTY

11. BECAUSE THE PROGRAM IS LICENSED FREE OF CHARGE, THERE IS NO WARRANTY FOR THE PROGRAM, TO THE EXTENT PERMITTED BY APPLICABLE LAW. EXCEPT WHEN OTHERWISE STATED IN WRITING THE COPYRIGHT HOLDERS AND/OR OTHER PARTIES PROVIDE THE PROGRAM "AS IS" WITHOUT WARRANTY OF ANY KIND, EITHER EXPRESSED OR IMPLIED, INCLUDING, BUT NOT LIMITED TO, THE IMPLIED WARRANTIES OF MERCHANTABILITY AND FITNESS FOR A PARTICULAR PURPOSE. THE ENTIRE RISK AS TO THE QUALITY AND PERFORMANCE OF THE PROGRAM IS WITH YOU. SHOULD THE PROGRAM PROVE DEFECTIVE, YOU ASSUME THE COST OF ALL NECESSARY SERVICING, REPAIR OR CORRECTION.

12. IN NO EVENT UNLESS REQUIRED BY APPLICABLE LAW OR AGREED TO IN WRITING WILL ANY COPYRIGHT HOLDER, OR ANY OTHER PARTY WHO MAY MODIFY AND/OR REDISTRIBUTE THE PROGRAM AS PERMITTED ABOVE, BE LIABLE TO YOU FOR DAMAGES, INCLUDING ANY GENERAL, SPECIAL, INCIDENTAL OR CONSEQUENTIAL DAMAGES ARISING OUT OF THE USE OR INABILITY TO USE THE PROGRAM (INCLUDING BUT NOT LIMITED TO LOSS OF DATA OR DATA BEING RENDERED INACCURATE OR LOSSES SUSTAINED BY YOU OR THIRD PARTIES OR A FAILURE OF THE PROGRAM TO OPERATE WITH ANY OTHER PROGRAMS), EVEN IF SUCH HOLDER OR OTHER PARTY HAS BEEN ADVISED OF THE POSSIBILITY OF SUCH DAMAGES.

END OF TERMS AND CONDITIONS

APPENDIX: HOW TO APPLY THESE TERMS TO YOUR NEW PROGRAMS

If you develop a new program, and you want it to be of the greatest possible use to the public, the best way to achieve this is to make it free software which everyone can redistribute and change under these terms.

To do so, attach the following notices to the program. It is safest to attach them to the start of each source file to most effectively convey the exclusion of warranty; and each file should have at least the "copyright" line and a pointer to where the full notice is found.

‹one line to give the program's name and a brief idea of what it does.›

Copyright © 19yy ‹name of author›

This program is free software; you can redistribute it and/or modify it under the terms of the GNU General Public License as published by the Free Software Foundation; either version 2 of the License, or (at your option) any later version.

This program is distributed in the hope that it will be useful, but WITHOUT ANY WARRANTY; without even the implied warranty of MERCHANTABILITY or FITNESS FOR A PARTICULAR PURPOSE. See the GNU General Public License for more details.

You should have received a copy of the GNU General Public License along with this program; if not, write to the Free Software Foundation, Inc., 675 Mass Ave., Cambridge, MA 02139, USA.

Also add information on how to contact you by electronic and paper mail.

If the program is interactive, make it output a short notice like this when it starts in an interactive mode:

```
Gnomovision version 69, Copyright © 19yy name of author

Gnomovision comes with ABSOLUTELY NO WARRANTY; for
details type 'show w'. This is free software, and you are
welcome to redistribute it under certain conditions; type
'show c' for details.
```

The hypothetical commands 'show w' and 'show c' should show the appropriate parts of the General Public License. Of course, the commands you use may be called something other than 'show w' and 'show c'; they could even be mouse-clicks or menu items—whatever suits your program.

You should also get your employer (if you work as a programmer) or your school, if any, to sign a "copyright disclaimer" for the program, if necessary. Here is a sample; alter the names:

Yoyodyne, Inc., hereby disclaims all copyright interest in the program 'Gnomovision' (which makes passes at compilers) written by James Hacker.

‹signature of Ty Coon›, 1 April 1989

Ty Coon, President of Vice

This General Public License does not permit incorporating your program into proprietary programs. If your program is a subroutine library, you may consider it more useful to permit linking proprietary applications with the library. If this is what you want to do, use the GNU Library General Public License instead of this License.

C

DOS AND UNIX EQUIVALENCES

DOS AND UNIX EQUIVALENCES

I f you take a close look at Unix and DOS commands, you'll find there are many parallels. This is true because DOS took much of its design from Unix, so if you have learned to use DOS, then you already know quite a bit about Unix.

The table that follows (courtesy of Mark Bolzern of Workgroup Solutions) shows the equivalences between common DOS and Unix commands. See earlier chapters in this book or use the **man** command to learn more about these Unix commands under Linux.

DOS	UNIX	DESCRIPTION
attrib	chmod chown chgrp	Change permissions or ownership of a file.
backup / restore	tar	Create a backup or archive backup/restore.
cd / chdir	cd	Change directory.
chkdsk	df du	Report on disk usage.
comp	diff cmp	Compare files or directories.
copy	cp	Copy files.
date/time	date	Set system time and/or date.
dir	ls	List a directory.
erase/del	rm	Remove a file.
exit	exit	Exit the current shell.
fdisk	fdisk	Define disk partitions.
format	mke2fs format	Format a file system or disk.
find	grep	Search for text inside files.
md / mkdir	md	Make a new directory.
mode/ctty	stty	Set modes on console, or serial and/or printer port.
more	more less pg	Display output screen by screen.
print	lpr	Print a file.
rename	mv	Move or rename a file.
rmdir	rmdir rm -r	Remove a directory.
sort	sort	Sort a file.
type	cat	Display a file on screen.
xcopy	cp -r	Copy files and directories recursively.

D

GLOSSARY

GLOSSARY

This glossary of terms will help as you explore Linux. You'll no doubt encounter many of these terms in your travels about Unix and the Internet, so bone up now on your geekspeak and you'll be prepared when the acronyms start flying.

ASCII (American Standard Code for Information Interchange) A set of 128 standard characters guaranteed to display the same way on any computer. The ASCII character set consists of numbers, letters, and other special characters that you can find on a standard U.S. keyboard. Examples of non-ASCII characters are ü, é, â, and £.

ANONYMOUS FTP A public archive of files that anyone can access without a user ID or password.

ARCHIE Internet-based software used to search for files at anonymous FTP sites.

ARTICLE A message posted to a Usenet newsgroup; see *Post*.

ATTACHMENT A file attached to an e-mail message. Attachments are often graphics, compressed documents, or programs.

BASH Acronym for "Bourne Again Shell," the default Linux shell.

BBS (bulletin board system) A computer you can dial to access files and participate in electronic discussions. Unlike the Internet, BBSs are not always networked, and often require that you have a password or membership before you can access them.

BACKGROUND A task that runs behind the scenes, allowing no user interaction. See also *Foreground*.

BANDWIDTH A measure of the amount of data a network can send or receive at one time. Think of bandwidth as the size of the pipe through which data flows from one computer to another.

BINARY FILE A file containing items other than plain text (ASCII characters), such as a program or graphics.

BIT The basic unit of data a computer processes. A bit may have a value of 1 or 0.

BOUNCE   An e-mail message that could not be delivered and is returned is said to have *bounced*.

BROWSER   As in World Wide Web browser: a piece of software like Netscape, Mosaic, or Lynx that displays World Wide Web documents.

CLIENT   Also called *client software*. Connects your computer to another (server) computer.

COMPRESSION   The compacting of files to save storage space and reduce transfer time. Common compression tools for Unix are **gzip** and **zip**. You will often find software packages distributed as compressed files on the Internet.

CROSS-POSTING   Posting the same message to several Usenet newsgroups.

CURRENT DIRECTORY   The directory in which you are currently working. You display its value with the **pwd** command.

CYBERSPACE   A term coined by William Gibson in the science-fiction novel *Neuromancer*. Though commonly used to refer to the Internet, it describes the virtual space one occupies when participating on any computer network.

DAEMON   (Pronounced like *demon*.) A background process that takes a predefined action when a certain event happens. An example is the printer daemon, which manages the print queue.

DIRECTORY   A place where related files are grouped. Directories may contain files or subdirectories (directories below the first level), resulting in a treelike organization of files.

DOMAIN NAME   The name assigned to a computer on the Internet (for example, *http://www.snarch.com*). The suffix on the domain name tells you the type of organization that operates the system (for example, **com** = business, **edu** = university, **gov** = government, **mil** = military, **org** = organization). Sometimes the organization type is followed by a two-character country code (au = Australia, for example, as in outback.edu.au).

DOWNLOAD   What you do when you transfer a file from another computer to your own. Common usage implies moving a file from a public library to one's personal space.

E-MAIL (electronic mail)   Electronic messages sent or received over the Internet, other online services, or computer networks.

ENCRYPTION   Scrambling a file so that it can't be read without special decoding software and a password. PGP is the most commonly used encryption software.

FAQ (frequently asked questions)   A document that provides answers to frequently asked questions on a specific topic. (Can be pronounced like *fact* without the final consonant.)

FTP (File Transfer Protocol or File Transfer Program)   A means of transferring files between computers on the Internet.

FILE PERMISSIONS   A set of permissions associated with a file or directory that tells who can read, write, or execute it.

FILE SYSTEM   A chunk of hard disk formatted so that Linux can use it, with a hierarchical (treelike) structure for storing files. This might be a hard disk drive or a partition on a disk drive.

FILTER   A program in a pipeline that reads a stream of data, performs some operation on each line, and sends out the modified lines.

FINGER   A program that displays information about another user on the network.

FLAME   Expression of a strong opinion or criticism, usually in an e-mail message or Usenet posting.

FOREGROUND   A program running in the foreground is one you can interact with. See also *Background*.

FREE SOFTWARE   Software that is covered under the GNU Public License (see Appendix C). Free refers to freedom and not cost in this context. Not to be confused with *freeware* or *shareware*.

FREEWARE   Software that is free of charge. Not to be confused with *free software* or *shareware*.

GIF (Graphic Interchange Format)   A graphics file format used on the World Wide Web. See also *JPEG*.

GEEK   Someone who enjoys being with computers as much as or more than being with people.

GOPHER   A menu-based interface to collections of information on the Internet.

HTML (HyperText Markup Language)   The language used to create and format documents for display by a World Wide Web browser.

HTTP (HyperText Transfer Protocol)   The way the computers on the World Wide Web communicate. When you type **http://** into a URL, you're telling your browser that the file you want resides on a Web server (as opposed to a Gopher or FTP server).

HEADER   The lines in an e-mail message that precede the message body. These lines identify the sender, the recipient, and the path traveled by the message.

HOME PAGE   A World Wide Web document that is the online home of a person, business, or organization. The first in a series of Web documents.

HOST   A computer on a network that provides access to files or information. See also *Server*.

HYPERTEXT   A way to link documents so they can be explored by selecting highlighted words or phrases (hypertext links) in Web documents. These links, in turn, are linked to other documents that display as you select each link.

IP (Internet protocol)   The rules that govern the way computers communicate on the Internet. Internet protocol allows large chunks of data to travel in small packets across computer networks before they're reassembled at their destinations.

ISP (Internet service provider)   A company that provides Internet access and services.

INTERNET   The set of networks that connects over a million computers and an estimated 40 million people worldwide.

IRC (Internet Relay Chat)   A multiuser system that allows people to chat live with other Internet users.

JPEG (Joint Photographic Experts Group)   An acronym for a file format that compresses graphics files to reduce their size. JPEG files are commonly found on the World Wide Web. See also *GIF*.

Kbps (Kilobits per second)   A measure of the speed at which data moves across a network or modem. A kilobit is equal to 1024 bits, or 128 bytes. The higher the number, the faster the transfer.

LISTSERV   Software that distributes e-mail to groups of mailing list subscribers. Majordomo and Listproc are similar programs.

Man page   A page from an online Unix manual.

MIME (Multipurpose Internet Mail Extension)   A way to encode and attach binary files to e-mail messages. You must have special MIME decoding software (or a mail reader that supports MIME) in order to decode a MIME-encoded attachment.

Mailing list   An e-mail discussion group. Mailing list subscribers automatically receive members' postings. Mailing lists are usually managed by automated software like LISTSERV or Majordomo.

Modem   Hardware your computer uses to communicate with another computer over a telephone line. Modems convert analog telephone signals to digital (a form your computer can process) and vice versa. Modem speeds are measured in bits per second (bps). The higher the bps, the faster the modem can send or receive data.

Mount   To make another file system available. One can mount a floppy disk, a CD-ROM, a partition on a hard drive, or a directory on a remote machine.

NNTP (Network News Transport Protocol)   The communication method used to distribute Usenet postings.

Nameserver   A networked computer that tracks the relationships between Internet domain names and their actual addresses. For example, a name server will know that the domain name *xyz.com* has the address *193.252.47.19*.

Nerd   A socially inept person, slavishly devoted to intellectual or academic pursuits—pocket protectors, taped glasses, and plaid shirts are optional.

Netiquette   Internet etiquette; a set of generally agreed upon rules for proper behavior on the Internet.

Newsgroup   A Usenet discussion group.

NEWSREADER   Software that reads and posts Usenet messages. Tin is commonly used on Unix for this purpose.

POP (Post Office Protocol)   A communication method used by SLIP/PPP software to send and receive e-mail. Also stands for Point of Presence—a computer system that accepts local dial-ins for a large regional network.

PPP (Point-to-Point Protocol)   A communication method that allows a personal computer to connect directly to the Internet using a standard telephone line. PPP is gradually replacing the older SLIP technology.

PACKET   A small chunk of data sent over a network. Packets include the message, the sender's and receiver's identities, and some error-control information.

PIPELINE   A sequence of programs through which a stream of data passes. Each stage or filter performs some operation on the data.

POST   What you do when you send a message or article to a network newsgroup.

POSTMASTER   The person who administers the e-mail system on a network and responds to users' questions and complaints.

PROTOCOL   A prescribed method of communication allowing different types of computers to exchange information over a network.

REGULAR EXPRESSION   A text string that includes special characters for pattern matching.

RFC (Request for Comments)   The standards that define the Internet and how it works. RFC also refers to the way these documents are discussed and approved by the Internet community.

REDIRECTION   Piping the output of a command to a file or another program, instead of having it display on screen.

ROOT DIRECTORY   The directory located at the top of the Linux file system, represented by the forward slash character.

SLIP (Serial Line Internet Protocol)   A communication method that allows a personal computer to connect directly to the Internet using a standard telephone line. See also *PPP*.

SERVER   A computer that responds to requests from a client computer. See also *host*.

SHAR FILE   The **shar** (shell archive) command bundles a bunch of program source code files together so they can be easily transmitted by e-mail.

SHAREWARE   Software you can try for free before buying it. See also *Freeware* and *Free software*.

SHELL   A program that acts as intermediary between the user and the operating system. Commands entered by the user are passed from the shell to the operating system for execution.

SHELL SCRIPT   A short program written in an interpreted language to automate routine command-line tasks.

SHELL PROMPT   A character at the start of the command line that indicates the shell is ready to receive your commands. In the **bash** shell, the prompt is a percent sign for normal users, and a pound sign for superusers.

SHELL ACCOUNT   A type of Internet account where you dial in to a service provider's system and use Unix commands there to access e-mail and Internet resources.

SIGNATURE   A brief, personal message or tag line at the end of an e-mail or Usenet message. A signature should generally not exceed four or five lines.

STANDARD INPUT   The source of input for a program. This is assumed to be the keyboard unless input is redirected from a file or another program.

STANDARD OUTPUT   The destination for output from a program. This is assumed to be the screen unless output is redirected to a file or another program.

TALK   A program for online chats between two users.

TAR FILE   The **tar** (tape archive) command bundles a bunch of files together and creates an archive (commonly called a *tar file*) on tape, disk, or floppy. The most common use is packaging multiple files or directories into a single file for easy transfer or archiving.

TCP/IP (Transmission Control Protocol/Internet Protocol)
A set of rules that enables different types of computers to communicate over a network. The basis for all Internet communications.

TELNET   Software that allows Internet users to log into another computer remotely.

UNIX   A generic term for any UNIX-like operating system. Linux is an implementation of Unix.

UNIX   An operating system developed by AT&T's Bell Labs, later sold to Novell, now owned by SCO. UNIX is a trademarked name, while Unix is a generic term.

URL (Universal Resource Locator)   The assortment of colons, slashes, and other funny characters that make up the address of a Web document—for example, *http://www.xyz.com/welcome.html.*

UPLOAD   What you do when you transfer a file from your computer to another.

USENET   An electronic conferencing system that enables millions of Internet users to wallow in dung. Also a place where you can post messages or read the messages posted on various topics by other users.

UUENCODING   A way to convert binary files to ASCII so they can be e-mailed to other Internet users. The **uuencode** program converts the binary file to ASCII, and the **uudecode** program returns the file to its original form. See also *MIME.*

VT100   A standard terminal type supported by many computer systems. Telnet programs emulate this type of terminal in order to connect to many Internet sites.

WEB   A common abbreviation for the World Wide Web.

WORLD WIDE WEB   Originally designed as a way for researchers to share documents, the World Wide Web (commonly referred to as the Web or WWW) has become the Internet's primary tool for storing, presenting, and researching information. The Web is a collection of electronic documents built on top of the Internet that is part data and part navigational aid. The Web uses hypertext links to tie together collections of documents, images, and sounds located on the Internet.

WWW   A common abbreviation for the World Wide Web.

INDEX

D

E

K

kernel (Linux), 208, 240, 294
    applications, 240
keyboard, Linux installation options for, 23
kill command, 41, 216
Korn shells, 32, 144

L

languages
    Linux's non-English features, 232, 244
    for programming, 242–243
laptops, Linux-compatible, 264–266
leased phone lines, 207
less command, 56
less-than (‹) symbol, 38
libraries, Linux, 245–246, 254
LILO (Linux loader), 23, 217
linking files, 82–83, 214
Linux
    application packages, 236–255
    binaries, 51
    calendar feature, 82
    configuration files, 51
    configuration with Control Panel, 137–138
    Documentation Project, 200, 232
    exiting, 31
    hardware compatible with, 14, 215, 258–291
    information sources for, 225–233
    installation, 12–25
    Lab Project, 286
    license, 6, 294–303
    Mall, 140
    origin and features of, 5–6
    partitions, 15–20
    printer configuration utilities, 72–74, 138
    pronounciation of, 4
    text editors, 88–105
    shells
        changing default, 32
        features of, 28–29
        See also bash shell
    utility, 5
    versions
        installing various, 12

    in languages other than English, 232
    for Macs and other special computers,
        232, 263–264
    warranty, 301–303
    X Window configuration, 22, 127
    See also Unix
Linux Encyclopedia, 5
Linux Hardware Survey, 258
Linux Journal, 233
Linux Network Administrator's Guide, 209
Linux Newsletter, 232
Linux Pro, 5
    components to install, 21
    installation commands, 17–18
    installing, 12
    kernel, 208, 240, 294
    optional components, 16, 21–22
    Web server, 208
Linux/SMP Project home page, 266
listing files. *See* ls command
listserves, Linux, 232
LMB (left mouse button), 128
ln command, 82–83, 214
loo (local loopback) interface, 195
log files
    /var/syslog/messages file, 195
    for X Window, 127
logging on and off Linux, 29–31
    multiple log-ins by one user, 30
    as root, 29, 61
log-in scripts
    PPP account, 194
    SLPP account, 191–194
logout command, 31
looping, 152–154
lowercase use in Linux, 33, 49
lpq command, 76
lpr command, 74–75
lprm command, 76
ls command, 25, 53–55, 61
Lynx, 202–203

M

Mac emulators, 221
Mac versions of Linux, 232, 264
Maclean, James, 218

P

paging, 8
parameters, 148–149
parent directory, 51
partition
    defined, 15
    mounting a DOS, 213–215
    root, 18
    swap, 18–19
partitioning
    repartitioning a hard drive, 15–17
passwd command, 30, 69–70
passwords, 69–70
    during Linux installation, 24
PATH variable, 42–43, 220
pattern matching, 111–112, 114–116, 117
PCMCIA cards, Linux-supported, 290–291
PCMCIA laptops, Linux-compatible, 265
PCPlus, 205
pdksh shell, 32
Perl, 156
permissions
    file access, 61–65, 182
        for shell scripts, 145–146
PGP (Pretty Good Privacy), 183
Pico editor, 100–105
PID (process ID), 40
pine command, 167
Pine Composer, 100–105
Pine e-mail program, 100, 166–171
Pine Information Center (PICO) website, 105
Ping (utility), 200–201
pipe (|) symbol, 39
pipelines. *See* pipes
pipes, 29, 38–39, 76, 121–122
    Pine e-mail, 171
    sending uuencoded files to mail program to, 182
Pkunzip (DOS) for Linux files, 179
Pkzip (DOS) files, creating, 179
pop-up menus
    changing, 134–136
    X Window, 130–131, *132*
ports. *See* serial ports
POSIX, 7
Postscript files, 77, 283
power savings protocol, 285

Powerglove, 287
powering off a machine, 31
PowerPCs, Linux for, 264
PPID (parent process ID), 40
PPP connections, 189–190, 194–195
ppp0 device, 195
pppd (utility), 190, 194–195
pppd command, 194
pr command, 75–76
print flag for find command, 79
print spooling, 74
printers, Linux-compatible, 282–284
printing
    configuring, 72–74, 138, 218
    Linux utilities for, 250
    output to screen, 76, 79, 109
    using awk command, 118
private files, 61–65
problems. *See* troubleshooting
processors. *See* computers
Procomm, 205
.profile (file), 37, 189, 201
Program Menu pop-up, 137
programming
    with Linux, 144–157, 302–303
    Linux packages for, 241–244
    not needed by Linux, 108
    shell variables, 44
Programming Perl (Larry Wall), 156
prompt, 28
ps command, 39–40, 216
PS1 variable, 42
PS/2 systems, 264
ps-f command, 41
publishing packages, Linux, 239
pwd command, 51, 61

Q

q command, 165, 166
question mark (?) wild card, 35
    in file names, 49
quotes, single and double (' and "), 147, 148

R

r flag, 58, 59
r (read) right, 62, 65
RAM. *See* memory
read right, 62, 65
rebooting after Linux installation, 24
Red Hat Linux, 5
redirection of program output, 29, 37–38
    background tasks, 40
regular expressions, 116, 117
relative file name, 52
removable drives, Linux-compatible, 281
rename command, Linux equivalent, 212–213
renaming files, 57, 60
repartitioning a hard drive, 15–17
repeating a command, 28, 35–36
reply command, 166
restart fvwm command, 135, 136
rights, file, 62
    changing, 64–65
rm command, 58–59
    dangers, 61
RMB (right mouse button), 128
rmdir command, 59
/root directory, 51, 52
root partition, 18
root user accounts, 29, 61
routers, 207
rpm utility, 22

S

S3 cards supported by XFree86, 288–289
Samba, 221
saving work
    in emacs text editor, 94, 96
    in Pico text editor, 102–103
    in vi text editor, 90–91, 92
/sbin directory, 51
scanners, Linux-compatible, 284–285
scheduling with Linux, 82, 239
SCO (Santa Cruz Operation), 7
screens. *See* consoles
scripts. *See* log-in scripts; shell scripts
scrolling through text, 129

SCSI controllers, 270–272, 291
SCSI hard drives
    Linux-compatible, 270–272, 278
    Linux installation option, 17
    mounting DOS partition on, 214
    partitioning, 19
SDL Communications RISCom/N2 adapter card, 207
search criteria for find command, 119–120
searching
    for files with find command, 119–120
    Pine e-mail, 170
    text with emacs editor, 98
sed command, 116–117
semicolons, double (;;), 152
serial ports
    configuring for DOSemu, 218
    raising speed of, 188
set command, 42
setserial command, 188–189
setterm command, 285
sh command, 180
shar (shell archive) files, 180
shell archives, 180
shell programming, 144–156
shell scripts
    for boot-up
        /etc/fstab file, 215
        /etc/profile file, 37, 189, 201
    vs. compiled programs, 144
    defined, 144
    writing, 145–156
shells
    defined, 28
    Linux, 248
shift command, 153
shutdown command, 31
single dot (.) notation, 52–53
single quote ('), 147, 148
sl0 device, 195
SLIP connections, 189–194
smileys, 162
software
    commercial Linux, 139–140, 221, 295
    downloading, 197
    emulators for Linux, 215–221
    "free" Linux, 294, 295, 302–303
    installing and removing, 137

W

X

WGS The Linux Shopping Mall
WORKGROUP SOLUTIONS, INC.

One user in 20 is mistaken about Linux.

Sadly, one user in twenty hits a snag while installing Linux and mistakenly concludes that it's not worth the effort. If you're among that unfortunate minority, chances are you've run across one of four easily solvable problems—and we've got the solutions! (By the way, these products are so useful, the 95% who don't have problems will love them too!)

Problem #1: Your hard drive is so full of DOS, Windows or OS/2 files that you're having trouble creating the necessary partition for Linux.

Solution: Partition Magic 3.0
Forget data-destructive utilities like FDISK. Now it's easy and safe to create, resize, move and format hard-disk partitions on the fly! You protect your

data while freeing up disk space that was wasted by inefficient FAT clusters. Plus, there are no TSRs or device drivers to create compatibility problems.
00380.....2 lbs......US$ 67

Problem #2: You want to have several operating systems installed at once, and be able to choose which one to boot at any given time.

Solution: System Commander
To keep your multiple-boot system running problem-free, you'll want the incredible utility that *BYTE* magazine called "a blooming miracle!" With System Commander, you can have up to a hundred operating systems installed on one machine, and can switch between them by simply rebooting.

Running an Internet server? Linux is unbeaten for reliable Internet and Intranet services.

Even Windows 95 will now coexist peacefully with Linux and other operating systems.
00096.............................1 lb...........................US$ 95

Problem #3: Your graphics card is not supported.

Solution: Accelerated-X Server 3.1 for Linux
This is the easiest X Server to install, and it's unbeatable for hardware support! It supports nearly every major video card available today, including most of the proprietary cards that Xfree86 may never support. It multiplies your system's GUI performance by 30x or better, making use of the acceleration features built into your video card. It also works on BSDI, FreeBSD, and NetBSD.
00359....2 lbs ...US$ 95

Problem #4: Your CD-ROM drive is not compatible.

Solution: IDE/ATAPI CD-ROM Drive
We thoroughly test every brand of CD-ROM drive we sell, to ensure it is compatible with Linux. Brand names will vary as we work to keep up with the latest technology. See our web pages for specifics.
00082.......... 2 lbs.............US$ 89

Still not sure about installing? View *Linux — Installation And Beyond*
Seeing the process on video before you try it yourself reduces frustration when setting up your Linux system. Once you've watched the complex installation of an older version of Linux, the newer, streamlined ones are a snap!
00117 ....1 lb ....US$ 22

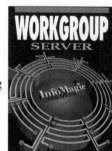

The Linux Shopping Mall

WORKGROUP SOLUTIONS, INC.

Linux is habit forming.

Archived treasures:
Linux libraries and archives on CD-ROM

The Internet contains mountains of information that's available free—*if* you have the time to sort through it all and download the data you want. Instead, you can buy gigabytes of Linux-related data already downloaded and conveniently stored on CD-ROMs.

Treasure chest for developers: InfoMagic Linux Developer's Resource

Superb for application development and research, this distribution packs six CDs with the Metro-X servers from MetroLink, several different distributions of Linux, archives, How-Tos, and a collection of commercial demos.

00384 ......1 lb......US$ 27

Red Hat Power Tools and Linux Archives

These six CDs include the Official Red Hat Linux along with compilers, networking software, source code, online documentation, and over 3 gigabytes of tools, utilities, applications and games.

00350 ....1 lb..........................US$ 29

Searchable text for instant answers:

Red Hat Linux Library

This single CD contains all texts and how-to's of the Linux Documentation Project, Internet Engineering RFCs, GNU docs, Usenet FAQ's, and much more.

00356 ....1 lb ....US$ 28

Eight disks of software from the Internet: Linux Internet Archives

Yggdrasil has compiled eight CDs' worth of software, including nine ready-to-install Linux distributions, the SunSite and TSX-11 archives, GNU, X11R6, and Internet RFC archives.

00122 ....1 lb................US$ 21

Linux does everything but make coffee and empty the wastebaskets.

As the popularity of Linux grows, software companies are realizing that they need to provide office applications for busy users. Whether they create them just for Linux, port them from their original operating system, or emulate their native OS, you'll find these applications more than equal to most office needs!

Want to resell our products, or have us sell yours?

Visit our web site to find out how!

You won't even miss your MS Office: Applixware

This is the complete GUI office suite for Linux. It includes a Word Processor, Spreadsheet, Presentation Graphics, and E-Mail to help you stay productive.

Applixware can access most file formats including HTML, Microsoft Word, PowerPoint, WordPerfect and more. Applixware was ported specifically for Red Hat Linux, and has been successfully tested by WGS on Linux Pro.

00168 ....4 lbs ....US$ 189

More on Applixware on the next page!

WGS The Linux Shopping Mall

WORKGROUP SOLUTIONS, INC.

Linux is great in the office.

Send us proof of your status as a full-time student or faculty/staff member, and you will be eligible for the **Educational Edition of Applixware:** not stripped-down, just priced for education.
00169 ....4 lbs ....US$ 69
For the technically minded, the **Developer's Version of Applixware** provides development tools and an extension language facility to let you add your own features.
00138 ....4 lbs ....US$ 475

All your favorites in one package:
Caldera Internet Office Suite
Caldera Internet Office Suite is a complete bundle of familiar business applications that include WordPerfect, Z-mail, NExS Spreadsheet, and Metrolink's

Executive Motif Libraries. With word processing, email, spreadsheet and more, this single suite can keep your whole office running smoothly.
00099 ....2 lbs ....US$ 209

Graphical word processing:
Caldera WordPerfect & Motif Bundle
Caldera combines the graphical word processor WordPerfect with Metrolink's Executive Motif run-time libraries. You can publish HTML documents directly to the Internet, while Motif makes the best use of your hardware investment.
00098 ....2 lbs ....US$ 122

Windows without the pane:
Wabi for Linux
If the thought of losing all your favorite 16-bit Windows applications has held you back from trying Linux, you've just run out of excuses! Wabi, Caldera's Microsoft Windows emulator, allows

Prices and availability are always subject to change. For the latest information on any product, see our web site:
www.wgs.com

you to install and run those familiar programs just as you would on a native Windows system, but with all the added benefits of Linux! Wabi runs as a Linux program, giving you a multitasking, secure, Internet-aware platform to run your favorite personal productivity applications. In fact, you may even find those apps running faster—up to *ten times faster*—than they did under Windows 3.x! A 200-page User Guide is included with the CD-ROM.
Sorry, support for Windows 95 applications is still under development.
00094.................1 lb....................US$ 196

Mac fans can use Linux too: Executor 2
ARDI started from scratch and rewrote the system services that are present on 68000-series Macintoshes. The resulting Mac emulator for Intel-compatible machines boasts unparalleled speed and versatility. Not only does it read and write Macintosh format files on floppies and hard drives, but it also runs many (not all) Macintosh applications flawlessly. In fact, Executor 2 on a Pentium will run many Mac-native applications up to one and a half times *faster* than the same application on a Quadra. Sorry, support for PowerPC applications is still under development. For limitations, see our web site.
00129 ....1 lb..........
$239

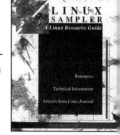

The Linux Shopping Mall

WGS

WORKGROUP SOLUTIONS, INC.

At WorkGroup Solutions, we want to be your One-Stop Linux Shop!

Don't see what you want? Browse the Mall.
No print ad can keep up with our rapidly expanding selection. If you have a product in mind and don't see it in this ad, that doesn't mean we don't carry it. Visit our web site, the Linux Mall, to see what we offer in operating systems, applications, developers' tools, reference materials, and other great Linux-related products!

In addition to the Linux Mall, our web site includes information on:

- Important new developments in Linux
- Trade shows
- Contests
- User groups
- Changes in the computer industry
- How to become a reseller of our products
- How to get your products into the Mall
- How to get on our contact lists
  for email or postal mail
- And much more!

Better deals elsewhere? Check with us.
When the manufacturer offers you a special deal, check with us. We will match any legitimate offer from the manufacturer of a product we sell. That's part of the deal when they sign up to be in our catalog.

WGS in the flesh
Look for us in person at trade shows, expos, and other computer-related events. We'll be happy to talk with you about Linux in general or any product in particular. At our discretion, we may even arrange your admission to any show we attend in exchange for a few hours helping us staff our booth. See the web site for details.

Your convenient source
The Linux Mall is your convenient source for all your Linux needs—truly a One-Stop Linux Shop!

Your choice of ways to order:
1. Use our secure on-line ordering direct from the web at http://www.LinuxMall.com
2. Order by e-mail at sales@wgs.com. Please reference offer #WB0011.
3. Order by phone at 1-800-234-7813. Please reference offer #WB0011.
4. Order by mail. By using the order form on the next page, you automatically become eligible for a 10% discount on the products you buy (shipping is not discounted). Mail to: WorkGroup Solutions, Inc., P.O. Box 460190, Aurora, CO 80046-0190, USA.
5. Order by fax at 303-699-2793. By using the order form on the next page, you automatically become eligible for a 10% discount on the products you buy (shipping is not discounted).

Payment
We accept checks, money orders, Visa, MasterCard, American Express, and Discover. With approval of credit, we also accept purchase orders (we must receive a hard copy by mail or fax). In all cases, please arrange payment in US funds.

Shipping
Our usual shipping method within the US is UPS Ground. Outside the US, shipping methods will vary according to what is most reliable and economical. When ordering by phone or email, you can specify the shipping method of your choice. Please allow up to two weeks for delivery. To compute shipping costs, multiply the product's shipping weight in pounds by:

$2.00 per pound for shipping within the U.S. ($5 minimum)

$3.00 per pound for shipping to Canada ($10 minimum)

$10.00 per pound for shipping to all other countries ($10 minimum).

We will contact you if the shipping cost will exceed what you have calculated by this formula, so please include your email address.

WorkGroup Solutions, Inc.

Order Form for Offer #WB0011

Please print clearly.

Name _____

Company Email _____

Personal Email _____

Company Name, if any _____

Shipping Address* _____

_____ Suite/Apt.# _____

City _____ State _____

Postal Code _____ Country _____

*Please note: if you supply an address with a P.O. box, then we can ship only by U.S. Mail.

Work Phone _____ Home Phone _____

Company Fax _____ Home Fax _____

Fill out this section if using a credit card.   Name on card _____

❑ Visa ❑ MC ❑ AmEx ❑ Discover Exp._____ Card number _____

Credit card billing address, if different from above: _____

_____

❑ Check here to subscribe to our emailed monthly *Linux Newsletter*. No purchase required.

Part No.	Item	Weight	Qty.	Price	Total

Total shipping weight [   ]   Subtotal [   ]

If you are mailing or faxing your order, deduct 10% from the subtotal [   ]

Multiply total shipping weight by $2 per pound USA (min. $5), $3 per pound to Canada (min. $10), $10 per pound to other countries. Enter the result here.   Shipping [   ]

Total [   ]

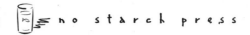
The No B.S. Guide to Windows NT

Just What You Need to Know to Upgrade, Install, Optimize, and Use Windows NT 4.0

Covers Workstation and Server

by JIM FORKNER

What looks and feels like Windows 95 but is really an industrial strength operating system in disguise? It's Windows NT 4.0, and unless you have the time to read an 800-page book to learn how to use it, you could end up wasting precious time just trying to install it. *The No B.S. Guide to Windows NT 4.0* is a step-by-step guide that shows you how to: get your system ready for a trouble-free installation; uninstall if you change your mind; install both Windows NT Workstation and Server—step-by-step; customize NT, get free productivity aids, and use RAS (Resource Access Permissions) to administer an NT system both on and off the network; control what others can do when logged on to your system; use an NT domain and work with shares; connect your NT system to a LAN or the Internet and work with routable and nonroutable protocols; install your own Web server, configure and administer World Wide Web services, even administer a Web server remotely; and plenty more tips guaranteed not to waste your time.

JIM FORKNER is a senior Windows 95 and Windows NT 4 administrator for advanced projects at the Pennsylvania State University, providing backup technical support to front-line consultants. A part-time computer science instructor, Forkner has helped to install Windows NT on over 1,000 PCs.

250 pp., $21.00 (Canada $29.75)
ISBN 1-886411-14-X

The No B.S. Guide to Windows 95

by SCOTT SPANBAUER

"*. . . a no-nonsense guide for people who already know how to use a mouse and double-click on an icon.*"—NEW YORK TIMES

If you can figure out how to launch programs from Windows 95, this book is for you. You'll find clear, pithy answers to questions like: How do I unclutter my desktop and manage long file names? How do I use Exchange and Microsoft Fax? What should I do with config.sys and autoexec.bat? How do I manage memory under Windows 95? How do I connect my laptop and desktop computers and synchronize files? How can I tweak the Registry safely? Where can I get free updates and add-ons, and which ones are worth downloading? All without the B.S.

SCOTT SPANBAUER is a *PC World* contributing editor, the author of *PC World's* "Help Line Q&A" column, and a contributor to *The PC Bible* (Peachpit Press). Visit Scott at *http://www.indra.com/~scott*.

190 pp., $19.00 (Canada $26.95)
ISBN 1-886411-05-0

The Book of SCSI
A Guide for Adventurers

by PETER RIDGE ET AL.

"A must-buy for everyone who wrestles with this touchiest of technologies."
—PC MAGAZINE

Acomprehensive book for all SCSI users with: plain English explanations of the basics of SCSI; how to work with SCSI IDs, LUNs, termination, parity checking, asynchronous and synchronous transfer, bus mastering, caching, and RAID; how to add SCSI to your PC; an explanation of how the SCSI bus works; overviews of ASPI and CAM programming; questions and answers from the major SCSI vendors; clear, uncomplicated drawings and diagrams of SCSI hardware and systems; tips, tricks, and troubleshooting help for SCSI systems; an extensive, plain English glossary of SCSI terms; and a comprehensive index.

400 pp., $34.95 (Canada $49.00)
ISBN 1-886411-02-6

Distributed to the book trade by Publishers Group West

If you can't find No Starch Press titles in your local bookstore, here's how to order directly from us (we accept MasterCard, Visa, and checks or money orders— sorry, no CODs):

Phone:
1 (800) 420-7240 or
(415) 284-9900
Monday through Friday,
8 a.m. to 5 p.m. (PST)

Fax:
(415) 284-9955
24 hours a day,
7 days a week

E-mail:
sales@nostarch.com

Web:
http://www.nostarch.com

Mail:
no starch press, Dept. LX97
401 China Basin St., Ste. 108
San Francisco, CA 94107-2192
USA